THE MEMOIRS OF A BIRMINGHAM

POLICEMAN

(1975-2005)

THE MEMOIRS OF A BIRMINGHAM

POLICEMAN

(1975-2005)

BY NIGEL WIER

authorHOUSE®

AuthorHouse™
1663 Liberty Drive
Bloomington, IN 47403
www.authorhouse.com
Phone: 1-800-839-8640

First published by AuthorHouse   07/25/2011

ISBN: 978-1-4567-7916-0 (sc)
ISBN: 978-1-4567-7917-7 (ebk)

Printed in the United States of America

CONTENTS

For Angie, of course.

For my son, Alex.

For my parents, Albert and Maisie

For Martha and in memory of Harry.

INTRODUCTION

Well here I am writing my first book, it is about my 30 years as a policeman in the West Midlands Police, why have I written a book about my memoirs or I suppose my diary of my career well it is just that they are my memoirs not all of them by far just a few, that even in retirement I still think about, many other things that happened could have gone into the book but perhaps I might just write a second book.

To write all of my memoirs I would probably have needed to write a book about each and every year of my service because so much happened in those 30 years most good, some very good, some excellent but some not so good, some even too horrible to even write about.

I have wanted to write a book for some time but it is the same old reason why you do not, you always say to yourself, I have not got the time and who would want to read my book anyway.

Well five years after re-tiring I have decided to make the time to write the book and as for who would want to read it, I certainly cannot answer that but hopefully some people out there might want to, they might want to read about the police service from a constables view point and from a constables experience. But I suppose the real reason for writing the book is I have written it for me.

Of course I have retired from the police service as a police man but six weeks after I retired I was re-employed by the West Midlands Police as a police support staff worker in my role as accredited financial investigator which is all about taking the money from criminals so I must be a devil for punishment and I am still employed in that role today but my powers of a policeman have long gone.

You will see that in the book some of the criminals and people I have dealt with during my time, I have decided to use letters instead of their correct or full names, I have also done this in relation to their respective companies. This is my choice and I have not done it out of any sympathy for them or to save them any potential embarrassment it is something that I have chosen to do.

I would presume anyway that none of the criminals I have dealt with over 30 years would ever buy this book but if they did they would know who they are and exactly who I was talking about.

Again with the police officers I have mentioned in the book some I have named others I have not, I suppose the best way to describe why I have chosen to write the book in this way is that the ones I have named have probably had a bigger influence on my career, but of course that is no disrespect to the ones I have not named.

I hope none of the policemen or policewomen mentioned in this book, mind that I have included them in my memoirs I am sure they do not.

The book also gives you examples of the some of the very boring and mundane work that you can experience as a police man but hopefully it will give you an inside into all aspects of the work that a police man deals with every day and of course it is from a constables view point.

I have included some of the more serious and violent crime in the book, that I was involved in and this is not meant to shock you it is so you can see and understand that some of our work is not pleasant and it often makes you wonder why and how one human being can commit such a crime on another human being, but I cannot answer that, but we the police are of course expected to deal with it.

I chose and perhaps the West Midlands police chose for me that I was to become a detective for over 23 years of my police career and I am most glad that this was my chosen route, I always wanted the CID from the day I joined in 1975 and when I became a detective in 1981 I was perhaps the happiest man in Birmingham.

I have to say that during my time I was a detective not once did I ever regret it, I never got up one morning and thought I do not like being a detective as I was one of the proudest detectives you will ever meet.

Some people have asked me did I have an hobby or indeed did I have time for a hobby, well I had three the first was reading, I have always as far as I can remember have read true crime thrillers or books based on the history of Ireland something I have always been interested in. My compulsive reading was probably one on the main reasons that I decided to take up writing.

My second hobby was and still is taking holidays with my family I love the chance to get away for a few days with the beautiful Cotswolds one of my favourites so quiet and peaceful, not at all what I am use to.

And thirdly my other hobby was and had to be the police, it took up a lot of my time and I loved doing it so as well as being my job it was also my hobby.

It was not easy and I would never say that it was, as a detective I often worked long hours often putting a strain on your marriage but it was what I wanted and I am proud to have become and ultimately served as a detective in the best force in the country.

Finally this is my book and in it are my views and my recollections and of course my experiences and are not the views of the West Midlands Police in any way.

ACKNOWLEDGEMENTS

I wish to thank every single police officer I have had the pleasure to work with and to meet in over the thirty years, I have met some very brave police officers in my time and now some of them are my best friends. Others I have not seen for years as we all headed off in a separate directions but none have I forgotten.

Every one of them has helped me in some way, some only in a small way, but others have directed my career path. I cannot thank each and every one of them it would take far too long but hopefully by writing this book I have managed to thank them in my own way.

I would also like to thank Birmingham Central Library Archives Department where I have spent many a long hour researching some of the more important dates to be included in my book.

ABBREVIATIONS

PC	Police Constable
DC	Detective Constable
PS	Police Sergeant
DS	Detective Sergeant
DI	Detective Inspector
CI	Chief Inspector
DCI	Detective Chief Inspector
D Supt	Detective Superintendent
C Supt	Chief Superintendent
DCS	Detective Chief Superintendent
CC	Chief Constable
CID	Criminal Investigation Department
SOCO	Scenes of Crime Officer
SPG	Special Patrol Group
IRA	Irish Republican Army
SFO	Serious Fraud Office
CPS	Crown Prosecution Service
OPRA	Occupational Pensions Regulatory Authority

ITS	Independent Trustees Services
PCB	Pensions Compensation Board
DTI	Department of Trade and Industry
OR	Official Receiver

CHAPTER ONE

The Beginning

I joined the West Midlands Police on Monday 10th March 1975 but the actual beginning was a long time before that, the real beginning was August 1970.

At this time I was working as a trainee joiner and carpenter at a small company called Castle Joinery situated in Webster Street, Aston. I had begun my working life there in July 1967 after leaving school. I remember leaving school at the beginning of July 1967 and I recall my father saying to me, 'Son on Monday you will leave this house and start walking down Kingstanding Road and do not come back until you have found work.'

Thanks dad I thought, well I did set out on that Monday and began walking, I tried several big companies on the way, Lucas, The Rover, IMI Kynock, Tufnell's absolutely nothing, I began walking down Newtown Row an area I didn't know that well when I had just past the Barton's Arms public house and just before a big store called the House that Jack Built a bit like a Woolworths.

I decided to turn left down Webster Street I could see a small factory there it was almost part of a row of terraced house, it said on a sign stuck to the window 'Vacancies for a trainee joiner and carpenter' I thought if you don't ask you don't get so in I went. I met one of three brothers who ran the company a lovely man called Reg Tooker, he asked me various questions including and most importantly, 'Why did you want to become a trainee joiner and carpenter?'

I thought of the first thing I could and said to him, 'I liked working with wood and making things out of wood and I think I am pretty good at it.' fingers crossed.

It done the trick I got the job and I started the following day, the hours of work were 8.00am until 5.30pm Monday to Friday and the weekly wage was to be £4 and 3 shillings (£4.15 pence in today's money) I didn't care it was a job. I got home and told my father and he was most impressed.

I started at Castle Joinery in mid July 1967 and I must admit I loved the work, there were two floors to the building downstairs made and cut all the window and door frames and upstairs which included me put them together as a finished article and painted them before they left the company.

I did enjoy it but at the back of my mind there was always something niggling at me I wanted to be a police man, why I don't know but it's something I had wanted to do it must have been the television programmes like 'Dixon of Dock Green' I just wanted to be him. There were no other police men in my family so if I were successful I would be the first, anyway I just had to give it a go I would never be satisfied if I did not even give it a try to become a policeman.

In 1970 it was the Birmingham City Police and its Chief Constable at the time was Sir Derek Capper, I made several telephone calls to the recruiting department of the Birmingham City Police and was eventually pointed in the direction of Tally Ho Police training centre in Pershore Road, Birmingham. The idea was for me to attend an informal interview and medical examination, in those days you had to be for a male at least 5' 10" inches tall and be between the age of 19 years and 30 years and of interest for a female officer you had to be 5' 4" tall.

I measured up fine in the height department but failed in the weight department I weighed 9 stone 7 pounds and the police sergeant in charge of the day informed me that I had to be at least 10 stone, I couldn't believe I had failed. He advised me to go home and drink as much water as I could and try again.

I felt so disappointed I walked out of Tally Ho feeling as if I was never going to become a policeman and perhaps I should I forget all about it, I was never the heaviest person in the world and how the hell was I going to put on half a stone. I thought I was tall enough, answered all the questions right, physically fit, did not wear glasses and I could drive a car, I had ticked most of the boxes but I was not heavy enough. You know how suddenly you lose interest I thought so what, it's there loss not mine I will get on with my life and forget about becoming a policeman. The stuffing was knocked right out of me.

So it was back to Castle Joinery which of course I never minded anyway, I learnt a lot there which would keep me in good stead for years to come but it was not to last, the area of Aston, Webster Street and its surrounding roads were being demolished for regeneration, the old pre-war houses, shops, factories and streets were disappearing fast amongst dust and rubble and new properties were to be built in their place.

The Tooker brothers who ran Castle Joinery announced they were to close after nearly 50 years in existence and that all the employees were to be made redundant as of February 1972, great I thought, anyway at the end of February 1972 I left with the company with my redundancy payment of £9.00.

I was lucky my mother's uncle worked at Birmingham City Council and he explained to me that they were looking for carpenters for some modernisation work to be done on council houses that they were proposing to repair in the Small Heath area of the City and was I interested, interested of course I was, I had been out of work albeit a matter of days so I said to my Uncle, 'Yes, I am definitely interested.'

So a couple of days later I attended an interview at a council depot in First Avenue, Bordesley Green, Birmingham where I met the area manager and my future foreman for an impromptu interview. I got the job I had to exaggerate my knowledge of joinery and carpentry to secure the job as they were expecting me to fit new front and rear wooden doors make and fit garden gates and fencing, fit casements windows, but hey I will give it a go as I was told that I was to be part a gang of people working on modernising council houses to a good and proper standard.

I was to be working in the main an area of Birmingham called Small Heath and this is true we worked out of a metal shed about ten foot square in the front garden of a house in Fosbrooke Road, and in a metal shed next to us we kept all the materials that we needed in order to do our work.

The work itself was very different to what I was use to but it was enjoyable and you worked on a bonus scheme which meant if you really worked hard say between 7.00am and 2.00pm then you could take the rest of the day off all in real terms you all went for a pint at the local pub called 'The Monica'

1972 for me had high points but there was a very low point when on 28th May 1972 which incidentally was also my mother's birthday, my brother Barrie who had been born physically handicapped and who had been admitted to Good Hope Hospital earlier in the week had now quite suddenly died of leukaemia. It was shattering news for all the family he was 23 years old and for all the different things he had suffered with he always had a smile on his face.

In July 1972 I met my wife Angela at a club known as Rebecca's in Birmingham City Centre I was there with my cousin and she was there with a friend anyway we hit it off and we are still together today after getting married in September 1974.

Job wise in the summer of 1972 it was going good the team of men I worked with were helpful and always willing to listen they were much older than myself and I have to say I was enjoying myself, most of the work I was now doing was outside so I had the best of both worlds doing a job I enjoy and working outside in the summer sun.

I had purchased my first car which was a light blue Ford Cortina Mark II registration number POP 203G things were going well.

There was trouble in Northern Ireland at this stage the British Troops had gone into Ireland at the request of the Irish in 1969 but after arriving as peace keepers they soon became the enemy and were subject of many attacks in the main by the Irish Republican Army, and by the middle of 1972 several British soldiers had been killed.

As part of their campaign against the British the IRA and in particular their supporters they were trying to disrupt the people's lives in England by setting off incendiary devices in shops and cinemas and causing as much mayhem and panic as they good.

On 14th September 1974 I married Angela Cook and we settled into our rented flat in Erdington.

On 21st November 1974 the worst British main land attack by the IRA occurred when they bombed two Birmingham Public Houses, The Mulberry Bush at the bottom of the Rotunda and The Tavern in the Town in nearby New Street both in the City Centre and the result of this attack left 21 dead and over 170 people injured, I can recall this night as we had been to Edgbaston to visit the wife's parents and we were driving back and we were stopped going our normal way by uniform police officer, they told us that there had been an incident in the town but said little else.

We got home about 10.00pm still not knowing what had happened when the telephone went it was my father enquiring if we were all right, he informed us that some bombs had gone off in the town and people were dead, over the next couple of days we found out how many had died it was horrendous attack on innocent people having a night out, committed by so called supporters of the IRA.

Of note just six weeks before the bombings I had held my stag night at The Tavern in the Town. But I know now why those policemen stopped me driving down Broad Street that night.

It's now December 1974 and a total of six men from Birmingham had been arrested and charged in connection with the bombings in Birmingham, I think what made me feel particularly bad was the fact that the men charged with the bombings all lived in the Birmingham area.

I now know what I needed to do I needed to join the police force, I wanted to help people and make sure these cowardly attacks did not happen again to innocent people and the best way to do that surely was to become a policeman.

So in early December 1974 I wrote to the Personnel and Training Department of the West Midlands Police, the West Midlands Police had recently been formed on 1st April 1974 following the reorganisation of local authority boundaries, the Birmingham City Police was amalgamated with the West Midlands Constabulary and parts of Warwickshire and Coventry police to form the new force.

I had a response and I was sent a Preliminary Application form, number 1086/74 I completed it, signed and dated it 27th December 1974 and sent the form back. The form asked amongst personal details to give three reasons why you wanted to join the police. I wrote (1) service to the community, (2) never a dull moment and would be full of interesting things happening and never a day the same and (3) job security no fear of being made redundant.

I was then notified to attend an entrance examination at Lloyd House, Birmingham on 11th January 1975, it was an educational type examination of multiple choice answers, I was successful in the exam gaining a pass mark of 92%. Things appeared to be going well I then received a full application form and in this they ask you for two references, previous details of employment which I completed, I then signed and dated the form 21st January 1975 and sent it back to Lloyd House, by this stage I was getting excited I was getting ever nearer to my goal of being a policeman.

On 31st January 1975 a uniform Inspector visited my in laws at their home address in Edgbaston and the same evening we were visited by Chief Inspector Longcroft and a uniform Inspector at our flat. New recruits at that time were always visited in their home surroundings. It is just to have a general chat with you as to why you want to join the police and it gives them a chance to get the views of your wife or partner.

Of note when I retired I had occasion to look through my personnel file that the police keep on all officers and on that file next to Chief Inspector Longcrofts report to Personnel and Training from January 1975, was a hand written note from the then Assistant Chief Constable of Personnel and Training, I will not mention his name and the note said, ***'Accept for training of limited ability, but could make grade provided he works hard.'***

It was always excepted when I joined that in the police that there preferred way of recruitment was through the police cadets. I was then notified to attend Lloyd House for a medical and second interview and on 18th February 1975, I attended for the medical and it went well by this time I was heavy enough not like in 1970, no doubt the married life was suiting me.

I even remember going to the Chest Clinic in Great Charles Street for various checks so it was a pretty thorough medical, the second interview was more of a final call up as I was excepted for training and told to report to Tally Ho Training Centre, Pershore Road on 3rd

March 1975 at 8.30am in the morning and to make sure I got a haircut as mine was too long.

The purpose of a one week induction course at Tally Ho was just that various lecturers visited along with more senior police officers and you discussed things like what was expected of you, the length of training that you were to embark on, various local Birmingham bylaws were explained to you that you were likely to use when you returned from your 10 week training at Ryton upon Dunsmore Police Training Centre.

It's a way of them deciding if they want you as a policeman or alternatively do you still want to be a policeman now you know what it's all about.

Ryton of course was to become my home for the next ten weeks they again reminded you to get a haircut and I suppose most importantly they told me as from 10th March 1975 I would be earning £1,632.00 per year.

But before all that could start I would need a uniform and that meant a visit to the uniform stores at Duke Street in the heart of Birmingham University, it was quite an experience to get your first uniform because from memory the only thing you tried on and that was likely to fit you properly was the trousers and they were made out of a serge type material, very comfortable I do not think.

We had two pair of trousers, 6 light blue shirts, two tunics, a gabardine mac, god that was awful and a cape along with two helmets, nothing fitted you properly but the uniform store's manager a Mr Greenslades always said the same thing to you, 'You will grow into son.' I got my numeric numbers that I had to put on my tunic, my cape and mac along with my epaulets for the shirts and that's when I realised I had arrived I was now Police Constable 3055 Wier.

During my various examinations and interviews over the previous few weeks particularly the last week I had become very friendly with a chap called Roy Fisher, he had previously been a police officer, but had left after two years and had joined the Royal Navy, he then left the Navy and had been I successful in re-joining the police, we had got on very well and he had a very good sense of humour so we sort of became good friends and he was useful to know because he had done it all before.

The arrangement was that on the evening of Sunday 9th March 1975 he would collect me from my parent's house in Kingstanding and we would travel in his car to Ryton, it was agreed we would take it in turns to drive each other to Ryton for the duration of the 10 week course.

The reason for collecting me from my parents' house is that during my ten weeks training my wife was going to stay there during the week, at the time she did not want to stay alone in our flat.

So that was it I was just about to embark on a career as a policeman and it was to start at the training centre at Ryton upon Dunsmore.

CHAPTER TWO

The Training

At about 7.30pm on the evening of Sunday 9th March 1975, Roy turned up at my parent's house in his Volkswagen Beetle it was light blue in colour, I'll never forget it. I said goodbye to my wife and parents and walked down the path to Roy's car I turned round and I waved goodbye to the wife and parents, I got in his car and off we went in the direction of the A45 towards Coventry and we arrived at the centre about 8.15pm.

We parked the car up in the car park and walked and reported to the main hall to await further instructions. We were met by what was called the duty officer and the duty squad and they showed us to our rooms that were going to be our homes for the next ten weeks.

How would I describe the buildings that were going to be our home, well they were something out of a World War Two prisoner of war camp, there were rows of long buildings with a corridor all the way through the building and leading off the corridor were 20 or so single rooms about 10 foot by 12 foot square, there was a single bed and a small dirty looking sink, the only heating was a large water pipe going all through the building about 6 inches from the floor and about 10 inches in diameter.

There were two showers and two baths and four toilets at the one end, the end with the entrance door of course, so taking a shower or bath was extremely cold work. That was it out home for the next ten weeks.

What had I walked into, Ryton on Dunsmore had been a police training centre since 1963 and it was now 1975 and nothing had changed I am no doubt it was still the same paint work. First impressions were it was dark, damp and depressing. But here I was, course 3/75 and ready to become a policeman.

Day one and it was off to the dining room where we had breakfast and of course where we started to meet with our new colleagues who were going to be our friends and class mates for the next ten weeks, after breakfast we made our way to our allocated classroom where we were introduced to our two class instructors, Police Sergeant Colin Harrison and Police Sergeant Adrian Adderley we were then give the house rules of what we could do and more importantly what we could not do, it was like being back at school.

We were told in no uncertain terms to keep away from Jean Law house, which was a modern purpose built block where the policewomen resided whilst on the training course it was not a bit like our building, also do not get found in passion alley, this was a walkway near to the men's block where apparently it was known that individuals of the opposite sex or even the same sex met up late at night for a chat!!!!.

We were told how we were expected to behave particularly in the students bar and no drunkenness was to be tolerated, otherwise you would be expected to attend to see the Commandant of the centre, told you, the Commandant of the centre it was just like the Second World War film.

The bar closed at 10.30pm and lights off were at 11.00pm, there would be a duty squad who made sure everyone was in his or her room by lights out. The duty squad were policeman and policewomen who had completed five weeks of their ten week course and were now known as seniors, we of course on day one were known as the juniors.

The course was to last ten weeks and on each and every Friday just after lunchtime you went home but you had to be back at the centre on the Sunday evening before lights out.

There would be an exam each Monday and a junior and senior exam at the beginning of the fifth and tenth weeks. If you failed any exam you could be back coursed literally meaning starting all over again. I was not the brightest person in the world I had even failed my 11 plus examination but I have to say that I did pass every exam whilst I was at Ryton, I was never in the top three but I was never in the bottom three either.

As I said after five weeks course 3/75 us, would become the senior course, courses 2/75 had completed their training and were being returned to their individual forces and 4/75 would arrive at the centre being the junior course.

Each and every morning we had to parade on the drill square at the front of the centre to learn how to march properly and march to music at that. The drill sergeant was Police Sergeant Tom Trickett and he was certainly a military looking individual with his short hair, and upright walk, his peak cap slit so the peak was straight down onto his forehead, so to see you he almost had to look upwards and into the air, his loud voice that early in the morning went straight though you, his boots bulled (polished) so much you could see your face in them, his uniform was immaculate and the crease down the front of his trousers had been stitched in so it was always there, but he did march with perfection and his job was to get us into some sort of marching group.

Well you could count on one finger the amount of time that I had marched in my life which was precisely none, never mind I was going to learn now. In its way it was good fun and it did make you more disciplined in your attitude something sadly missing today.

On the Wednesday of the first week the 12th March 1975 it was a bus ride back to Lloyd House in Birmingham where I was sworn in as a constable before a Justice of the Peace. The words of the oath were, *'I do solemnly and sincerely declare and affirm that I will well and truly serve our sovereign lady the Queen in the office of constable, without favour or affection malice or ill will and that I will to the best of my power cause the peace to be kept and preserved and prevent all offences against the person and properties of her majesty's subjects and that while I continue to hold the said office I will do the best of my skill and knowledge, discharge all duties and there off faithfully accord to law'*

I was handed my police warrant card with my picture on and my collar number of 3055 that had been allocated to me and it was something that I would retain for the next thirty years.

Sport was also a big thing in police training and they openly encouraged it, there was a decent gym and a fairly modern swimming pool at the centre, you could also get involved in football and rugby so there was plenty to choose from.

In the second week I did my first cross country run and finished fifth which I was pleased with. I have always enjoyed cross country and back in my school years I actually ran in the Northern England Schools cross county completion and I finished fifteenth out of four hundred and eighty runners and our school was placed second overall, I got a medal for that.

The training was now gathering pace and I must say I was getting use to the whole scenario a lot more, we were shown how to use a police radio of course in those days in was a 'Pye' two piece radio, you held one piece to your ear to listen and spoke into the other piece how things have changed. I believe you can still see these radios in the West Midlands Police museum.

The instructors would also stage so called real life incidents for us like drunks, robberies, fights, domestic disputes and car accidents and we would be asked to respond to them like a policeman or policewoman would. Everybody was petty useless to begin with but in fairness we all got better and some were quite good at the end of ten weeks but as the songs goes, 'there ain't nothing like the real thing' and that was still some way off.

I recall one occasion when Sergeant Harrison was acting the part of a drunk allegedly urinating against a wall, in truth he had a fairly liquid bottle filled with water and he was standing in such a way he had his back to me and holding this bottle in such a position to all intents and purpose it looked like he was urinating against a wall, 'PC Wier deal with it.' shouted Sergeant Adderley.

So over I walked not really having a clue what to do and tapped the instructor on the shoulder and said, 'Excuse me.'

He immediately turned round and sprayed me in the face from the bottle and me thinking what it could have been and acting like any sane person would, I sprung into action I grabbed hold of him and dragged him as hard as I could to the floor and began to pull him along the ground he was shouting, 'Let go we are only acting.' I never heard that and so I carried on dragging him to the police station some twenty yards away at this the other instructor at the top of his voice shouted,

'For God's sake stop, what the hell you doing?'

I said, 'Nobody but nobody urinates on me.'

He reminded me that I was only training to be a policeman and it was not the real thing and why did I not arrest him, 'I forgot to.' I said quietly, the rest of the class had a good laugh, I do not suppose I was the first to react like that and I am certain I would not be the last.

I recall another practical when I am writing out a parking ticket and it is raining very, very heavily, I eventually finished writing the ticket out which is now is soaking wet and which by now you can hardly read. I handed it to the driver who promptly throws it on the floor so I tell him, 'Pick it up' and he ignored me. I then said to him, 'That I would also be summonsing him for depositing litter on a public highway as well as the parking offence.'

I am thinking I am doing quite well here, when he turns round looks at me and starts to laugh and then runs off shouting, 'It's not even my car I stole it.'

He promptly disappears out of sight leaving me holding a sodden piece of paper which I had just picked up and thinking that did not go to plan and looking sheepishly around I could see the rest of the class sheltering from the rain trying not to kill themselves laughing at me.

As the weeks went on the training seemed to get easier and you got more confident, the weekly examinations were going well you were getting to know everyone else that bit better and dare I say it, it was becoming enjoyable.

On the fifth week I sat the junior exam and made above the class average so I was pleased with that, then after that week end we came back on week six and we were now the senior course and with that more responsibility around the centre, you took it in turns to be part of the duty squad that had its own responsibilities you had to make sure that the students bar was shut on time at 10.30pm and that lights out went without any problem at 11.00pm, obviously check passion alley, you as duty squad would also look after the front gate of the centre to make sure only the right people were allowed access and some of you formed part of the fire duty squad checking the fire extinguishers were in order.

Another role was that of bar staff at the students bar so all in all you were given more and varied rolls within the centre I suppose it was done in the main to give you confidence. I think one of the less enjoyable roles as a senior student was that one who was asked to ring the bell at the start of lessons for the day and again to ring it to finish the lessons for the day, your timing had to be perfect and you had to have a watch that worked as the rest of us did not want to either start the lessons earlier than we should or more importantly finish later than we should.

You of course as the senior course had to be on your best behaviour because you needed to set an example to the junior course because they would look up to you for advice just as we did when we were the junior course. The practical's seemed to became more purposeful because by now everybody in the class had made complete fools of themselves, so we had gone through that and we were getting more and more professional in the way we dealt with them. In other words you became one big happy family all with the same goal.

Our class consisted of about 15 men and 5 women because at this time mid 1975 policewomen were earning less money than policemen so for that reason there were always less of them wanting to join the police service. In total out of my class of twenty or so I think there were about eight of us from the West Midlands, the others would have come from surrounding forces with exception of the Metropolitan Police who have their own training centre at Hendon in North London.

The days were generally mixed between theory, studying the law from law books in the class room and practical's trying to put the theory into practice sometimes it worked other times it did not. But what you always remembered was that everyone was in the same position of you, by now I was coming towards the end of the ninth week and for the first time I could see light at the end of the tunnel and week ten would probably be the week where I would get most pleasure from.

The Monday of the tenth week began with the final examination I passed it just above class average again, what a relief I could now happily say that I had passed all ten exams, I never finished in the top three once but equally I never finished in the bottom three either so that was good enough for me.

After the examination it was time to prepare for the dining in night, it's almost a tradition with the police that when you come to the end of a residential course you have a dining in night which consists normally of a dinner and dance and you dressing up in formal dress.

But before that I had to hire my dinner suit I remember I hired it from Dormer Hire, I think they came to the centre. Suit hired, Wednesday was dining in night it was just the senior course involved it was their end of course dinner and we were waited on by the instructors who had been putting us through hell for the last ten weeks. It was an excellent evening and everyone had plenty to eat and drink and I can say that everyone enjoyed themselves because it was the end in sight.

The following morning the Thursday was the day of the passing out parade not quite what it sounds like, this is the day that we march to music in front of our wives, husbands, girlfriends, boyfriends, moms and dads we were now going to see if the last nine weeks or so of marching practice would come together and that the drill sergeant Police Sergeant Tom Trickett had done his job properly.

I remember the day was fine and dry and there I was standing in class formation in best uniform with white gloves, with others from the senior course waiting for the music and out of the corner of my eye I noticed my wife standing there. She had travelled from Birmingham by bus to see this so I better not make a mistake.

The music started and off we went marching to music it went well I think we were marching for about thirty minutes or so criss-crossing the drill square, but I swear it seemed like all day, but we got through it without any major hiccups.

I remember people were taking photographs and cheering at the right time. We finished and people clapped so hopefully they had enjoyed it we certainly did, we went then and met with our respective partners, relatives and friends and really that was it, the passing out parade was finished. We said our good byes but it would not be long before we saw then again as we only had a day left.

We had almost reached the end of our training it was not long to go before I would be walking along the High Street in uniform as a policeman hopefully doing the job I always wanted to do.

It was the 16th May 1975 the last day the Friday, it was a day of good byes at the centre we had made good friends some I would see again others I would not. Overall it had been a good ten week adventure into a world I knew nothing about I had now come out of the adventure at the other end and I was now almost ready to face the world in my new job.

But I still had a further two weeks of training to complete this was to be at Tally Ho Police Training Centre in Birmingham and was known as the Local Procedure Course. But first things first after the good byes it was a quick dash to the room to collect your belongings which you had already thrown into a suitcase and another even quicker dash to the car and we drove out of the centre onto the A45 and home. I was looking forward to a relaxing weekend before Monday at Tally Ho.

I began the Local Procedure Course on Monday 19th May 1975, this was to be a two week course on local procedures which would include local bye laws that you may come across whilst you were out and about. Silly little things to do with ice cream musical tones and only a certain time of day that they can use them, or you cannot throw human waste out of a window onto the street below, do people do that?

All the way up to vehicles parking or driving on the grass verge and dogs barking. Normally these were bye laws that had been passed as law by the local councils relevant to their local areas many, many years ago some in the nineteenth century and not at all often used.

One of the days we visited Birmingham Magistrates Court and were introduced to Police Sergeant Tom Hurley who was in charge of policing the courts, and of course when you went to court with your own cases he was also in charge of you. You had to book on and off in the duty room and in a corridor facing the duty room PS Hurley would have you stand to attention to make sure you were properly dressed for court. It was all very regimental and disciplined but it did you no harm. We were told to respect our senior officers and if the senior officer had his or her cap on then we would be expected to salute them. It was a good insight to what was expected of you certainly in the early days.

Of note up until 31st December 1975 a total of 3,891 applications were received by the West Midlands Police from people of both sexes wishing to join the force, of that a total of 553 were accepted and most completed the training and I was one of those. Of interest out of the 553, 116 were women, so almost 1 in 5 joining the West Midlands Police was now women.

And of course on 29th December 1975 the Sex Discrimination Act became law which would lead to the demise of the Policewomen's Department as we knew it, the new law would now give female officers the same opportunities as men and would give them what they had strived for in the past and that was of course equal pay. The downside for them was they would now have to work the same shift systems as the men which they did not have to do prior to the act coming into force.

All I knew was that Monday 2nd June 1975 was fast approaching and my first day at Queens Road Police Station was almost here.

CHAPTER THREE
Queens Road Police Station

The day of reckoning was here this is the one I had waited a long time for in was Monday 2nd June 1975 and at about 8.30am I walked through the front door of Queens Road Police Station. The police station its self was known as the 'D' Division Headquarters which incorporated both the D1 sub division based at Queens Road and the D2 sub division which was based at Sutton Coldfield, I was to be working on the D1 sub division.

I suppose the police station was built in the early 1960's and covered such diverse areas as Nechells, Witton, Aston, Erdington, Perry Common Kingstanding and through to Great Barr and Sutton Coldfield and it had boundaries with both Warwickshire Police and Staffordshire Police. If you looked at a map of the West Midlands Police area then the 'D' Division was to the North East of the region.

I introduced myself to the office sergeant and he directed me to the administration block at the back of the police station, I was to work 9.00am x 5.00pm on the first day, as my unit 'D' unit were just about to start a week of nights I would be joining up with them on the Tuesday of nights. Today was all about getting yourself familiar with the police station and its surroundings; you would be allocated a locker to keep you uniform in and generally shown around the station.

The administration block is where the Divisional Chief Superintendent had his office and at this time it what DCS Bagnall a ferocious man who's face got redder and redder the more he shouted at you and I did see that red face a few times over the next two or three years, the Divisional Detective Superintendent also had his office there, at this time it was Detective Superintendent Colin Holloway, he was head of the Criminal Investigation Department for the 'D' Division.

I also recall there was a secretary and a typist, and the plan drawer was also based in the administration block and then of course there was the admin staff itself which consisted of a Police Sergeant, PS Leytham and a Police Constable, PC Dave Todd, I remember Dave Todd well he was a big man over six foot who enjoyed his golf and he was coming to the end of his thirty years with the police, sadly he is no longer with us he died many years ago.

The first place I was showed was the canteen where I was told to sit and wait, have a cup of tea and somebody will be with you in a minute. Over the next couple of hours I was shown round the police station, I first met with the uniform Chief Inspector 'Wryleybird' Wilson he was so named because he was always flapping about over something or nothing and constantly running around the station, he gave me a welcoming to D1 chat, I was then shown the locker room, the parade room, the CID office, the plan drawers office, the front office, the controller's office, the collators office, and lastly the cell block area. It was all very fascinating and of course it was all very real.

I was told to go and have some lunch and then to make my way to the parade room for 1.45pm and I could go out with one of the more experienced officers in a police car or a 'panda car' as they were known. I had bought sandwiches so I sat in the canteen and had them, had a drink and then prepared myself for the afternoon, 'C' unit were on afternoons.

In 1975 a sub division had police officers working four separate units, 'A' 'B' 'C' and 'D' and that would give cover 24 hours a day, 7 days a week 52 weeks a year, they would work a shift pattern 6.00am x 2.00pm, 2.00pm x 10.00pm and 10.00pm x 6.00am, to supplement those officers a sub division would have possibly sixteen or so resident or permanent beat officers as they were known, they would all have their own allocated area or beat and would work that particular area for many years almost a 'Dixon of Dock Green' type of police, in all my dealings with them they had a mountain of knowledge on all the local individuals, they were expected to know their area well and all of them did.

Most of them are what I describe as experienced police officers who did not want the hassle of driving from place to place in police cars, and dealing with all the many and varied incidents that came with it and the enormous amount of paperwork each incident generated and of course they did not have to work nights either, so I suppose it had its advantages. But at this stage of my career day one, it was most certainly not for me.

I was put with Mike 7, Police Constable Henry Nevin and his area was mainly Kingstanding, an area I knew well as my parents lived there and I had spent many years of my early life there. So by about ten past two on that Monday afternoon 2nd June 1975, I was sat in a police car or panda car as there were more affectionally known waiting for my life as a policeman to begin properly, this was the real world I was entering into.

I remember my first journey as if it was yesterday, we drove out of the police station yard left into Queens Road left into Grosvenor Road right into Aston Hall Road left into Electric Avenue, right onto Brookvale Park Road left in to the Ridgeway heading towards Kingstanding, when

I heard the controller on the police radio say, 'Delta 1, Mike 7, Mike 7.' PC Nevin answered and the controller at Queens Road directed us he said, 'Mike 7, to make the College Arms Licensed House, College Road to a report of an automatic alarm.'

And off we went at last I was going to my first real job as a real policeman. I had waited years for this moment, was I going to arrest my first burglar breaking into the public house sadly no we got there and it was the licensee locking up after the dinner time trade. It made it worse, PC Nevin knew him it was if this was a regular occurrence, 'Hello Tommy.' he said,

'Hello Mr Nevin.' said the licensee.

Well that was it my first job as a police officer in the West Midlands Police was a false alarm.

The rest of the afternoon was pretty quiet, he stopped a vehicle for me so that I could issue the driver with a HORT1, which is a form which requires a driver of a vehicle to produce at a police station of his choice a valid driving licence a valid certificate of insurance and a MOT if needed for the vehicle, the driver had five days from midnight to produce those documents.

He took me to Kingstanding Police Station which was part of the D1 sub division and working from there was a regular office man, a small team of detectives led by a Detective Sergeant and about five of the resident beat officers that covered the area of Kingstanding and Great Barr. PC Nevin drove me back to Queens Road for about 5.00pm and I went home.

I had to prepare for the following day Tuesday as I would be going to work with my own unit and we were on nights, 'D' unit would be my home for the next few years and some people have always asked me what part of the thirty years gave me the most pleasure and the most enjoyment and I have to say my four or so years on 'D' unit at Queens Road would be certainly near the top.

Tuesday arrived, I had never worked a night shift in my life and people were advising me to stay in bed till 2.00pm, well I could not sleep past my normal getting up time so I just lay there till about 10.00am and got up, it is a very strange feeling being at home during the day when most people were at work and then of thinking of going to work when most people were sitting at home watching the television after an evening meal. I was very nervous on that Tuesday, as I was going to meet my new work colleagues for the very first time, were they going to like me, was I going to like them, all these things go through your mind but I would soon be find out.

I got ready and drove to Queens Road and parked my car in the rear car park of the station. I had got rid of the Cortina by now I had sold it to a neighbour, I was now the proud owner of a bright red Ford Consul 2.5L registration number EXC 350L, I locked my car and began the short walk although it seemed like a long walk to the locker room.

I saw other policemen arriving and changing into their uniform, these people were 'D' unit I am sure, one or two of them sort of nodded in my direction and one said, 'You the new pro con?' short for probationary constable.

I told him, 'I was.'

Another said, 'Welcome to 'D' unit.'

I acknowledged them and with helmet in one hand and my brand new pocket book and wooden truncheon in the other I walked in to the parade room.

Some were already sitting down around this rather large dirty looking wooden table which was covered with newspapers, clip boards, bits of uniform, pens, cigarettes and the odd broken ash tray, some were smoking, but we were all waiting for the same thing and that was for the Inspector and Sergeant to enter the room and when they did you all stood up, that's until the Inspector said, 'You can all sit now.'

I was introduced to the rest of the unit by the Sergeant and then he began to read out the postings for the night, he said, 'Mike 1, PC Field with PC Wier, 2.00am refs.'

The room suddenly went quiet and before the Sergeant could say Mike 2, PC Field said with a serious looking face, 'Not another pro con.' looking at me, of course I did not know which way to look, but by the time the rest of the postings had been read out and we all made our way up to the canteen for a quick cup of tea, I quickly found out that PC Field or Tony was one of the units comedians and over the next few weeks and months and years I found Tony to be one of the most competent and courageous policemen I ever met and had the pleasure to work with. I owe him a lot and I learnt so much from him, I was proud to know him and what a sense of humour to go with it.

At the time Queens Road had nine mobile areas Mike 1 through to Mike 9, the area I was to work on with Tony for the next four weeks was Mike 1, this area covered most of Nechells which was a mixture of houses and factories and a small part of Aston where Ansell's Brewery and the HP Sauce factories were.

Each mobile area would normally have two resident beat officers or walkers allocated to it. I remember the first night because it was very quiet I think we had a couple of false burglary alarms at factories and prowlers in the back garden of a house that we never found and that was about it. We drove back into Queens Road at about quarter to six, handed the radios back along with the car keys said our goodbyes and went home.

The following night Wednesday was totally different as I had my first prisoner it was for an offence known as Burglary other Buildings. I was with Tony again on Mike 1 and at about 12.30am we were driving up Nechells Park Road towards Thimble Mill Road and Tony shouted to me, 'Look the shoe shop has been done.'

I looked towards this shop and could see that the front display window was smashed and property which was obviously shoes had been stolen. Tony immediately contacted the controller informed him what we had found and asked the controller to contact the nearest key holder for the shop. In the first instance were both standing outside the shop waiting for the key holder to arrive and we were both having a cigarette.

Just then both of our attentions were drawn to three figures dressed in dark clothing about 200/250 yards away from us walking down Nechells Park Road, the pretty obvious thing that caught our eyes were they appeared to be carrying boxes, perhaps boxes of shoes.

They seemed to have come out of nowhere and onto the pavement they then they disappeared as quickly again, Tony shouted, 'Come on I know where they have gone they will have run into Elliot Street across the waste ground.' we both jumped into the police car and Tony reversed it down Nechells Park Road to the junction of Elliot Street, we could now see the same three figures this time they were on the waste ground and a hell of a lot nearer to us then when we had first saw them.

The police car ground to an halt and without the need for Tony to say anything to me we both ran as fast as our little legs would take us after the three figures who were still carrying boxes of shoes, you would have thought that of the very least they would have dropped the boxes but no they preferred to run with them safely tucked into their arms.

We both ran after them and after about 50 yards or so I made a grab for one of the figures which I now know as a young male and I dragged him to the floor, the boxes of shoes went everywhere but I know he was not going anywhere apart from the back seat of the police car and that is where I took him to, I remember he kept shouting at me, 'I've done nothing, put me down, leave me alone.'

I was catching my breath back standing by the police car when Tony returned with his prisoner and he too was put into the rear of the police car, and both were then arrested on suspicion of burglary, they continued to protest their innocence despite sitting in the back of a police car surrounded with boxes of shoes.

We had two two prisoners for burglary and we had recovered about 15 boxes of shoes, the third person had escaped but I was reliably informed the day staff CID would arrest him as we knew he was the brother of one of our two prisoners.

We were joined by another police officer who would await the arrival of the key holder and to establish exactly what property had been taken and the value of it.

Our two prisoners were taken to Queens Road Police Station to be processed. You drove into a secured area behind the police station which allowed you access to the custody area it would save you walking with your prisoners through the police station and through the front office.

The custody sergeant was in fact also the office sergeant, it was Police Sergeant Lew Kellman, I stood with Tony with our prisoners in front of the sergeant who would now process them, and their details would be recorded on a custody record which in those days was a carbonated A5 sheet of paper, now of course it's all on computer. In turn he would ask the prisoner his details, name, age, address date of birth etc . . . then one by one he turned to Tony and me and we had to give him the place, time, date of arrest and for what for. They were searched and details of their property and cash was recorded on the custody record then placed in a bag with a security tag that was then locked away until they were ready to be bailed or released or of course going straight before the courts.

The two prisoners were both interviewed by Tony and myself, with me doing more listening then talking and it came as no surprise that they eventually admitted the offence; they apparently were going to sell the shoes in the local pubs the following day. The elected to make a written statement which we took down at their dictation and on completion they were both invited to write a caption on the bottom of the statement themselves.

That went *'I have read the above statement and I have been told that I can correct alter or add anything I wish. This statement is true I have made it of my own free will.'*

They both then signed their respective statements, the next part of the process was to complete some forms they were called CRO 74 forms these forms would contain the prisoner details, the offence, the modus operandi, the time date place of the offence, the prisoners habits, employment, schooling, parents, brothers and sisters, hobbies, marks scars and tattoos and loads of information like that.

The forms were also carbonated and you had to type the details onto the forms, using a very old well-worn typewriter. Had I ever used a typewriter before, no, but there was always a first time, one finger at a time very slowly it was going to take me for ever, but I had to learn.

These forms when completed would be submitted with the prisoner's fingerprints and photograph to the Criminal Records Office in New Scotland Yard and copies would be kept in MIDCRO, the Midland Criminal Record Office at Police Headquarters, Lloyd House. I suppose taking my first set of finger prints were the most hilarious thing I had seen for ages, as you could not believe where you get the fingerprint ink, shirt and face were two of the most popular places.

But I managed, you take two sets of fingerprints, if the offence is burglary like ours was then you take a third set on what was called a 'breakers card' this would allow the fingerprint experts at Lloyd House an opportunity to search your prisoners fingerprints against any outstanding fingerprints. If your prisoner was Irish you completed two 'breakers cards.' one for Lloyd House and one for IrishCRO, the Irish Criminal Record Office, again all this is now computerised but it was not in 1975.

A charge sheet was then typed which would contain details of the offence and the sergeant then read the charge over to the prisoner and would then ask the prisoner if he wanted to say anything in relation to the charge, he would then be asked to sign and he was given a copy, it would also contain the court time and date. They were then either bailed from the station or taken to Steelhouse Lane Police Station to remain in custody to appear at court later that morning or the following morning.

There was of course was other paperwork to complete like the crime report which again was a carbonated form and you would obtain the crime number normally from the office sergeant and all the paperwork would now go into the sergeant's basket for checking. I made my pocket book up with the circumstances surrounding the offence and arrest and the Inspector signed it. Even way back in 1975 there seemed to be lots of paperwork to be completed for each time you arrested someone.

The rest of the week went without any further prisoners for me and pretty much nothing exiting happened. I remained with Tony for the rest of the week and I was to be with him in total for four weeks.

I remember putting on my application form when I joined as for one of the reasons I wanted to be a policemen and I said 'Never a dull moment full of interesting things to do and no day the same.' How wrong can you be never mind more was to come. The first set of nights was over we finished them on Monday morning at 6.00am and we were next due on duty on the Wednesday for 2.00pm x

10.00pm shift, where you had to parade at a quarter to the hour.

The Monday I had off was a waste of time I was in bed most of the day but never mind nobody said it was going to be easy I was after all doing the job I had wanted to do.

Nights was a funny time to be working they always use to say the only people out of a night were policemen and criminals, I think that might be a bit unfair to the taxi drivers, bus drivers and delivery drivers who sometimes work through the night. It did effect your life balance at times particularly until you got use to them because you were asleep when most people were awake you would be eating in the middle of the night, which in itself seemed strange having a sandwich of ham and pickle at 3.00am in the morning and you would be at work when most people were asleep. But it is like everything you get used to it.

Wednesday arrived it was if you have never been away and 2.00pm x 10.00pm came with its different problems, early evening rush hour traffic with its normal array of accidents and people arriving home from work finding that their house had been broken into, or to a lesser extent the garden shed. Disputes in shops and the early evening drunk who the licensee wanted out of his public house, you sometimes had the occasional domestic dispute between husband and wife, boyfriend and girlfriend.

Domestic disputes were the worst of all case scenarios because whatever you did was wrong, and although in most cases they were the persons who had called the police when you got there they use to turn round to you and say, 'What has it got to do with you?'

But you had to deal with them as best and as understanding as you could, domestics can be very violent and I am sure you all know of people who have been injured perhaps seriously as a result of a domestic dispute. But you had to tread carefully always listening to both sides of the story or argument but be careful who you listen to or talk to or worse still agree with more because you will then be accused of taking sides.

You were a referee trying to keep the peace. Sometimes an arrest had to be made when the only way to solve it was to remove one of the parties away from the scene and nine times out of ten it was the male. During my time in uniform I went to literally hundreds of domestics and some of them were really violent and most of them were over nothing at all.

I will tell you about one of the first domestic disputes that I went to and it will give you an idea of what can happen and how they can become out of hand very quickly. Mike 4 (PC Dick Marchant) was called to an address in Minstead Road, Erdington, the call was to a domestic dispute between father and sons was in progress, it ended some two hours later with a father his four sons aged between 15 years and 20 years involved in an all-out attack on the police.

The end result was a total of six police officers attended at the house yours truly being one, three police officers being assaulted, with one ending up with a broken wrist and all five members of the family being arrested and they were unceremoniously thrown into the back of a police transit van, we left the wife and mother of four at home even though she was screaming abuse at us doubting that any of us had parents.

What was it all over I have no idea, I had no idea then and over thirty years later I still do not know what it was about. That in police terms was a 'domestic' later in my career I went to another domestic in Kingtsanding, this particular couple were so violent towards each other that they would always send two policemen, although it did not stop them abusing you when you turned up.

One night I got the call, can you go to such and such they are at it again, I arrived quickly followed by another police car and we entered the house by the smashed open front door and what I saw next I could not believe, this was a couple who had lived together for over 30 years and for that period of time they had regularly fought one another.

This particular night was alcohol induced as was normal and as myself and my colleague entered the lounge we saw the male sitting on a chair in front of the television covered head to toe in hot chip fat, his partner had tipped the whole pan of oil over him and it was now starting to solidify and it looked like he was wearing a greasy hat, jumper and trousers, god did it smell, she on the other hand was standing in the kitchen trying to remove a pen knife that was embedded into the back of her head and I will never forget what she said to us, 'What the fuck do you want?'

They were both arrested for a Section 18 wounding on each other and were firstly taken to hospital then to the police station. They survived and fought many another day.

They would never give evidence against one another and when they appeared at the magistrate's court a few days later they were both were bound over for twelve months to keep the peace.

That was just another domestic dispute.

Anyway I was on the 2.00pm x 10.00pm week, some Saturdays were busy because very close to Queens Road was Villa Park and normally every other Saturday there was a home game, now when you were on 2.00pm x

10.00pm you would sometimes be busy from work initiating from the game, mainly theft of and theft from motor vehicles, sometimes you would get involved in the crowd trouble but not often because most matches were covered by the Special Patrol Group and it was never left up to the local police to police.

However, there is always an exception and I was involved on this occasion, the date was 11th October 1977, there was an exhibition match at Villa Park, it was Aston Villa v Glasgow Rangers, which was a Saturday afternoon to remember.

I recall I was working 2.00pm x 10.00pm and Villa were playing Rangers in a friendly game, the Rangers supporters had started to arrive early for the game and when I got to work at about 1.30pm they were actually sitting on the grassed area in front of the police station drinking beer as they were causing no problems, it was decided to let them stay there as they would be going to the match soon.

I was on Mike 5 that day, but because the match was on we were told to keep local in case there were any problems with the crowd, particular outside the ground because by now the SPG were mainly inside of the ground.

The match itself erupted when Villa scored a second goal to go 2-0 up in the match, the Rangers fans ran onto the pitch in their hundreds and they began to head towards the Holte End where the Villa fans were and on their way to the Villa fans they pulled the goal posts down.

The referee of the day Mr Derek Civil decided to abandon the game on 53 minutes and the players were taken off the pitch. It was now up to the police to remove the fans from the ground and get them to different railway stations as soon as they could and naturally away from the area.

But they fought, Villa fans and Rangers fans, the police bought their dogs in and police reinforcements were being bought in from other police stations and we as the afternoon shift helped as much as we could, but I have to say it was chaos. I recall driving down Witton Road heading towards Witton Railway station where other police officers were calling for assistance and as I drove slowly past these Rangers fans some of them threw a giant Rangers flag over the police car, for a few moments I could not see out of any window of the car.

I stopped the car and with the flag completely covering the whole of the police car, I now felt the car being rocked from side to side they were intent on turning the vehicle over with me inside.

I could only think of one thing to do, I am going to put the car into gear and drive forward in the hope that the flag would come off, and that's what I did, I put the car into first gear and moved off very quickly I travelled about 20 yards and the flag came off and as I looked in the rear view mirror I could see some of the Rangers fans just getting up off the floor, had I hit them or had they jumped out of the way when I drove off, I do now know and certainly at the time I did not care.

Public houses were closing, shops were closing, they were causing chaos, I eventually finished my shift at about 3.00am the following morning, and when I arrived at work the following day, the Sunday, some Rangers fans were still sitting on the grass outside the police station but this time they were not drinking any beer they were waiting for their friends to be released from the police station after being arrested the day before.

The end result was over ninety arrested.

Your 2.00pm x 10.00pm week finished on a Sunday night, but the shock was the following day the Monday when you were on 6.00am x 2.00pm, so normally you finished work on the Sunday night at about 10.00pm, you would go for a drink at the Adventurers public house next door to the police station and get home about 11.30pm and go to bed, the following morning you would have to be up at about 4.30am to get to work for parade at quarter to six. It was called a 'quick changeover' I wonder why.

Earlies was for me week three and earlies was completely different to everything else and when I was sitting on parade at quarter to six most people were still in bed was I mad or what. I was still with Tony on Mike 1, I recall we had a quick cup of tea in the canteen got into the police car drove out of Queens Road down Grosvenor Road right into Lichfield Road and left into Bourne Road and when we reached the bottom of Bourne Road with Thimble Mill Lane Tony stopped the police car and switched off, turned to me and said, 'You feeling hungry?'

I said, 'Yes why?'

'Come on then.' He said, and at that we both made a short walk to Brian's Café, and what a wonderful place that turned out to be as it was open from about 6.30am in the morning and would close around three in the afternoon Monday to Saturday. I had my favourite sandwich of sausage and tomato; I have to add it was the first of many.

First watch is a strange shift you cannot really drive around your area too much because people are going to work so the roads are busy and parents taking their children to school, so in truth you would normally park up somewhere conspicuous and wait for the work to come to you. You would not normally wait too long as the popular job on first watch was when people were arriving for work and finding their factories, shop premises had been broken into or perhaps just damage caused. Possibly a caretaker opening the school and finding the school broken into so there were always jobs to be done.

With burglaries you would always inform the controller to put them in the SOCO book, (scene of crime officer's book) and they, the SOCO would in turn decide if it warranted a visit by them in order to see if the alleged suspect had left any tell tail signs. You could get lucky sometimes and the burglar left a fingerprint but we as uniform officers would probably never get a result it would normally go to the CID to deal with and to arrest the burglar.

In relation to burglaries whether at a house, factory or school building you were expected to tell a CID officer about the crime. I remember the first visit I made to the CID office. It was a burglary at a second hand shop on the Lichfield Road in Aston and sometime during the night someone had thrown a brick or something through the front window which caused the glass to smash and it would seem that they had stolen some electrical stuff from the front window.

A lady called Maureen owned it she was a good friend of the CID I was told. I took details of the crime and made a list of the property that had been stolen and when I returned to Queens Road I asked the station sergeant,

PS Kellman the whereabouts of the CID office, he said, 'Top of the stairs on your right and knock on the door and do not go in to the office until they call you they can be a funny lot.'

So off I went I had my details of the crime and now I was going to inform the CID about it. I reached the door of the CID office and as instructed I knocked the door and waited, a few minutes later somebody from inside the office shouted, 'Come in then.'

I opened the door and walked in to be met by five or six detectives laughing hysterically at me and one of them said, 'Look another pro con they never learn.' I had been set up once again but never mind I was learning all the time.

The Sunday of first watch was the last first watch before you entered relief week, this was a week which consisted of two days of 2.00pm x 10.00pm, followed by two days of 6.00am x 2.00pm, followed by your long week end of three days off then you would be back onto nights. That last Sunday was the day the pro con washed the police cars or as many as he could owing to what was happening in the world of policing, a horrible job but the rewards were good as the Inspector would normally let you finish at midday and you could go home, so all in all it was not too bad.

I was now coming into week four of being a policeman was it like I thought it would be, no it was not, but I can assure you it did get better over the next 30 years.

The fourth week came and went without any exciting incidents just run of the mill stuff but now I was to look forward to three days off before I start nights again.

I had now been at Queens Road for four weeks and I now thought that I was becoming part of a team, I suppose the my shift had about ten police constables, three sergeants and one inspector and I seemed to get on with them all which of course is always a good feeling. I suppose I was enjoying it and that is always good if you enjoy your work but I was constantly reminded there were plenty of not so enjoyable jobs to be done and on week five on the Monday of nights I found out the less pleasant side of being a policeman.

On that Monday I was put with another officer PC Dickie George, another very experienced officer and we were allocated Mike 7, this covered a large part of Kingstanding and Great Barr much more residential than the previous area I worked, I suppose it was to get you used of both ends of the sub division from factories to houses. After parade we had a quick cup of tea and started to make our way to Kingstanding just then the radio went and the controller said, 'Delta 1, Mike 7, Mike 7, can you call me from Kingtsanding.'

PC George drove us to Kingstanding Police Station and called the controller from a telephone booth which was situated in the front office. I could see him writing something down and then I heard him say to the controller, 'Is it expected?' I guessed now what it was, it was to be my first insight into what police call 'death messages' basically informing people that someone probably very near to them has died.

It could be a natural death, sudden, suspicious or as a result of an accident they came in a variety of different reasons. PC George said, 'Watch and listen what I do and you can do the next one.' People being people react differently on receipt of such a message.

We drove to the house and walked up to the front door and PC George knocked on the door it was answered by a middle aged lady who instantly said, 'What's happened what's wrong?' The theory is that policemen do not come with good news, they only come with bad news and I think that theory is probably right. PC George delivered the message and we gave the lady as much detail as we could including contact telephone numbers. It was sadly her mother who lived outside the Birmingham area who had been found dead at home. It was a horrible feeling but it was the first of many death messages that I did during my career.

The Tuesday of nights I had another prisoner, I was with PC George on Mike 7 when at about 11.00pm we were directed to Rochells Butchers on Kingstanding Circle where the automatic alarm had just been activated. We arrived within minutes and could see that the glass front door had been smashed in, there was glass everywhere and as we got into the shop we could see a male obviously drunk standing or should I say staggering by the open fridge door stuffing frozen meat into plastic carrier bags.

He was promptly arrested after a bit of a struggle as he did not want to come with us he just wanted to take the meat home and we were in his way but eventually with some general persuasion from both of us we got him into the police car and he was taken to Queens Road to be processed.

I think it was later that same week I had my first visit to the Central Mortuary in Birmingham its virtually next door to the main police station at Steelhouse Lane. There were times when the mortuary would have to be opened outside normal office hours, in instances where a person has been found dead in a public place and there are no obvious suspicious circumstances, in that at first view it appeared to be natural causes and not as a result of violence, then the hospital would not normally except a dead body so you would have to go with the ambulance or meet the ambulance staff at the mortuary.

The role of the policeman was to collect the keys from Steelhouse Lane Police Station and open the mortuary, assist in carrying the body inside then undress the poor victim, bag his property and belongings and take them to Steelhouse Lane for safe keeping until the victim had been positively identified and his or hers relatives informed. Normally the ambulance crew would assist you. The body was then placed on a steel tray and pushed into a very large refrigerator.

A pathologist would then complete a post mortem on the body within the next day or so. It was horrible there must have been about 12 or 14 bodies in there and I am convinced to this day that they were watching us or watching me because they knew I was the pro con. That was my first visit to the mortuary but it certainly would not be my last.

The rest of nights finished without any major incident of note, there were plenty of routine jobs, fights at public houses but they had normally always finished when the police arrived there, reports of prowlers in back gardens, people trying car doors and general drunks shouting and swearing on the way home.

My sixth week consisted of the 2.00pm x 10.00pm shift which I think was my least favourite shift of the lot, you could not really do much in the morning as you had to get something to eat then get ready for work and when you finished and got home the only thing you wanted to do was to go to bed. Anyway the week passed without any real excitement and here I was Monday 14th July 1975 at 5.45am in the morning on parade waiting to go out on my own for the very first time, this is what the training was all about. Parade was taken and PS Jones said, 'PC Wier, Witton Road straight, refs at 9.00 office at 10.00.'

That roughly translated meant you were to walk Witton Road from its start at Witton Island up to where it finished at Six Ways Island, Aston and back again keeping to the main road, you were not expected to wander off into the side roads unless you were sent or you had a valid reason and the controller would know where you were. You took your refreshment break at 9.00am and you would then assist or relieve the office staff at 10.00am to allow one of them to take their refreshment. In truth you answered the telephone and dealt with people at the front counter and made the sergeant a cup of tea.

Witton Road was a mixture of shops and terraced houses and three public houses. To get to Witton Road from the police station was a fifteen minute walk that took you past Villa Park the home of Aston Villa Football Club, the two main tea spots on Witton Road or somewhere to hide when it was pouring with rain were the security office at the IMI Kynock works and an old lady we would always refer to as Ma.

Situated halfway up Witton Road was Lodge Road where at number 14 Lodge Road, Ozzy Osbourne founder of the world renowned rock group Black Sabbath was born in 1948.

A little bit of history now Ozzy was born John Michael Osbourne on 3rd December 1948, he had two brothers and three sisters, his parents both worked, his dad at the GEC Witton and his mom at Lucas, Farm Street, at the time both very large Birmingham companies.

Ozzy then formed Black Sabbath in 1969 and never looked back he now of course spends most of his time in Los Angeles.

Anyway back to Witton Road as a policeman you walked slowly and tried to be as polite as you can, but in the real world even back in 1975 not too many people would stop and chat with you, sometimes the best you could get was a nod of the head. I walked past the electrical shop that Leslie Smith the former Villa player owned, he had played in their historic win in the FA Cup Final of 1957 over Manchester United

I suppose it must have been about half eight by now I was near to the junction with Trinity Road when a woman stopped me and asked for help. She informed me that during the night somebody had stolen her son's pedal cycle from the back garden, my first job.

I proceeded to take all the details of the cycle I could think of including the best description I could get, because you had to fill in a cycle descriptive form because all found cycles or cycles handed in to the police would end up at the cycle store at Digbeth Police Station, and the form that you gave to the loser of the cycle allowed him or her access to the all the cycles held there to see if they could find their missing or stolen cycle. I took down that many details of the cycle I think I could recognise it myself.

Anyway job done and off she walked back along Trinity Road but not before I informed her that I would drop off the cycle form to allow her to go to Digbeth, by this time I was walking back to the station for my refreshments.

At 10.00am I was in the front office and an ideal time to fill in the crime report and cycle descriptive forms both of which were carbonated. Off I went, I was writing offence as reported, easy Theft of pedal cycle, next came time date stolen, time date reported and by who, losers details, and place where stolen. I had a problem I had spent so much time taking down the details of the cycle I did not ask who the woman her name or the name of her son or more importantly where she and her son lived.

I looked in the direction of PS Kellman and he looked at me and said, 'Got a problem son?'

I told him what I had forgotten to do; I explained to him I did not know even where the woman lived.

He said, 'Don't worry, just get yourself back down there to where she first approached you and start knocking on some doors you are bound to find her eventually.'

I remember that she was wearing slippers so she would not have walked too far and when we parted she was walking along Trinity Road towards Villa Park, not bad only about 60 houses to call at, so where do I start well I will start at the beginning of Trinity Road with its junction with Witton Road. What would I say to people when they answered the door I know, 'I am investigating the theft of a pedal cycle from a house further down the road where the offenders obviously climbed over the back gate and into the garden, I wonder if you saw or hear anything it was during darkness?'

I began knocking doors after I had knocked about six doors when an elderly lady answered the door I explained to her what I was doing and she said to me, 'The poor lad he has only just had the cycle they must have got over the fence or something.' and pointed to the last house of a row of four further down the road, I thanked her and walked straight to the house that she had indicated to me and I knocked on the door, the door opened and standing there was the same woman who told me about her sons cycle about three hours earlier I said, 'Just wanted to drop the form in on my way round.'

'Many thanks.' she said, and off I went and continued on my first day on my own, I think the only other job I had that day was when a lorry driver stopped and asked the way to a local factory which I was able to help with.

And that was it day one complete.

Over the next few months I walked Witton Road, Lichfield Road, Slade Road, Hawthorn Road, Kingstanding Circle and the worst walk of the lot Tyburn Road. The thing is when you are walking you do not get sent to many jobs so as far as I was concerned I was not really learning much, the jobs you had were minor and not very interesting. But I was told this from day one it will get better and it will get more interesting just be patient.

There were other roles as a probationer that you always got, one was traffic duty, we had two major traffic junctions, one Kingtsanding Road at Aldridge Road by the Boars Head Public House in Great Barr and the other at Gravelly Hill North with its junction with Kingsbury Road in Erdington. There were many times when I had to put my white gloves on and direct traffic and you are not really shown what to do, you are normally told once and you get on with it. What I will say is that the many times I did traffic duty I never caused an argument between drivers or more importantly never caused an accident.

The other job I did not like in fact I hated it was called 'hospital watch' this is when someone who is either in the custody of the police that is when they have already been arrested but have been taken ill, or the other time is when they are a suspect in a crime and as soon as the hospital say he is fit to be discharged you would arrest him.

But it was so very boring because the person lying in the bed never spoke to you in case he incriminated himself, his steady flow of relatives and visitors did not speak with you because they knew in due course you would be more than likely be arresting their relative or friend who was lying in the bed, nurses occasionally spoke but they were always too busy and doctors never spoke.

All sorts of things went through your mind, what if I want to use the toilet, and if I do use the toilet what happens if he escapes, so you would sit there for hours with your legs sometimes crossed until the next shift sent someone to relieve you, frightened to go to the toilet or indeed to have a drink because if you did that you would need the toilet. So I would count hospital watch as one of the boring things as a probationer constable that you were expected to do.

What did I want to do, of course I wanted to drive a police car every policeman does, so I kept asking my Inspector for a one day's unit beat vehicle course and if successful I could drive police cars up to a certain cc, panda cars as they called them. I got my wish and in November 1975 I went to Chelmsley Wood Police Station for the day's course. It went well there was some classroom work where they explained the do's and the don'ts about driving police vehicles trying to instil into you that it was a marked car everybody knew it was a police car and everybody would be staring at you when you were in the car.

When to use the blue light and siren, and how to stop cars safely and correctly. I then went and sat in a police car and drove one for the first time with a police driving instructor sitting next to me to monitor me, I drove out of the police station and I drove around Chemsley Wood for a little over an hour then it was back to the classroom.

At the end of the day the instructor told me I had passed the day's course and could now drive police cars up to a certain cc, and he handed me a small card the size of a credit card and that was to be my authorisation to drive it was called a grade 4 pass. I was over the moon now when policeman were missing off my shift if they were on annual leave or on a training course I might I just might get the chance to drive.

I did not have to wait long about two weeks later one of the policemen on our unit had reported sick with a heavy cold, so one day on parade PS Jones said, 'PC Wier, Mike 5, 7 o'clock refs.' and I was raring to go I collected a radio and a set of car keys and walked into the rear yard to make sure everything was in order with the police car.

I am so sad I even remember the make and registration number of the car, it was an Austin Allegro registration number HOF 832N at the time one of British Leyland's finest cars. I had my police radio, I had my A to Z street guide and off I drove into the world of Mike 5 certainly an area I knew very little about, I suppose it was midway between Nechells and Kingstanding it was mainly an area called Perry Common a particular large residential area of the sub division. It was also the quietest of the mobile areas and I found that out the next three days I hardly had a job and the one's I did have were minor but never mind I was driving.

The following week I was back on nights and back walking as the policeman had returned from sick leave. Christmas 1975 and New Year came and went I was driving a police car now and again but all this time my wife was still not that happy with my new chosen career,

I think it was mainly when I was on nights that she felt the most vulnerable and lonely and then she suggested something I had never thought of she said, 'I want a dog.' Now I had never ever owned a dog but my wife had when she was living at home her parents so my view was if you want one, go ahead have one it will keep you company.

So we went out and bought our first dog a West Highland Terrier who we named Dee.

During the early part of 1976 I was getting traffic duty at Kingstanding Road at Aldridge Road quite often; we actually called it Boars Head traffic for short, as there was a pub of that name very close to where the traffic post was. The traffic post was on first watch only so you could get it seven times in a month if you were unlucky.

To get there you walked from Queens Road probably about 2 ½ miles in distance, you did the traffic post from 8.00am until 9.00am, 9.15am, then you were expected to walk back to the station, then you would have refreshments and also to cover the front office. Then one day I was on the traffic post it never stopped raining and I got back to the station drenched through I always remember people telling me a 'good policeman never gets wet' well I must have been a right bad policeman because I was soaked it was dripping off me. It felt as if I had fallen in a canal and just got out.

I finished my refreshments and dried out but I was still shivering I thought I will take a crafty look at the daily posting sheet which I knew after parade was kept in the controller's office as he would need to know where each of the policemen on duty were posted to. You shouldn't look at but our controller at the time PS Bill Twamley did not mind. I needed to know if I was on Boars Head traffic the following day so I could get some warmer and more suitable clothing on, so I picked the posting sheet up and as I was looking at it PS Jones walked in and demanded to know why I was looking at the posting sheet, I told him my reason and he said, 'PC Wier, not only are you doing it tomorrow but you will be doing it for the next three months, alright.'

I looked at him and said, 'Yes Sergeant.'

He then walked out leaving me holding the posting sheet and feeling a complete idiot. And I will tell you something he was right, every first watch for the next three months I did Boars Head traffic even the motorists were getting to know me. I never looked at the posting sheet again.

I was still awaiting my first Crown Court appearance I had been to the Magistrates Court several times with fairly minor things like traffic offences all the way up to a not guilty drunk but Crown Court was so much more different, there was a Judge, barristers, solicitors and of course the jury made up of 12 members of the public. But my time was not far away and the incident that was to lead to my first Crown Court appearance had occurred just before Christmas 1975.

I was on nights and was walking Witton Road it was about 11.00pm when the controller directed me to some waste ground near to the Bulls Head Public House, on Birchfield Road apparently an ambulance had been called to a man found collapsed with head injuries. I suppose I was about five minutes away so I decided to jog to the scene carrying my helmet as I ran, I was aware that Mike 3, PC Mick Martin was on his way as well. As I was steadily running toward the waste ground I heard that Mike 3 had arrived and was calling for Scenes of Crime Officers and a Police Photographer to be informed.

Now both SOCO and the police photographer had to be called out from home so it had to be serious. I reached the waste ground and saw both PC Martin and two ambulance bending over this male, who was lying on his back on waste ground next to a busy road I walked over and looked at him and I felt sick he was covered in blood particularly round the face, head and upper body it was clear he had taken an almighty beating about the head and face. He was trying to speak but he was very quiet but what could be made out was that he was walking home when he was attacked by two or three young white men.

Just then another police car pulled up it was a brown coloured Austin Allegro and a tall bearded man with slightly receding hair, wearing a smart suit and an overcoat got out of the car it was of course the night CID man, DC Harrison, I had never seen him before but he apparently worked from Sutton Coldfield on the D2, I later found out that the night detective covered both D1 and D2, on this occasion it was a D2 detective.

By this time the ambulance crew had put the injured man into the ambulance and the night CID man said to me, 'You will have to go with the ambulance and the injured man to the hospital.'

'Why?' I asked.

'In case he dies.' Was the reply.

So I did as I was told. The ambulance drove at speed to the Birmingham General Hospital in Steelhouse Lane and arrived within minutes and I just followed the ambulance men into the hospital as they carried this badly injured male on a stretcher, I did not really know what to do but I was happy in the thought that the night CID said he would be along in a few minutes. I got so far when I was stopped by a nurse who informed me that I could not go any further and would have to go and wait in the police room for the time being.

The police room was a very small untidy room near to the accident and emergency department towards the front of the hospital, it contained a desk, seat, phone, kettle, a couple of dirty looking cups and a small metal filing cabinet with police paperwork in there and that was about it. So here I went and waited, I telephoned the controller and kept him informed of what was happening at the hospital and there I waited not knowing what was going to happen next.

It seemed like hours but I am certain it was not a nurse then came in and handed me a brown paper bag with the man's clothing and personal belongings in there and she asked me, 'Has the gentleman's next of kin or family been told?'

I had not got a clue nobody had told me anything so I said, 'I would find out.' so I made a quick call to the controller who confirmed that the man's wife and son were on their way to the hospital. I informed the nurse of this and enquired how the man was and all the nurse would tell was that he has suffered serious head injuries which are now being operated on. I felt so sorry for him I did not know the circumstances of the incident but what I did know was that there was an elderly Asian man lying in the hospital badly injured.

I carried on waiting by this stage I suppose it is about 4.00am in the morning and I am getting hungry but my sandwiches were lying peacefully in my sandwich box in my locker at Queens Road and I never did get to eat them.

Just then the door to this very little room opened and there like something out of a cow boy film stood the night detective, he said, 'I have spoken with the doctor and have been told that the old chap with live but it is still a good section18 wounding, or maybe even an attempt murder, so when you finish here come back to Queens Road to the CID office we will need to speak.'

I said, 'Alright then I'll see you later.' and off he went into the night just like the midnight cowboy the only thing missing was the horse all he had was a dirty brown Allegro.

A policeman from first watch came to replace me at the hospital and by 6.20am or so I was back in the CID office at Queens Road where the same detective was sitting at a desk, overcoat and suit jacket off, tie undone and smoking like a trooper and sat with his head bowed over a very old and ancient looking typewriter. 'Right' he said, 'I am doing the night note for the day staff CID, can you get some brown paper from that cupboard lie it flat on that spare desk and lay out all the clothes we need them to dry out.'

I did what was asked and then completed an exhibit label for each and every item of this man's property and each item had its own separate identification number allocated beginning with NW/1 and so on.

The detective asked me to complete a witness statement which I wrote out there and then and left with him. Just then the cleaner walked in and said 'Tea anybody?' The detective had a cup but I declined I just wanted to go home it was about 8.00am now and I was getting tired and feeling hungry, I also felt dirty being in that hospital and messing with the man's blood stained clothes. Shower and bed that's what I wanted. I felt quite confident in what I was doing and after a few minutes I said, 'I think I have finished.'

The detective said, 'Thanks you can go home now but let day staff CID have your inconvenient dates as this will go to the Crown Court I am sure.'

It was now the summer of 1976 and what a hot summer it was, I had for many years suffered with hay fever bought on by the pollen in the air and what a sight I must have looked as I walked along the roads, sweat dripping off me in the heat of the sun, a helmet perched on my head like a ton weight, my constant sneezing, eyes watering and nose dripping like a tap, I must have looked a force to be dealt with and when I took my helmet of it always left a red line on my forehead which took ages to go.

During this long hot summer I had plenty of opportunities to drive police cars what with officers taking annual leave and various courses, I was actually getting a week here and a week there so I was getting through plenty of work and was having my fair share of prisoners mainly for crime, including theft, damage, burglary and theft of motor vehicles or take without consent as there were more commonly known. I was putting through a few summons's like parking on the approach to a zebra crossing, parking on double yellow lines, no tax, no MOT and general things like that.

But I still wanted that Crown Court appearance and I was still waiting for it. I did arrest prisoners for serious crime like assault, wounding's and burglary dwelling houses but once you had taken your prisoner to the station the CID would normally continue with the investigation, to allow you to get back out on the road where of course you should be.

In October 1976 I was back at Ryton for a refresher course for two weeks again it was a residential course. It was to give you an input to any new legislation that had come into force and generally to see how after 18 months as a policeman you were coping. It was a fairly relaxed course and you were treated like a grownup which was a pleasant change from the previous courses.

With the course now completed it was back to Queens Road. Christmas 1976 was with us and our unit had arranged a Christmas function at the Night Out restaurant and club in Birmingham, Dickie Henderson was the main cabaret star that night, I wonder how many of you readers remember him. He was described as a singer, dancer and all round entertainer and I have to admit without hopefully sounding too old fashioned that he was good. It was a good night for the unit and their respective wives, husbands and partners.

We were now heading into 1977 I was getting more and more confident and I was coming up to two years' service which meant I would no longer be a probationer constable. Then it came the telephone call to say I was to be at Birmingham Crown Court, court number 5, at 10.00am in the morning to give evidence in the case of the man who was savagely beaten up many, many months before, the CID officer who dealt with the case had charged three local men with Section 18 Wounding and Making an Affray.

I was to give my evidence on the Thursday the fourth day of the trial, the victim had given his evidence for nearly two days and then a doctor who treated him at the hospital gave his evidence, until we are called to give evidence as a potential witness we cannot go into court so instead we just hang about outside the court and of course not talking to anyone else who was involved in the case and who also was likely to be called to give evidence.

At just after 10.30am on that Thursday an usher came out of Court 5 and shouts, 'PC Wier please.' and in I went. Court 5, I had seen the court before when it was empty but now of course it was full of people, at the front was the Judge who seemed to sit ten feet in the air, then in front of him, the court clerk, then there was two rows of barristers and solicitors for all parties in the court, then the dock area where the three men who had been charged sat and next to them were two policemen.

I walked slowly to the witness box, stood straight up and took the oath **'I swear by almighty god that the evidence I give shall be the truth the whole truth and nothing but the truth'** Nigel Wier, Police Constable 3055 with the West Midlands Police.

The first barrister to stand up is the prosecution barrister, the good guy as we call him and he normally just leads you through your statement and evidence as he did with me, when he has finished the second barrister will stand up and he would be representing the people charged with the offence, in this case we had three charged so we had three barristers one for each defendant and each asked me questions.

There were no problems and I just reiterated what I had done that night. The Judge can ask questions but in my case he did not, then the prosecution barrister stood up once more and said, 'Thank you officer you can stand down now.' and I walked from the witness box and out of court. My God was I glad that was over my first taster of the Crown Court it was quite frightening and I was extremely nervous but I had got through it and over the years there was plenty more appearances at the Crown Court to follow and anyone including police officers who tell you that they are not nervous when giving evidence at the Crown Court are liars, believe me.

February 1977 I was posted to the CID office at Queens Road for two weeks as part of my probationary training. So I turned up on the Monday morning not this time in uniform but in a suit, I remember it was actually my wedding suit complete with waist coat. If nothing else I looked the part. My first taste of the CID what would I think of it and would I enjoy it or like some other uniform officers would say about the CID is that all they do is sit and talk football and then go to the pub, well I was now to find out.

Of course two weeks was not a long time so you were not going to get heavily involved in an investigation but it would give you an insight to what they do and what work they investigate, I was convinced I would enjoy it. Their shifts were strange you would work either a 9.00am x 5.00pm or 9.00pm x 1.00pm, finish and go home and then return to complete your shift working from 6.00pm x 10.00pm and that was called a 'split shift.'

Not a favourite of mine because when I went home I did not really want to come back to work not many people would.

However I loved the two weeks it went so quick I went to court with them, visited serious crime incidents, took several witness statements from both witnesses and victims of crime and of course posed in the local pubs in my three piece suit.

Of an evening towards the end of the split shift you would always go for a drink to wind down I was told that's where the CID get most of their information from most people talk more after a couple of pints, you were actually drinking in the same pubs as people you had previously dealt with for crime. I sensed an attraction to this type of work in actual fact as early as February 1977 I had decided that I wanted to be a detective, but I had a long way to go yet.

After two weeks it was back to the real thing I was on nights on the Monday on parade PS Jones said, 'PC Wier, Lichfield Road, refs at 3.'

Lichfield Road began at Spaghetti Junction or to give it its proper name the Gravelly Hill Interchange, it is one of the biggest road junctions in the world and it was built in 1972 it currently carries in excess of 200,000 motor vehicles a day, it is a massive piece of engineering and from the air it looks like a bowl of spaghetti with all the different roads criss-crossing each other, hence it got the name Spaghetti Junction.

The other end of Lichfield Road finished at Aston Cross which was a cross roads, it had Aston Road North which would take you into Birmingham City Centre, Rocky Lane that took you into Nechells and Park Lane that took you into Newtown, incidentally about a mile from where I worked at Castle Joinery all those years ago.

On the one corner of Aston Cross was the Aston Cross pub which incidentally is still there today, and on the other corner stretching down Lichfield Road was the famous HP Sauce factory that was originally built in 1924 but sadly closed in 2007 and had now been demolished.

In between Spaghetti Junction and Aston Cross I suppose you had a walk of some two miles that took you past the famous Ansell's Brewery that incidentally was built in 1903 and closed in 1981, you had six public houses, some terraced houses, a few shops and Salford Park with its massive lake that encouraged fisherman, a railway station and last but not least Thompsons Butchers with its own abattoir on site. If you were really lucky at about 4.00am in the morning you could hear the pigs screaming as they were taken from Lorries into the rear of the butchers shop to meet their death.

By March 1977 I had completed my two years as a probationer and I was glad to have done so, I was no longer the pro con on the shift we now had two new pro cons, who by the way became very good friends of mine and I worked with them several times during my career particularly on the CID and even in the same office.

7th June 1977 was a day to remember for me for all the wrong reasons we were on nights and this particular day was the Queens Silver Jubilee day, the Queen had now been our head of state for 25 years, the day was to be full of celebrations, there were to be street parties, parties in pubs and clubs and parties in houses or anywhere that people could find to hold a party. I even remember various roads throughout the West Midlands area were closed off to traffic to allow the street parties to go ahead.

Of course parties mean beer and I will explain that further in the chapter, anyway we were on nights and it was a Tuesday night, on parade PS Jones said, 'PC Wier, Mike 8, refs if you can get them at 3.'

We were obviously expecting a very busy night and I must say we were not disappointed. Mike 8 was the furthest mobile away from Queens Road and it covered the far end of Kingstanding near to the boundary with Sutton Coldfield. It also bordered the adjoining division the 'H' division, Aldridge. It had with it plenty of houses and plenty of pubs.

Parade finished and the Inspector told us there would be no time for tea, he wanted all mobiles out of the station and on their respective areas as soon as possible that sounded ominous to me no doubt trouble was expected. Pubs that would normally shut at 10.30pm were allowed to stay open a lot longer, nearly every road you turned down was full of people in the street having a party and consuming very large amounts of alcohol, and I was steadily driving around my area praying there would be no trouble and praying everybody would sooner or later go home peacefully.

From the start of the shift at ten o'clock you were sent from one job to another, fighting here, drunks there, a disturbance here, a domestic there, we had several pub fights and every incident appeared to be alcohol related, but what I will say is that in most cases when you arrived they had normally calmed down and in a lot of cases all the people wanted was to shake your hand, strange I know, but true.

The thing was you let a lot go that normally you would have arrested for, because if you started arresting people for drunk or shouting and swearing in the street, you would then be taking yourself off the street to deal with the prisoner so instead of nine mobiles we would now be reduced to eight mobiles, thus making the job more difficult for the policemen still out there so unless it was absolutely necessary you would not arrest but advise, because you knew eventually they would all go home.

However saying all that my day or should I say night ended at 2.30am in the morning, and I had no choice in doing what I did. I was called to a domestic dispute in Longford Road, Kingstanding, the controller gave me the number and off I went I was at Kingstanding Circle so it took me less than two or three minutes to get to the house, I stopped outside the house and before getting out the police car I informed the controller that I had arrived at the scene, I got out the car and could see lights on in the house both downstairs and upstairs, I walked down the path and knocked on the front door my world was about to change.

The door opened and standing there was a middle aged man obviously drunk, holding a rather large kitchen knife with a blade about ten inches long in his right hand, he was swaying from side to and could hardly stand upright and as I moved towards him urging him to put the knife down he moved towards me and there we were face to face and nose to nose with each other, and with him pressing this rather large knife against my breast bone, my first thought was that I do not really want to be here.

I began talking with him trying to say all the right things but he wasn't listening he seemed quite intent to spend all night there, we were like a pair of statues and I thought where the hell was his wife, as the initial call was to a domestic between husband and wife and she had made the call.

I am stood here thinking with all these parties around somebody was bound to walk past us and say something or better still see this idiot with a knife in his hand but no nobody passed and it was all quite apart from I could hear singing and shouting in the distance.

Now I know the controller would call me up at some stage if he heard nothing from me, but that literally could be ten minutes away, and I did not fancy the wait, so thinking on my feet, I thought I had my police radio in my right hand at that time there were 'Burndept' radios and they had a red button on the top which we pressed down to speak, so if I press the button down and start a conversation about something with this man perhaps the controller would realise something was wrong, and send another mobile to me.

You never know, if I talked long enough hopefully this man would get bored and go back inside his house, anyway pressing the button down was my first choice and I knew then I was going to use my radio at least twice.

The first time I moved the radio so the red button was facing the man and the radio was by my right hand trouser pocket and off I went, I pressed the button down and began to speak, I was telling the man to put the knife down, did he know that you don't point knives at policemen, why don't you go back inside the house, I was just talking about anything that came into my head but I did keep mentioning the knife.

This man kept reminding me that he hated all policemen and several times he doubted that I had parents, I have to say I was not particularly very keen on him. I kept releasing the button to hear if the controller was speaking to other mobiles, I thought I have been here ages and any longer and the milkman will be here.

But then I heard the magic words from the controller, 'Delta I, Mike 6, Mike 6, phone me now.' this of course is a time before mobile telephones so Mike 6 would need to find a public call box, and then he would radio in the phone number to the controller who would then telephone Mike 6 at the telephone box, I know it sounds long winded but it did work honest. I waited and waited still trying to talk this man out of being stupid.

Then after about four or five minutes, it seemed like hours, I could see out of my left eye PC Phil Dewan walking in front of the windows of the houses to the left of me and towards me, I still wondered when and how this would be sorted but PC Dewan was one of the more senior officers on the shift and I was in no doubt he had a plan even if I did not.

PC Dewan got to about two houses from me and shouted at the top of his voice, 'Hey you.' My knifeman was totally startled as to who was shouting at him and he suddenly looked to the right from where this shouting had come from, his body began to move to the right and with it his right arm and with his right arm went the large looking knife, and this gave me the opportunity to use my radio for a second time, I swung the radio round bought it level with the top of my head and bought it down as fast and as hard as I could and I proceeded to hit this man's right forearm, with all the power I could muster and at the same time screaming at him, 'Drop the knife, drop the knife, damn you.'

And as I hit him the knife fell to the floor and this man now suddenly within seconds had two policemen firmly on top of him as all three of us fell to the floor together.

He was dragged unceremoniously along the floor by his arms to the waiting police car and literally thrown into the back head first and he landed half on the back seat and half on the floor behind the front seats. I locked the door leant against the vehicle with PC Dewan and I remember we both had a cigarette,

PC Dewan informed the controller that one male was coming in for drunk.

You would never guess that my radio still worked after that and whilst we were finishing our cigarette a woman came out of the house and demanded to know what I was doing with her husband. I did not go into all the details I just said he was under arrest for being drunk and he would go before the court in the morning. She sort of yawned, turned round picked up the knife and went back in the house.

The prisoner was taken to Queens Road and processed, as I was to take the case at court myself later that morning, so when I had finished with him he went to the cell for a sleep and I went home for a sleep, we would next meet one another at 10.00am at the magistrate's court.

At the court he was bought up into the dock from the cells downstairs and the charge was put to him by the clerk of the court who said to him, 'At 2.45am this morning you were drunk and disorderly in Longford Road, Kingstanding how do you plead Guilty or Not Guilty?'

He replied, 'Guilty sir.'

I was called to the witness box where after swearing the oath I gave the brief circumstances of what had occurred and when I had finished the Stipendiary magistrate told him to stand up and said, 'Have you anything to say firstly to the policeman and secondly to this court?'

He said, 'I am sorry, I was drunk.' and he looked towards the floor.

He was fined £25.00 and that was it, what a Silver Jubilee.

I was driving more and more regularly now and I normally got Mike 5 which was an area known as Perry Common it was sort of midway between Aston and Kingstanding and was mainly residential and I was enjoying every minute of it. The next thing of note was in the autumn of 1977 the Fire Brigade went on strike, it was the first national fire brigade strike ever known, it was a Labour Government at the time and when the fire brigade walked out the government bought in the army, and the army bought with them their own fire engines and they were called the 'Green Goddesses.'

To give them their correct name they were a Bedford RLHZ self-propelled pump, it was a fire engine that had previously been used by Auxiliary Fire Service and later used by Armed Forces, they had apparently been built in the 1950's.

The fire brigade had pickets outside most of the fire stations and for some reason not known to me was that the army did not or were not allowed to drive the normal fire engines. On the 'D' division we had the army and their green goddesses based at St Georges Barracks in Sutton Coldfield which was on the D2 and on the D1 we had them based in the grounds of Fentham Road children's home in Erdington.

Each base had attached to them a police motor cyclist and when the army had to respond to an emergency, then the police motor cyclist would not only escort the army with their green goddesses to the incident but naturally he had to show them where the emergency was as most of the army personnel were not from the Birmingham area.

The strike went on for many weeks and I believe that the army and their green goddesses performed admirably. I recall one such incident involving them and it was a report of a car on fire in Electric Avenue in Witton, I was on Mike 5 and I was also asked to attend the incident as it had probably been set on fire deliberately and as such was a criminal act that needed investigation. I arrived and saw that the army had just finished putting the fire out so I began to walk towards them as I needed the name of the officer in charge as I needed this for my report.

I suppose I was about 20 feet away and you know when something is going to happen and you cannot do much about it well low and behold how right I was, the one holding the hose turned round faced me, smiled and decided he wanted to hose down a policeman which he promptly did, fortunately for me the hose was not on full pressure but it soaked me and the four soldiers standing there began to laugh as did the police motor cyclist, me I did not know whether to laugh or cry. I decided to laugh with them and then I crawled back into my police car drove to Queens Road and dried off as best as I could.

What I would say greatly in their favour is that they did a mean breakfast, and you were always welcome the food was good and plentiful, and I always think of those breakfasts when I hear that famous saying 'the army always marches on its stomach,' and it was right once you had managed to eat one of their breakfasts, you did not want to eat anything else for the rest of the day.

They were a fantastic bunch of people doing a very difficult job to the best of their ability but you could never replace a fully trained fireman.

CHAPTER FOUR
CID or Uniform

It was the beginning of 1978 now and I was getting itchy feet I had completed nearly three years in the police. I had done the walking and had done the driving but I now wanted something different, a new challenge I did not want to be a walker or a police car driver all my service.

But what could I do I had only known uniform and a very short two weeks on the CID but I was years away from the CID, so I put a report in to my Inspector, Inspector Ron Chapman asking for an attachment with the Special Patrol Group, the SPG as they were known, they would work a police van with a sergeant and seven policemen and cover all different sorts of disorder throughout the force area.

They would also cover the football matches at grounds in the West Midlands and do not forget we had six football teams, Aston Villa, Birmingham City, West Bromwich Albion, Wolverhampton Wanders, Coventry

City and Walsall so you would be covering at least two matches a week.

The Inspector called me in to his office and queried why if I loved the CID so much why was I was putting in for another uniform post, I explained that I had had three years' service and I did not think that the CID would even look at me as I was still too young in service for them. He suggested that I just put in for a three month attachment, that way I could see if I still liked the CID work or not and they, the CID could see if they might want me as a detective in the years to come and that is what he advised me to do, so I went with him and submitted a report asking for a three month attachment to the CID the report for the SPG was filed, in the paper bin.

I waited for only about a week or so and then I was told to report to the Detective Chief Inspectors office for an interview as to my suitability and of course it allowed them to see if I was up for the role. I knew working for the CID; my normal hours of work would go out the window because when you were on the CID you were expected to work all sorts of different hours including large amounts of overtime.

I met with Detective Chief Inspector Joe Frazier and Detective Inspector Roy Bunn and was given a short interview in which they asked loads of questions, as to why I wanted the attachment, what the CID did, why would I make a good detective, why should we have you on attachment, what have you got to offer us, what do you want from us, I answered every question as truefully as I could, and further told them that in due course I wanted to be a detective and a three month attachment to me was the first stage of reaching that goal.

I was told later in the day that I had been accepted for the attachment and was to start the following Monday in February 1978. I got home and told the wife and the best way to put it was she was very happy for me because she knew I wanted to become a detective.

Things were going well for us we had not long found out that my wife was pregnant and I had got my attachment to the CID, life was extremely good.

I turned up on the Monday morning this time wearing not my wedding suit but a new suit that I had bought off the peg from John Collier, a tailors in Erdington High Street and here I was in an office surrounded by detective's, I first met with my DS, Brian Davis who was going to look after me for the next three months and I was introduced to the detectives that I was going to work with.

First things first I was shown the tea making facilities and by ten past nine had made my first cup of tea for those who wanted one, I found out later that a lot of detectives would go out of the station and to a local café for breakfast.

I was allocated a chair and desk and almost immediately became involved there was a report of an aggravated burglary overnight. It was where four men had broken into an old ladies house in Erdington and threatened her with a knife and had stolen some of her personal belongings, including jewellery, a couple of rings and other bits and bobs.

One of the detectives in the office had just received a telephone call from one of his informants.

An informant otherwise known as 'sarbut' 'snout' or 'grass' is a person who gives information to the police about people committing crime in exchange for favour from the police and that favour would normally mean money.

Anyway as a result of this telephone call, myself and three of the detectives ran downstairs from the CID office jumped into the CID car and drove to a second hand shop situated on the Lichfield Road, the detective whose informant it was, left the vehicle and went into the shop, the three of us remained in the car. He was gone about five minutes and came out to tell us the suspects had disappeared but not before selling two rings for £40.00.

The owner of the shop allowed us to keep the jewellery to try and identify it and of course she had made a record of the names and addresses of the persons who had sold her the jewellery, but in most cases both the name and address were false and made up. The address given by the suspects in this case was near to the aggravated burglary so you never know. The names given by the suspects were not known by any of the detectives.

Decisions were made, the one detective returned to Queens Road to liaise with the collator, the collator being the officer who quite literally collated all information coming into the police station about criminals and crime effecting our sub division, I was sent with the jewellery to the old ladies house and the other two detectives went off in search of the informant who had first made the telephone call.

What happened next is what happens on the television in programmes like 'The Sweeney' I knocked on the door and a man answered who introduced himself as the ladies son and I was invited in, I told them the reason for my visit and showed them the jewellery that we had recovered which consisted of a wedding ring, a dress ring and a couple of non-descript bracelets, in moments her little eyes lit up, 'They're mine.' she said, I needed to know how she had recognised them, she then showed me a picture of herself and her late husband at a dinner and dance in the early seventies and on her left hand were the bracelets, the dress ring and wedding ring, she was over the moon and so was I.

I sat down and wrote out a witness statement outlining firstly the offence itself, then the identification of the jewellery and included in the statement was reference to the picture and I took the picture with me as an exhibit and part of the evidence and I left the house saying that we would be in touch.

I walked out the front door and radioed the controller as I wanted a lift back to the police station, I waited a few moments and the CID car pulled up with two of the other detectives in, they quickly informed me that they have two suspects in custody so get in we need a de-brief at the station. The two in custody had been put in by the informant as being on the burglary but not having the knife so the knifeman was still outstanding.

We got back to the CID office and the four of us sat there and discussed the plan of action, and we then split into two teams in order to go and interview our two suspects, it was barely midday and we had so far achieved so much, remember this was only my first day on the CID.

The interviews went well, both youths in custody were 17 years old and they readily admitted being involved in the burglary at the old ladies house and stealing the jewellery and selling it, but both adamantly denied having a knife or even seeing a knife, they both then elected to make written statements under caution admitting their part and saying that they were sorry.

The two youths were returned to separate cells, and the four of us had a further de-brief in the CID office.

We still had a lot of work to do, we still had two suspects outstanding, we still had property outstanding and we still had a knife outstanding so we could not yet rest on our laurels just yet.

The detectives went out and spoke with their informants, the collators were re-visited and now we were looking for friends or associates of the two we had in custody, we knocked on doors near to where the burglary had taken place to see of anyone had heard or seen anything, a lot of my work was looking and learning and I suppose we got back to the office for about 5.30pm and all had a quick bite to eat in the canteen.

Back in the CID office we had a cigarette, with the exception of one detective who continually smoked Hamlet cigars, and we took time to telephone our respective wives and partners to let them know that we would be late home, there's me day one, late home.

Phase two kicked in we had spent most of the afternoon attempting to identify the other two men in this burglary and we think we now we know who they were and where they were going to be in the next hour. They were going to be in a local pub The Armarda which was at the bottom of Slade Road near to Spaghetti Junction not a mile away from the burglary, what had we got to go on, we think we knew their names, we think we knew what they looked like, colour, age height sort of stuff and that was it, oh and of course the detectives nose.

So off we went the four of us plus we now had been joined by the Detective Sergeant, Brian Davis in two CID cars to The Armarda pub and in we went into the lounge that's where they will be we were told, we all walked up to the bar and tried to make ourselves not look like the police, an impossible task. The DS bought us all a half pint of beer, he always drank halves, and we stood by the bar, we talked and we waited and could we blend in with the locals no, we all had suits, collars and ties and either the statutory Crombie overcoat or Sheepskin coat, I still have my sheepskin although it's now very tatty and lies in a box in the loft, anyway we did our best not to look like policeman and more like businessmen.

We had just finished the first half a pint and one of the senior detectives had just ordered the second when the lounge door opened and two white males walked in, was they our suspects you bet your life they were but hang on we have just got our second half a pint, we will all look to the DS for out next move, the look on his face was a picture and with a little twinkle in his eye he said,

'Let's finish the beer first, it would be a shame to waste it.'

Our two suspects also bought a pint each and they walked over to the far end of the lounge and stood by the one armed bandit and proceeded to feed it 10p coins.

The plan was that the DS and one detective would walk towards the two men introduce themselves and advise them to walk to the door where we were waiting for them, so myself with the other two detectives went and stood by the door to the lounge and waited. The plan was perfect and went without problem the two men walked towards us being followed by the DS and the detective, the youths came up to us they were detained, arrested and in one foul movement they were escorted out the pub and into the CID cars and within no time they were both at Queens Road in separate cells.

God was I enjoying this, this was good, one of my favourite television programmes at the time and no doubt a favourite of many a policeman was The Sweeney, a DI and DS who worked on the Flying Squad of the Metropolitan Police, purely a fictional story but they always got their man and today was beginning to feel like that for us and especially me.

We again split into our two teams and interviewed both men, they too admitted being involved in the burglary and to stealing the jewellery but again denied seeing or having a knife; they too elected to make written statements under caution admitting their parts.

They were then returned to the cells, a visit to one of their addresses gave us the rest of the property that they had stolen during the burglary.

All four were later that evening charged with Aggravated Burglary Dwelling House and remained in custody until their appearance at the magistrate's court the following morning.

The officer in charge of the case was to be the one who would be going to court with them and I would go with him in order to learn some more about CID work. The following day I went with him to court and the four defendants were bought into the dock from the cells below, the detective got into the witness box, then took the oath gave brief circumstances of the case and asked that all four to be remanded in custody. One by one their defence solicitors stood up and argued the case for their client and asked the court that he be allowed bail with conditions.

However all four were refused bail and were remanded in custody for seven days. We left the court happy knowing they were off the streets for now anyway and we returned to the office for day two of my three month attachment what an amazing 24 hours I had.

Was it all to be the same no was the answer?

The only downside to the job was that we never found out who had the knife when they committed the burglary although we did have our suspicions, and for that reason we never recovered a knife. In due course all four appeared before Birmingham Crown Court and were sentenced to various terms of imprisonment for their parts in the offence.

There of course was a lot of routine work on the CID you had your various crime reports booked to you, and it was your responsibility to investigate the crime on that report and they varied from thefts through to damage and all the way up to burglaries and assaults and wounding's so there was plenty of variation.

You were also expected to take statements off victims and witnesses in crimes and on occasions if the crime warranted it or perhaps a suspect had been seen by a witness then you would take that witness to the photographic department at Lloyd House, so that they could be shown photographs of potential suspects. Ferrying officers to and from court, regular visits to the Forensic Science Laboratory, taking exhibits to be examined and that could be anything from a pair of trousers to blood or even particles of hair.

You were also involved in the investigation of serious crime like indecency offences up to Rapes. But at the moment life was good to me I knew in the long run I wanted to be a detective, and at the moment I was doing the job that I wanted to do that is being a policeman, but I was in plain clothes and not in uniform so I had the best of both worlds.

I knew I was to finish my three month attachment towards the end of April and here we were in the first week of April it had gone so fast but I was now about to enter the longest week of my life.

Easter was early in 1978 and over the Easter period my wife who was pregnant was not feeling very well, so we decided to telephone for a doctor who in turn advised us to go to the local hospital which we did, it was Wednesday 5th April a date neither my wife nor I will ever forget. The visit to the hospital was for my wife to have an ultra sound scan, everything after that happened so quickly. My wife was taken off for the scan and by mid-afternoon she had been admitted to hospital and had given birth to our still born daughter of 26 weeks.

What had we done wrong to deserve this I asked, it was a horrific moment and it left both of us totally distraught and in bits.

I went and telephoned my DS, Brian Davis, who knew I was taking some time off to go to the hospital but I now had to tell him what had happened to us, me like an idiot was worried about asking for some more time off, my DS was wonderful and he said go home look after your wife and telephone me next week, and forget about work it's a distant second place at the moment, I thanked him for being so considerate and understanding.

My wife was discharged and we both went home not really knowing what to do we literally just sat at home wondering why us.

On the Monday morning there was a knock at the door and it was the DS he had come round to the flat armed with a large bunch of flowers for the wife and a bottle of Bells whisky for me, he told me the lads in the office had had a quick whip round for me, it was great feeling bearing in mind I hardly knew these people.

I returned to work the following day I had barely three weeks left of my attachment but I knew day by day what I wanted to do in the police force but I also knew I still had a long time to go to for fill that ambition. The DI, a tall straight backed man who always wore a pork pie hat called me into his office one morning and told me that the Chief Superintendent had heard about what had happened with my wife and said that he would have no objections to me stopping on for a couple of weeks more, if that is what I wanted enquired the DI,

I said, 'Yes I would like that.'

I left the office feeling very pleased.

The Chief Superintendent was Chief Superintendent Jack Bagnall who could be a bit of a ferocious man when upset, he was in charge of the whole of the 'D' Division which included both CID officers and uniform officers and at this stage in my career I was still a uniform officer so I was very grateful for his decision.

Anyway the days turned into weeks and it is as if I had become the forgotten man, I was still working on the CID, my uniform inspector was not shouting for me to go back on to the shift and my DS said, 'Just keep your head down and don't worry about it.' So that's exactly what I did.

On 25th July 1978 a 13 year old girl called Candice Williams was found brutally murdered on a stairwell in a block of flats in Bleak Hill Road, Erdington she had last been seen alive the day before on the Monday. An incident room was set up at Erdington Police Station to investigate the murder and detectives from Queens Road were seconded onto the incident room for a while, I was left at Queens Road to carry on as before.

A month after the murder a £500.00 reward was put up by a local newspaper, the Birmingham Evening Mail but despite the reward the murderer remained at large for many years.

The murder of this young girl was not finalised until 1992 as a result of new advances in DNA profiling which were not available to the police in 1978 and as a result a local man, Patrick Joseph Hassett who had been

19 years old at the time of the murder was arrested and charged.

He was later convicted of her murder after a trial at Birmingham Crown Court and was quite rightly sentenced to life imprisonment.

My time on the CID was coming to a close in August 1978, I was sitting in the canteen at Queens Road it was about 5.30pm one night and I was having something to eat when Chief Superintendent Bagnall appeared through the far door of the canteen, from the direction of his office and he started to walk towards where I was sitting, I thought he never comes into the canteen he does not have to, no he is heading towards where I am, am I in for a ticking off I thought, no I had not done nothing wrong as far as I was aware, but in the real world I knew what he was coming to tell me,

He looked at me and said, 'Son.'

I said, 'Yes sir.'

He went on, 'It has been a long three months and I am no doubt you have enjoyed it.'

I said, 'Yes sir it's been good and can I thank you for letting me have the extra time.'

He said, 'That's alright but back to your unit on Monday son.'

I said, 'Yes, okay.'

I am in no doubt he sensed the disappointment in my voice but that was it, that was it the end of my attachment which initially was for three months and ran into nearly seven months, I thought all good things must come to an end.

I went and told the DS and DI and they both said, 'Let's go and have a sharp half to say good bye.' So we did we went next door to the Adventures pub and had a few pints but for me it was back to uniform on 'D' unit.

But not before I thought I want to be a detective and I will.

CHAPTER FIVE

Queens Road Police Station (2)

Well here I was back on my old unit at Queens Road and my first day back was first watch, and I was on parade at 5.45am, and PS Jones said, 'PC Wier, Mike 5, refs at 10.00.' it was as if I had never been away, the same faces, the same moans, but I believed I had made my first inroads into becoming a detective I had got on with the rest of the CID staff well so I now had to continue and carry on and impress them as much as I could.

I was very confident that I could do that but in the back of my mind I remember someone saying to me the only way you become a detective on this division is if one of them leaves or one of them dies.

I recall one set of nights that our unit had, we ended up having several prisoners for crime, I think we were averaging about four or five a night and it seemed that every time you left the station and drove down the road within the next minute you would drive back up the road with a prisoner

To such an extent that for that one week of seven nights the whole of the unit received a Chief Superintendents commendation, which is something to be proud of. For me it was brilliant because I only wanted prisoners for crime because I wanted to be a detective and the best way for me to achieve that was to keep arresting people for crime and hopefully get noticed by the CID, I certainly would not get noticed by them if I kept reporting speeders by way of a summons or knocking off motorist parked on double yellow lines.

As the end of 1978 approached I reflected on the year, it had been a mixed year for me personally of course it was the year my wife gave birth to out still born daughter. It was the year I had a three month CID attachment that lasted the best part of seven months.

Other memories for me during 1978 was my first taste of a major and serious public disorder as a policeman, I had been to many fights but this was the real thing this was serious disorder and during 1978 the West Midlands Police had four major demonstrations to police.

On 10th June 1978 there was an Anti-Racist march in Wolverhampton, on 2nd September 1978 there was a march by the Anti-Nazi league and on the 18th November 1978 as a result of the visit of Miss Indria Ghandi there was a mass protest and demonstration, but with these three demonstrations, although there were some problems with pockets of disorder and there were many arrests it was nothing like the demonstration outside Digbeth Civic Hall in High Street, Birmingham, on 18th February 1978, just days before my CID attachment began.

Inside the hall there was a meeting being held by the Young National Front, and those opposed to their views were going to hold a counter demonstration and this is the one serious disorder that I was directly involved in and it became known as 'The Battle of Digbeth'

The streets around Digbeth were deserted to the public but it was soon to become a battleground as anti-fascist demonstrators targeted a meeting of right-wing supporters and although their politics appeared dubious to most people the Young National Front had a democratic right to meet, and the police lined the streets to stop and to prevent opposing groups fighting.

The police as normal were well and truly stuck in the middle of both sides, we had the meeting inside the hall and a police cordon outside, totally protecting the hall and its occupants and facing us on the opposite side of the road were the protesters and there were thousands of them.

As normal most were well behaved but in excess of 300 or so were hell bent on trouble.

I remember we were in place early in the morning around 8.00am and the meeting was to be held later that same morning, and through the early part of the day there was sporadic violence with the usual throwing of missiles that included stones and bricks at the police, damage was being caused to buildings and property, litter bins were being thrown and general abuse being shouted at us. I was to the far left of the police lines and you can imagine what was happening they were pushing us and we in turn were pushing them back and then at around 2.00pm there was a massive barrage of missiles being launched at the police this included larger bricks and broken paving slabs and probably for the first time in my life I was afraid that I might die.

We were not properly protected and most of us only had our normal police issue helmets and there were certainly no proper shields to protect us, it was frightening and the looks on the faces of these so called protesters were that they wanted to kill you.

A colleague of mine PC Alden was struck on the head by a brick thrown by one of these protesters, he fell to the floor with blood streaming from a head wound and he had to be unceremoniously dragged away from the crowd by some of us and it was later discovered he had suffered a fractured skull, it was quite horrendous.

To this day I do not think that the protester was positively identified and arrested by the police.

As the day progressed I assume the protesters were getting hungry like us because they all started to disappear but obviously we could not go until more or less everyone single protester had gone. I recall the Assistant Chief Constable of the day a big man called Bill McDonald was standing with us on the lines and he managed to get a local licensee to open the pub to allow us a few of a time to go into the pub to use the toilet and to grab a drink of water and a bag of crisps and to have a rest for a few minutes.

Eventually the day finished after about 12 hours and what a mess was left behind, there was damage to buildings, and vehicles, there was rubbish, bricks, stones, litter bins up turned and thrown everywhere and broken glass everywhere, many arrests had been made and a few policeman injured, PC Alden being the worst of the injured.

On that day a total of 2,210 police officers were involved and the West Midlands Police were assisted by officers from Staffordshire, West Mercia and Warwickshire, all leave for us was cancelled and the only food we managed to get was a police packed lunch, I am convinced that the pork pie that is always in the packed lunch was harder to eat than some of the bricks that were being thrown at you.

It was also remembered as being one of the first demonstrations where the police used a helicopter to assist.

And the last thing I remember of 1978 was the Lord Justice Edmund-Davies commission on enhanced pay for police officers which went in our favour and the officers both men and women of the police service had a decent pay rise for the first time in many a year.

1979 arrived and we had found out that my wife was pregnant, I was still on the same unit at Queens Road and on most days I would be driving a panda car normally covering Mike 5, Perry Common, things I suppose were going along alright and I was still getting my fair share of prisoners for crime and I can recall once such incident very fondly.

I was on nights on Mike 5, two of the Aston cars had prisoners so by about 1.00am I was effectively covering the mobile areas of Mike 1-5 and we had two police cars covering the Kingstanding area, it's not unusual and it normally happens when we get prisoners, and it is quite normal to cover more than one area when other officers are at the police station dealing with their prisoners, but tonight it was my turn to cover more than one mobile area.

It was about 1.30am and I was due in for my refreshments in actual fact I was thirty minutes or so

117

late, so I decided on the way in I would call at the chip shop in Nechells Park Road as he normally stayed open till about 2.00am and of course his fish and chips were very good.

I parked outside and checked with the controller to find out if anybody else wanted me to bring them something in, and the controller would normally ask by use of the following message, 'Delta 1 control to all mobiles any despatch required?'

Nothing heard so I got my own food and set off back to Queens Road for my late dinner. I was on Lichfield Road out of town at the junction with Church Road, it was a junction controlled by traffic lights and it was my intention to turn left towards the police station, the lights as normal were on red and even though it was nearly 2.00am in the morning I was not going to drive through a red light, because someone somewhere would see you, so I stopped and waited for the green light and you seem to wait for ever.

I was of course in the near side lane when just then a vehicle pulled up in the outside lane and stopped it was a dark coloured Morris or Austin 1100 with three young men on board, it stopped at the red light and there we both sat, we were both waiting for the thing the green light, the only thing on my mind was fish and chips and the wonderful smell that was drifting around the inside of the police car, mind you not so much fun for the person on first watch I thought.

Then for no apparent reason off went the 1100, straight through the red light and down Lichfield Road towards Spaghetti Junction at speed, why oh why, what is he playing at I thought. I have now got to go and stop the vehicle and find out why he does not like the colour red. So off I went in pursuit I called the controller, 'Mike 5 Delta I, moving vehicle check please'

'Go ahead,' PS Twamley answered.

I said, 'It's an Austin 1100 dark blue number ABC-123 travelling at speed down Lichfield Road towards Spaghetti.'

The controller came back confirming it was a stolen car from Erdington Hall Road earlier that night, and so I thought he is driving back to where he stole it from, which of course is normally the case for car thieves because if you drop a stolen vehicle you are not going to walk five miles to go home are you?, in truth you drop it around the corner.

I followed it down Lichfield Road around Spaghetti Junction and right in to Tyburn Road and it then turned left into Hawksyard Road, I suppose he was travelling between 50mph and 60 mph, the controller then put the radios on talk through which meant I could speak to the other policemen without going through the controller the next thing I heard was, 'Mike 6, I am on Tyburn Road, where do you want me?'

I said, 'Carry on along Tyburn Road and towards the Navigation and wait there.'

The Navigation was a large pub at the junction with Tyburn Road and Bromford Lane. The stolen vehicle turned right into Wheelwright Road and left into Croydon Road and I was relaying this to Mike 6 and also Mike 1 who had come out of refreshments to assist me. In Croydon Road the vehicle was still travelling at speed, and I could now quiet clearly see three on board and just then it the driver appeared to lose control of the vehicle and collided with parked vehicles, on his left hand side of the road, what a noise it made but the stolen car ground to a halt and the three occupants managed to get out and began to run up Croydon Road away from the crashed vehicle.

I am still relaying commentary and by the time I stopped I could see both Mike 1 and 6 turn into Croydon Road. Who do I run after?, well the driver of course he is always your first target, the passengers can always say 'I did not know the car was stolen' but that is always more difficult for the driver to say. So off I went with the driver in view I ran about 200 yards and he stopped he turned round and said, 'Look I'm knackered, I'm not running anymore.'

He just stood there, breathing heavily, mind you so was I, I then took hold of him and walked him back to the police car.

The other two were quickly arrested by the other policemen and all three were taken to Queens Road. With the assistance of another officer the three youths were processed, charged and bailed to Birmingham Magistrates Court.

Why did they go through the red light, well they panicked and assumed that because of the time of night or should I say time of the morning that I would automatically check the vehicle out so they decided to make a dash. Little did they know I was not about to check it out, I was actually heading for my refreshments with my fish and chip supper albeit it was a 2.00am supper.

It was nearly time to book off so I went back to the police car which was still parked in the secure rear yard at the back of the station, this was actually the prisoners exercise yard, but when you were bringing prisoners under arrest to the station we made use of this space particularly if you had someone who was violent or non-compliant. You could drive them straight into the yard, which was surrounded by walls of at least 30 feet high and you could lock a big steel gate behind you.

It was my intention to remove my cap, gloves and torch and paperwork from the car and to re-park it in a normal police bay, but as I opened the door, there it was my fish and chip supper, but it was not neatly wrapped up it was in fact all over the floor of the car, fish and chips were everywhere so as well as not eating them, I now had to pick them up off the floor stone cold and dump them.

The unit had some sad news in March 1979, PC Hughie Moreland was found dead at home on the 8th March, Hughie had been on 'D' unit for several years and was one of the more experienced officers, he was a typical police man he had a barrel chest, moustache and always had a smile on his face. He was sadly missed by all of us.

I continued working hard and trying to get my face known by the CID upstairs and whenever I had a prisoner for crime I would go straight up and tell them, I suppose you would call it brown nosing.

I suffered my first assault in 1979, not badly thankfully, but an assault on police never the less. I was working Mike 5 and was on nights when I was sent to a report of a disturbance at the British Steel Social Club in Bromford Lane, Erdington. The information from the controller was that there was a wedding reception being held there and towards the end of the night there was some sort of disturbance, various individuals including the groom appeared to be involved in a fight.

I arrived at the scene and it looked like most of the guests probably some eighty or so from the reception, were now outside in the street trying their best to separate two men who were throwing punches at each other, there were some younger women involved and they were shouting and screaming abuse, there was hair pulling, punching and kicking and that was just the young women.

Enter Mike 5, don't forget I am the good guy who has been sent to sort out whatever the problem is or so I thought. The two men fighting was where I went to first, I assumed that once they saw me they might calm down but I could not be so far wrong, I attempted to talk to both men and that did not work, then I tried pulling them apart and telling them to grow up as it was a wedding they were wrecking. The taller of the two men shouted at me, 'I know it's my wedding you pratt.'

I am still trying to pull them apart and by now the groom has calmed down and is being dusted down by his family but the other man wanted now to fight me, he started to prod me with his finger into my chest and I have to admit that I hate that, so I warned him about his behaviour, it made no difference and for some reason the younger women who had been fighting also turned their attentions towards me, and I now had three or four of these drunken women plus the man pushing me backwards and laughing as they did so.

I then made a decision probably the wrong one probably due to the circumstances, but I looked straight at the man and said, 'I am arresting you for being drunk and disorderly.'

He said, 'No you're fucking not.'

He then began to run off along Bromford Lane in the general direction of where I had parked the police car.

I chased him only for about thirty yards and caught up with him I grabbed hold of his arm and began to drag him towards the police car, I opened the driver's door lifted forward the front seat and began to push him into the back of the car. But it was not going to plan he grabbed hold of my tunic and pulled me towards him and this resulted in two or three of my tunic buttons being ripped off and with him still trying to pull me into the back of the police car.

He was kicking out at me and caught me several times on the upper legs and once in the stomach, and just when I thought it could not get any worse two or three of the drunken women returned and had now decided to pull me away from the police car altogether, to allow their friend who by now was half in and half out of the car get away.

I thought I need some assistance here, I am getting surrounded by drunken people who want a fight, I was shouting at some of the other guests to drag their friends away but they continually ignored me, I guess they thought it was funny, there was only one thing left for me to do I needed to get the arrested man away from the scene so I got on the radio and said to the controller PS Twamley, 'Mike 5, Delta I, assistance please at the Bromford Club.'

It seemed like hours but I know it wasn't, police cars began to arrive from every direction and the junction of Bromford Lane and Wheelwright Road was now a sea of blue flashing lights and police officers.

What a glorious sight it made.

My arrested man was removed from the scene and taken to Queens Road and two of the four or so women were also arrested, as even when all the police were there, they could not keep their mouths shut they had to shout abuse.

The arrested man was later charged with Drunk and Disorderly and appeared at court on the Monday morning where he was fined £15.00, he was not charged with Assault Police, as to me it was part of my job and I was not badly hurt, in fact the only thing hurt was my pride.

The two women spent the night in the cells and were released with a headache on the Sunday morning.

The man, I won't name him but after that we became quite good friends job wise, and sometime later I was called to a fight at the Navigation pub in Erdington and he helped me and prevented me from being attacked by some drunks, so at least some good came out of his arrest.

My tunic buttons well I had to put a report in to the uniform stores, Mr Greenslades, remember I mentioned him earlier in the book; well he reluctantly gave me some replacements which I had to sow on myself.

On 3rd May 1979 there was a general election and it was an unusual one as it was won by a woman, Mrs Margaret Thatcher, the daughter of a grocer from Lincoln and she was to be the first woman prime minister that this country had ever had and she was to remain as prime minister until 1990.

Another brilliant part of 1979 was the birth of my son Alexander James Wier on the 20th June that year.

By nature police forces are always changing and the West Midlands Police is no different, and during 1979 work was being done on Erdington Police Station to increase the size of it, the plan was to make it another sub division within the 'D' division, we had D1 and D2 this was to be D3 and it was to cover the areas of Pype Hayes, Erdington, Perry Common, Kingstanding and Great Barr.

The police station at Erdington had since 1975 been part of the D2 Sutton Coldfield sub division, but that was about to change. It would be a sub division in its own right and it would take over the police stations of Erdington from D2 and Kingstanding from D1.

The building work was behind schedule because of the bad winter of 1978/79 but it was due to open as D3 in September 1979. I had always enjoyed my work in Perry Common because for the last few months I had been driving Mike 5 the Perry Common car and I had always liked the work at Kingstanding so I decided to ask to go to D3 on its formation.

I suppose after four years I needed a change and D3 I thought could give me a new challenge. Was I getting a bit stale? Yes, I suppose I was, do I want a new challenge? Yes, well let's go then. I had to submit a report to my Inspector requesting that I be considered for the move to D3, obviously staffing the new sub division was now a priority but it could not be done to the demise of the D1 and D2.

There were already officers based at Erdington and no doubt some would want to stay so all I could do was ask. After waiting a few weeks my move was authorised, D3, Erdington here I come.

CHAPTER SIX

Erdington Police Station

I was due to start at Erdington Police Station on the D3 sub division; on Monday 18th September 1979 I was posted to 'A' unit who were on relief week, so on my first day I was due to work on a 2.00pm x 10.00pm shift.

I knew I was going to like it here because I could even walk to work, I lived about 15 minutes' walk away which was good so now my wife with our 4 month old son could use the car, so from that point of view the move was good.

I had changed my car by now and I had a green Morris Marina estate car registration number BNX 468T I had bought that from Startins Garage in Erdington not far from where we were living.

I was on parade by 1.30pm I did not know anyone on the parade and as is normal the Inspector and Sergeant came in and I did not know them so quite literally it was like starting again. The makeup of police vehicles on the D3 were four Unit Beat vehicles or panda cars and two fast response cars or Zulus as they were known as. Was I going to be a driver on day one? I doubt it as all the officers on my new unit had previously worked the area when based at D2, Sutton Coldfield and some of them had even previously worked at Erdington itself.

But with four years plus service I was more experienced than most of them, so did I drive on the first day? Well you know what the answer is to that question it was; no, I did not drive on the first day.

The Inspector and Sergeant walked in and we stood up on parade and the Inspector motioned to us to sit down, I was then introduced to the rest of the shift along with the newly promoted sergeant, Police Sergeant Kelvin Roberts who in the years to come became a very good friend of mine, we were both starting Erdington, new on the same day.

PS Roberts said, 'PC Wier, High Street, refs at 7.00pm see me after parade please.'

I said, 'Yes Sgt.'

I was thinking to myself it looks like I am going to be walking Erdington High Street with all those shops and what goes with shops, shoplifters loads of them, I couldn't bear the thought of it. Anyway to the Sergeants office, we sat and we talked and I was told that for the next couple of days I would be walking the High Street but as from Monday of nights I would be driving, it's just that all the postings for the unit have been completed until Thursday and we did not want to change anybody about, I thought fair enough I can wait.

The first day I did not even reach the High Street until after my refreshments, as I was getting to know the police station and where everything was and sorting myself a locker out. The rest of the week went fairly quickly and fortunately for me I never had a shoplifter.

Nights arrived and when I first started driving on the D3 I was given Mike 19 which I hated, the reason for that was that Mike 19 covered the dreaded High Street with its shoplifters again, so I was very grateful when I was moved onto Mike 22 which covered Great Barr and parts of Kingstanding I was back on the area I knew best.

I was at Erdington as a uniform officer from 18th September 1979 until 5th April 1981 and I have to say it was one of the best times that I had with the police, the work was varied and you were always busy, the men and woman at the station and particularly on my shift were great and both myself and my wife met some good friends when I was there and some we still have today.

I was the second most senior policeman on the shift and with that went a lot more responsibility and on several occasions running up to Christmas 1980, I was given the role of acting sergeant in the front office and that meant that basically you were in charge of the front office, also when prisoners were bought in you had to look after their welfare, you would first record their details of the custody record and you in fact became their guardian whilst they were in custody, so with all that went a lot of responsibility but no extra money I'm afraid.

I was very fortunate when I was doing the acting sergeant role for assisting me at that time in the office was a young probationer, PC Michael 'Mick' Saunders, we got on like a house on fire, we hit it off straight away, we seemed to be able to read each other's minds and we seemed to know what each other was planning to do next. We assisted one another and we respected one another. It was a good working relationship whilst it lasted but being a probationer he would have to complete other roles on the unit and of course it seemed that every other week he was on training.

Sadly several years Mick tragically died of a serious illness whilst working at Sutton Coldfield Police Station.

I know it seems a strange thing to say but during my period in uniform at Erdington I seemed to do more, and learn more than at any time in my career and being one of the more experienced officers it seemed so much was expected of me and I think I rose to the occasion.

Cafes and police officers always go together well, you remember when I was on the D1 we used Brian's café in

Bourne Road and now when I was on the D3 we had two cafes that were regularly used by the police, I also know that on occasions the CID used them as well.

The first café was known as the Pype Hayes transport café which was situated on the Chester Road and this café was particularly well used by officers who covered the Erdington area, I think in all my time on D3 I only went to the café on maybe three or four occasions.

Above the café was a self-contained flat which the proprietor of the café use to rent out and I know on a few occasions his tenants had in fact been police officers from Erdington.

This changed on Boxing Day 1980 when the then proprietor was found hanging in the kitchen area of the café; he had been seen by a member of public who was walking past the front of the café and she contacted the police and I remember that the policeman who attended the death was a regular at the café and still used it after this tragic event. It became known then as 'the hanging café' and I certainly never went in again.

A new proprietor came in and it is still a café today after all those years but I have never set foot in the place again.

The second café was known as The Ridgeway and it was in College Road, Kingstanding, this was the café I used for many years, it was a brilliant place with a brilliant and nutty proprietor called Bob, he ran the café with the assistance of his wife and her sister.

Bob was mad he was so full of life it makes you wonder if he ever switched off when he finished, the café had been used by police for several years and when you walked in he would always greet you in the same way, he would say, 'What the fuck do you want.' or 'Hurry up; I am losing customers with you lot in here.'

I am glad to say he never meant it, that was his sense of humour, we knew it but you should have seen the look on the faces of some of his customers as Bob verbally attacked us.

We had several probationers on the unit I think at one stage we had about five which is quite a lot for such a small unit but in fairness to them I never met a bad one.

Throughout my period at Erdington I got the nickname of 'doctor death' now I will tell you that is not unusual as several policemen I knew had the same nickname and mine came from the fact that nearly every week a death of some sort would happen when I was on duty, most of them were not suspicious but some were.

My prize for that was that when there was a report of a sudden or suspicious death, I would be asked to take along a probationer and of course it was sometimes their first view of a dead body or dealing in anyway with a dead body, but they had to learn because in the future they would be doing my job and taking probationers to sudden or suspicious deaths.

I recall one afternoon I was on Mike 22 with a probationer, who I will not name to save any embarrassment for him and we were sent to an address in Kingstanding to a report that the gentlemen who lived in the ground floor maisonette had not been seen for some weeks. On arrival we walked around the back of the house after first knocking on the front door and getting no answer and when I lifted the letter box I got that smell of death I knew it was going to be a bad day and I would have to break into the property.

I stood outside the bedroom window at the back of the house and stared thinking those curtains are moving, I got my truncheon out and smashed a pane of glass in the window and discovered very quickly that it was not curtains I was looking at, it was in fact thousands and thousands of blue bottles up at the window and of course when I smashed the glass they all wanted to leave and I have never seen nothing like that to this day, thousands of them leaving this house by a smashed window.

We stood back we had to and watched this cloud of blue bottles leave us heading in the direction of College Road, I then very gently opened the window and climbed in, I suggested to the probationer to follow me in which he did but he did not stop too long.

There lying on the bed is what I can only describe as a skeleton of a man with some rags hanging off him, quite literally most of his flesh appeared to have been eaten away, I looked at him he had no eyes just holes in his face, the sight was horrific and the smell was even worse, I turned to talk to the probationer but I was too late he had left by the same window and was being violently sick in the back garden.

I informed the controller and requested a police surgeon to attend as they have to formally confirm death before the body can be moved to the mortuary. I know it was part of your job but you still have feelings although you cannot always show them.

They called me 'doctor death' because that is the weird sense of humour policemen have, there is nothing funny whatsoever in death but we had to deal with it in our own way and this is the way we did and no offence was meant by anybody.

But at times I did wonder why I ever joined the police but deep down I joined because I wanted to help people and if you can help people in their darkest hour then it is all worthwhile. When you arrived at these deaths as a policeman you were expected to know all the answers to all the questions and of course sometimes you did not, but what you did do as a policeman is you learnt very quickly and in a very short space of time of course you had to.

I recall another sudden or suspicious death I went to in Kingstanding, I was called to an address in Danesbury Crescent at about 5.30pm one evening, a mother had returned home from work and found her 14 year old son hanging from a curtain rail in the bedroom. What the hell do I do next Nigel; start thinking you have a mother who is totally and utterly devastated being comforted by neighbours and they had called the ambulance and police, and you arrive first and you must know the answers because you are the police.

You keep them out of the room because what happens next is not always pleasant because when people hang themselves, normally their body muscle's relax and bodily fluids leek out, so it is not pleasant and you must get the body down but retain the knot in the material that he has hung himself with.

Because forensically that piece of material or knot will have to be examined to ascertain whether he did or could tie the knot himself or whether he could not, then you would be looking for a third party, all this is going through your mind literally a thousand times a minute.

Sometimes you need help and you ask for another police officer to attend, but he could be fifteen or so minutes away and are you going to stand still and wait, of course you are not you have to get on with it. In this particular case the ambulance arrived and between us we got the body down and I saved the knot.

The young lad was dead but the mother is shouting at the ambulance men to take her son to hospital but now she turns to me, officer make them, make them take my son to hospital. I now had to tell her to sit down and listen to me and to give her the news that she suspected but did not want to hear.

I explained that nothing further could be done and we are awaiting a police surgeon, I am thinking at this time where's my bloody sergeant, I asked for him to attend hours ago, I did not it was probably five minutes ago but it seemed like hours and he is coming from Erdington in the rush hour.

Her neighbours were brilliant, because after the police surgeon has gone and after the ambulance men have gone, all that is left is me and possibly a neighbour if we are lucky and what am I going to be talking to the mother about, well I needed full details about her son, name, age, school and whether or not he had any problems that she knew about in particular was he perhaps being bullied at school and finally did she want the police to arrange a funeral director, none of it very pleasant but it had to be done and I needed to give her answers.

I did it methodically but with sympathy.

There is no way of explaining why we do this job, but at the end of the day I left her waiting for a funeral director that I had arranged for her, the neighbour was still there and her husband was on his way to the house from work. I returned to Erdington, completed a coroners form for the information of HM Coroner and then I booked off and went to the Swan pub across the road from the police station and had a drink with the rest of my unit then I walked home after picking up fish and chips on the way.

Her life would never be the same but mine would be because the next day I was back at work doing the job surprisingly I loved.

As a police officer you are also asked to do things, I suppose you would call them favours for next of kin or relatives, one I do remember is that an elderly gent had collapsed and died in the front garden of his house in Kingstanding, and after the police surgeon had confirmed death and a funeral director had been contacted by me, the gents wife asked me if I could move the body and take it to their bedroom and lie it on the bed.

How did I move that body I have no idea, but I did because she wanted me to, it was not a pleasant sight as I had to drag him by his arms up a flight of stairs, I might add with the assistance of a kind neighbour but we managed it between us and if nothing more, I had helped her in her hour of need.

Another one I attended is where an elderly gent had died in the armchair during the night, I attended on first watch and there was no problems the death was expected and the local GP had confirmed death, relatives were there and everybody was waiting for the funeral director to arrive.

In cases like this where death is expected and the deceased has been ill and has been seen by his or her doctor in the last 14 days, then normally a post mortem is not required as in this particular case.

The wife turned to me and said, 'Can you take his wedding ring off please as none of us want to touch the body?'

Okay I thought no problem, could I get the wedding ring off most certainly I could not and I thought for a moment it had been super glued on, but never mind I will try and thinking on my feet I said to his wife, 'Have you got any fairly liquid?'

She nodded in agreement and went into the kitchen and returned with a plastic bottle of washing up liquid which she handed to me, I thought just squirt a bit on his finger and I am certain the ring will come off. The first thing to come off was the top off the bottle and fairly liquid went everywhere all over the deceased body, and all over my hands and arms, what the hell have you done I thought, anyway not wanting to give up I did get the wedding ring off and walked into the kitchen and handed the ring to the old lady and apologised for the mess.

I had left fairly liquid all over the lounge carpet and all over her husband. I took some details for the coroners form and left quickly with the old lady waving goodbye to me from the window. So even in death there are lighter moments.

And talking of lighter moments there are one or two I remember quite fondly, one was early in 1980 and I was on first watch on Mike 22 and it started to snow, it was rush hour perhaps about 8.00am I really did not think too much about it, but down it kept coming the snowflakes were the size of dinner plates and the ground quickly covered but the longer it snowed the deeper it was getting and there was no let up and by 9.00am traffic was virtually at a standstill,the snow must have been five or six inches deep.

The controller advised us to park the police vehicles up wherever was safe and walk towards the nearest police station, there was little point in us driving anywhere, I was on Kingstanding Road near to its junction with Hawthorn Road and by now people were abandoning their vehicles everywhere, so I thought I will be smart here and park the police vehicle on the central reservation out of other motorist way, so on I drove I parked up and opened the driver's door to get out remembering to pick my helmet up from the passenger seat because if I was going to walk to Kingstanding Police Station some mile and half away I would need my helmet and not my flat cap.

I got out the vehicle walked one pace away and was about to turn round in order to shut and lock the driver's door and then it happened I lost my footing in the deep snow, and promptly fell backwards and landed on my back in the snow with my arms and legs in the air like a dying fly, my helmet had landed about ten feet away.

I shut my eyes briefly and when I opened them I could see that a number 90 bus appeared to have stopped a few feet away from me and everyone on the bus had their faces glued to the windows, laughing at me lying on the floor, not content with that a group of old people at the bus stop started to throw, I have to say quite gently snowballs in my direction, did anyone help me to my feet? no was the answer, I think instead most people in Kingstanding were laughing at the sight of a policeman in uniform trying to get to his feet whilst not looking embarrassed, and of course not trying to make eye contact with anyone. I eventually got to my feet picked up my snow covered helmet placed it upon my head and began to walk up Kingstanding Road with bits of snow dropping off me, did I look back? no I did not.

Another moment I recall and quite often smile to myself about was one night or should I say in the early hours of the morning probably about 1.45am, I was driving along Chester Road towards Erdington Police Station, I was on my way in for refreshments, the weather was awful the whole of Birmingham appeared to be covered in a layer of thick fog quite literally you could not see far in front of you may be about 10 or 15 yards at the most, there were no people about and very few cars about, it was like London at the time of Jack the Ripper in the 1880s.

I was making my way along Chester Road and was aware of two other cars behind me now I know from experience that in really bad fog you do tend to follow the vehicle in front, it makes you job easier, anyway there were two of them I could see them through my interior mirror and the only thing I could make out was their headlights, I reached Sutton New Road and turned right, they turned right with me I suppose we were travelling no more than 20mph.

I went through the traffic lights at Station Road, what's strange is you can always see traffic lights in fog, still the two cars were behind me I turned right into Wilton Road left by the side of the police station, and then left into Osbourne Road, still with them behind and after about 25 yards I turned left into the rear yard of the station drove up to the top right hand corner and parked the police car.

I got out to find the same two cars that had followed me down the Chester Road and half way across Erdington were now stationary in the rear yard of the police station, they had followed me from Kingstanding all the way through Erdington and into the rear of Erdington Police Station, I had to smile as I walked towards the first car as the driver wound the window down and said, 'Where am I?' I explained that he was in the car park at the rear of the police station, 'I wanted to go to Shard End.' He said and he cautiously began to turn round, the second vehicle I did not know where he wanted to go he just reversed out of the yard and disappeared into the fog no doubt very embarrassed.

With lighter moments come some very strange moments I remember one time it was a Sunday morning I was on first watch, it would have been about 10.00am and I was directed to St Margaret Mary Church, Perry Common Road, there is a report of a fight in progress, I got the call and thought that's going to be a false and malicious call, a fight at a church, no way.

I arrived and parked the police car out the front and there were people running everywhere I recall one man shouting, 'I think his gone mad.' I had no idea who he was talking about at this stage.

I walked into the church and it was like a film set, the father of the church was shouting and throwing things about, anything he could get his hands on, people were trying to calm him down but he would not have none of it he was shouting, screaming and swearing at everybody inside the church. He was pushing furniture over and throwing books about. I tried to calm him down but he was having nothing to do with me, I do not know what had upset him but he was not listening to any reason.

I needed to get him out of this church, but what should I do I had tried talking to him without any joy, I had tried to persuade him to leave by putting my arm around his shoulder, but that did not work either, other members of his congregation who knew him better than me tried, but no he would not listen to anybody, in truth I thought he had gone mad.

I needed to get him to hospital but how, he was not going to walk to the police car, I was now waiting now for an ambulance, it seemed ages but it eventually arrived but even they could not persuade him into the ambulance. I felt that he needed to go to a police station first be seen by a police surgeon, so a decision could be made, with a bit of talking and a bit of pushing and shoving, he was slowly and gently persuaded into the back of the police car.

He seemed to have calmed down a lot now but I still needed him at Erdington. Another mobile had joined the scene by now and the officer sat in the back of my police car and off to Erdington we drove the ambulance followed us.

At the police station a police surgeon was called out and it was decided that the best place for treatment for him would be Highcroft Hospital in Erdington, which is a specialised hospital, we got him to the hospital eventually and with even more persuasion where almost immediately a hospital doctor sedated him and he was escorted into a secure ward by hospital staff. I never know what happened to him and I suppose I never will. But how strange can anyone else remember a father of the church acting like that.

I have mentioned some lighter moments and strange moments whilst I was at Erdington I can now think of a scary moment, after all I am only human.

It was just after 9.00am I was driving back from Sutton Coldfield Police Station and I was with my patrol sergeant, PS Roberts we had just dropped off some papers for court. We were travelling along Birmingham Road towards its junction with Chester Road and we were heading back to the station.

The controller informed us that Zulu 7 and 8, the two fast response cars were making the post office in High Street, Erdington to a report of an armed robbery in progress, could we head towards the surrounding roads and work loose, rather than go to the scene, the idea being you can bet by the time the police had arrived at the post office the robbers would have driven off, so the idea being that us together with other mobiles would look at likely escape routes of the robbers vehicle which we had now been told was a white Ford Escort van possible a 'P' or 'R' reg.

Most robbers once they have committed the robbery drive their vehicle perhaps no more than half a mile, then change vehicles because they know as in this case everybody will be looking for the Escort van and not the changeover vehicle, particularly if we have no witnesses to the changeover vehicle

I drove to the roads that run parallel to the rear of the High Street, they were residential roads and the robbers in my mind were more likely to change over vehicles there, well that was my view anyway. We were looking for three men wearing 'old men' masks, one armed with a shot gun and the others with pick axe handles; they had apparently left the car park at the rear of the post office and drove through the Co-op car park and right into Mason Road, they were certainly driving into the area I was heading for.

I headed for Holly Lane probably some half or three quarters a mile from the post office, I drove down Holly Lane turned round drove back up and then turned right in Avalon Close, because I knew from living in Holly Lane that at the rear of the houses and maisonettes there were garages, and you could drive past the garages in to the park and off into Grange Road. So they could have gone that way, or was their changeover vehicle parked in the little car park situated within the park, I was about to find out.

I drove into Avalon Close to the top turned left into where the garages were and there it was the third garage on the right, the up and over door was open and I could clearly see the back of an 'R' registration white Escort van, was this the robbers car? of course I believed it was, but what the hell do we do now.

I looked at the sergeant and he looked at me and I drove at speed and parked the police car across the rear of the van, so at least now they could not reverse out, the sergeant opened the passenger side of the police car and that's the side we both got out of very cautiously, and then stupidly we both walked up to the van and looked in to see if our robbers were in there, there was nobody in the van, they had gone.

Thank god for that I thought, they had only just gone and this was confirmed because the bonnet of the car was still hot, meaning they had not long left the vehicle. I informed the controller and we waited for the arrival of the scenes of crime officers and then I drove the van back to Erdington Police Station and into a covered garage so it could be examined in greater detail.

The CID was at the post office taking witness statements and to begin their investigation into the robbery.

I later found at that the robbers had escaped with about £8,000.

The whole armed robbery was later featured on a police programme on ATV News called Police Five, the host of the show was Mr Shaw Taylor, I was even asked by the CID if I wanted to play the part of one of the robbers in the old man mask, I did however decline the invitation.

Some years later as part of a wider investigation into robberies, I do know that local persons were charged and convicted over the post office robbery and sent to prison. I have been to other robberies but some you always remember and that one was one of the robberies I instantly recall, I think it was due to the fact that I found the robbers van within four or five minutes of the actual robbery.

So lighter moments, strange moments, scary moments, all part of the policeman's life, I would say if you asked any policeman he could also recall those sorts of moments and then of course there was the tragic moments and unfortunately being a policeman for thirty years there have been too many tragic moments.

It was during 1980 that I was lucky enough to get a six month attachment to the CID; applications had come out for any officer who was interested in applying to submit a report to the Chief Inspector, who at Erdington at this time was Detective Chief Inspector Joe Rees. I submitted my report; it was another chance for me to reach my goal of being a detective, because to be a detective you had to have completed a successful six month attachment first.

The report went in to the Chief Inspector and I was fortunate to be given a time and date for an interview, now of course the only thing against me and it was a big thing was that I did not know the CID staff at Erdington like I knew them at Queens Road, but of course that's a risk you take when you move police stations.

The interview went well but I also knew the DCI had others to interview and at this time there was only one vacancy so it was a case of fingers crossed. A few days later I was asked to attend the DCI's office which I did and he congratulated me on being successful at the interview and after consultation with my unit inspector a start date in September 1980 was agreed.

In my mind I was thinking this is the next stage in my route to become a detective constable, I was going to work hard on the six month attachment but still enjoy it, but to me it was a make or break attachment, if I failed this I could wait for years to get another opportunity because all the time capable and good policemen and policewomen are coming through who of course want to be a detective like me.

I was to do three months of my attachment at Erdington and three months at Kingstanding. I started first at Erdington I turned up on the Monday bright and early, and I was allocated a desk, a chair and a diary. The diary was a book that all CID officers kept and it was where we recorded our day to day record of what we had done.

I was given my postings for the next month and off I went. The three months went very quickly you spent a lot of the day visiting crimes, taking statements and interviewing prisoners who had been arrested for crime. One of the biggest crimes in Erdington was shoplifting and if CID staff were available they would be expected to interview the prisoner and of course to search their house. It was to allow the uniform officer back onto the street as soon as possible.

I hated shoplifting and shoplifters, as I have explained before it was quite literally people going into a shop picking something up and leaving without paying for it that's shoplifting or to give it its proper name Theft Shops and Stalls and I hated everything about it and I will give you two examples of what I mean.

The first was an elderly man in his sixties who had been arrested for stealing a roll of bin liners from a local supermarket, he had been observed putting the bin liners inside of his coat and leaving the store without paying for them at a cost of about 50p.

I went to the interview room with the arresting officer and if he admitted the offence and had no like previous convictions, I was looking at the idea of getting him an Inspectors caution and the whole matter could be dealt with in under an hour.

He admitted the offence stating he was very sorry, a PNC check revealed no recent previous conviction and the last thing to do before the caution was to have a quick search of his home address.

He lived with his mother who was in her eighties so we had to be careful in the way we dealt with it. Anyway with the arresting officer I went to this man's house and we were invited in by his mother who was a very nice and friendly person, the search of the house was quickly made and nothing was found, we had left the man's bedroom till last and when we managed to force open the door, we walked in and we both stopped in our tracks and looked at each other.

We were surrounded by wall to ceiling rolls of bin liners, all colours; I said to his mother, 'Why does your son have all these bin liners in his bedroom?'

She quietly replied, 'He says there is going to be a shortage of them so every time he goes out he comes back with a roll.'

What could I say it took me and the other officer about three hours to collect up all the rolls and take them back to Erdington to be booked into the crime property store, in total there were over 250 rolls of bin liners.

We had another interview with him and he admitted stealing them over a period of 12 months or so from numerous shops all over Birmingham. We were never going to find out who owned them all, so he still had his Inspectors caution and the rolls of bin liners went to a local church jumble sale.

What was going to take an hour took about five hours and I remember telephoning the wife and telling her that I would be late home because I was dealing with an elderly man who had stolen 250 rolls of bin liners, she never said but I bet she did not believe me?

Another time was a 15 year old youth, he had walked into Boots the chemist on the High Street in Erdington and stole four deodorants, worth about a £1, he was seen by the store detective, and he was stopped outside the shop and escorted back into the shop and to the manager's office where they called the police.

Two police officers attended and they searched the youth and found the four deodorants in his coat pocket, he was arrested and bought to Erdington and placed in the juvenile detention room to await a parent. Juveniles were never placed in cells. The store detective attends at Erdington and hands over her witness statement and tells me that the value of the goods stolen is about £1, the statement of course is handed to the CID, me, and it is me who is going to interview him when a parent arrives. In this case I would interview him with one of the arresting officers so allowing the other officer to return to his normal duties.

How did it go, 'never a dull moment'

The PC checks the youth out and finds he has three previous convictions for shoplifting; I sought advice from the uniform Inspector who said the youth would be charged and bailed to the juvenile court.

His mother arrived and so to the interview room we all went, I explained to his mother the reason for his arrest and I cautioned the youth and I began to read out part of the store detectives statement to him and halfway through I said, 'Have you anything to say?'

He said, 'It's a lie I never stole nothing.'

I said, 'The property was found on you, in your coat by the police.'

'He shouted, 'She put them in my coat.'

I said, 'Why would she do that?'

'Don't know don't care.' He replied.

What a horrible little boy, I thought I know what he wants but I cannot do it, but looking towards his mother I think she was just about to do what I was thinking.

Just then his mother turned to her right and slapped her lovely son straight across the face, I could feel it from where I was sitting it shook his head from one side to the other and she then said, 'Now you tell these officers the truth, they have better things to do than listen to your lies.'

I looked towards him, and he now had his head bowed and I could see a nice red mark on the side of his cheek and he promptly told me he did steal the deodorants and he was going to sell them at school the following day.

I actually met that same youth several times after that and he graduated from shop lifting to burglaries, I wonder what he is doing now.

In December I moved to Kingstanding Police Station where I immediately noticed a big change in the work you were a lot busier and there were virtually no shoplifters to be seen anywhere. I remember seeing some graffiti on the side of a shop on Kingstanding Circle it said, *'Don't go to Burtons for a suit let the local CID stitch you up'*

Christmas 1980 came and went, the CID had their Christmas party in the CID office at Erdington, where local business men and women, licensees and friends were invited and plenty of drink was available. When we had our Christmas party, Queens Road CID would cover us and when they had their party, we would cover them so at all times there would be CID on duty and of course sober.

Christmas parties in CID offices soon became a thing of the past.

December 1980 ended on a sad note really on 8th December 1980 John Lennon, one of the famous Beatles was shot dead outside his apartment, the Dakota Buildings in Upper West Side, New York. I had grown up with the Beatles like millions of other people and to end a life like this was truly horrific. Of course the man who did this act was caught and later sentenced to life imprisonment and is still inside today.

There is a garden of remembrance to John Lennon called Strawberry Fields after one of their famous songs and it is situated in Central Park just across the road from where he died.

I have actually been lucky enough to have been to New York and visited both the place where he was shot dead and the remembrance garden Central Park, it is very poignant to say the least.

1981 arrived and by February I had completed my six month attachment to the CID, no extension for me this time. I finished on the CID on the Friday and on the Monday I was back in uniform still on my old unit, so I was back with my friends and I have to say nothing had changed and on parade on that Monday, it was relief week so I was working 2.00pm x 10.00pm, and it was PC Wier, Mike 22, 7.00 refs and off I went as if I had never been away.

But of course I had and I had just finished another six months in the job I wanted to do more now than anything. I was told by the Detective Chief Inspector that I had received an excellent report from both the Sergeants who had mentored me during my attachment, but now he explained I would have to sit and wait and I maybe considered for the next vacancy.

What concerned me was that the longer you waited the more policemen and women were having attachments and the longer the list of people waiting to transfer to the CID grew, my question was would you become a distant memory and the only one that they remember was the last one. It was a strange feeling I was looking at the detective's daily thinking why don't you retire or why don't you leave the job, I want your job.

At this time and the D3 in particular were having a spate of burglaries at social clubs namely working men's clubs and ex-servicemen's clubs, where they were being broken into and the contents of the gaming and cigarette machines were being stolen, all in coins. Often the alarms would be activated but by the time the police had got there the burglary had been committed and the offenders long gone, the times of the burglaries varied but they could be as late as 5.30am in the morning.

I was asked by the DCI, Mr Rees to work with another officer and to try and solve the burglaries. So the two of us were given virtually free rein to find these burglars as soon as possible. We were allowed to work our own shifts, wear plain clothes we also had the use of a plain car and the DCI said 'Do what you can in two weeks.' So that was our remit.

Day one, intelligence gathering and what do we know about the crimes and the suspects, there would be only one place to start that was the collators office at Erdington, in there we had PC Bob 'Flash' Boyce and PC Derek 'Griff' Griffin, total police service in excess of 100 years, only joking, they both appeared to have been about for years but they were friendly, helpful and knowledgeable and that was the place to start.

Of course the collator's office did what it said on the tin, it collated information from various sources in the main from other policemen and women. Today they have a new name they are called intelligence cells but they still do the same role.

So what did we know about these burglaries, well they were all committed in the very early hours of the morning normally between 4.00am and 5.00am, entry was rough and ready there was no style to it, it was just smashing a pane of glass in a window or door or forcing a door including fire doors, there was nothing skilful or clever about how they entered the property and once inside they smashed open the fruit and gaming machines and emptying the contents, which of course in the main were coins and tokens, they would force open the cigarette machines and steal all the cigarettes and coins from there as well.

Then when finished they would leave the premises normally the same way as they had entered and would always leave the scene in a dark blue van of some description, this van had apparently been seen driving at speed shortly after the offences but up till now the police had not stopped or got a full registration number for the van.

At some of the working men's clubs and ex-service men's clubs we had some poor quality CCTV, which showed us at best, there were two offenders both white, normal build and one had curly hair and they were aged between 20 to 30 years, and the van they left in was or looked like a dark blue Morris Marina van with the numbers 33 and a letter 'V' in the registration. They had left no forensics, no fingerprints and to date no clues.

The D3 had suffered five such burglaries, the DI had suffered two, and the D2 had also suffered two burglaries, so in total we were looking at nine similar burglaries on the whole of the 'D' division and as the DCI quite often said to me 'It is not funny anymore I want you to go and catch them.'

The D3 had taken the lead in attempting to solve the burglaries purely based on the fact that we had suffered the most and for no other reason.

Were there any suspects of course there always is, we had received several names that fitted the modus operandi and two of the list of suspects lived on the D3, so that's where we would start. I put all my eggs into one basket and convinced all the police officers on the D3 these are the two we are looking at.

This was done because I knew now that the police in their general day to day work particularly when I and my colleague were not on duty they would be looking around the sub division for us, and they would leave us notes if they saw or heard anything particularly in relation to the van. We also had good information that on the morning of the burglary they would leave the scene of the burglary and park the van up in some side road and return to the van later in the day when more people were about.

Now my view was if you are going to park the van up and walk back to where you live and return to the van later that day, then the van was going to be parked not far from where you live. Most people certainly criminals do not like walking, and that's all the intelligence we had in total, it was more to work on intelligence wise than some jobs I had.

Myself and my colleague normally worked 7.00am x 3.00pm in plain clothes and every morning we checked with the collators on all three sub divisions to see if there had been a burglary during the early morning.

We would then drive to Kingstanding and begin to make our enquiries, speak with potential witnesses, re-visit the scenes of the burglaries to see if we, the police had missed anything, speak with our informants, visit cafes, betting shops and public houses to see if anybody had been offered any cigarettes on the cheap, or had people been in these places buying stuff or placing bets and using more coins that most people would normally use.

I thought finding the van would be the best way forward because the information was that they never took any of the stolen property to their respective addresses, we had our two suspect's they were good burglars and there was no in point arresting them without some good evidence. So I looked at the geographic area of where they both lived and decided that the van would be parked somewhere in the middle of where they lived, and they probably would not have a garage.

We had one suspect living in Finchley Road and one living in Parkeston Crescent, my bet was that the van would be in the Twickenham Road area or very close by, perhaps parked in one of the groves off the main road.

It was time to have a walk round and see what we could find, well the answer to the walk is we found nothing, I had lost round one to them, I needed that van and after about a day or so of looking and following my so called hunches I found it, a dark blue tatty Morris Marina van with the registration number ending in ABC 123 V, that was it I was convinced, the van was parked in a row of other cars in Brackenbury Road near to the junction with College Road not too far from where they both lived.

We had a walk past the vehicle, there was no tax on it, it was unlocked and it looked abandoned, that was going to be our van. We now had the full registration number and a PNC check revealed that the last owner had sold the vehicle about two months ago so it was time to pay him a visit.

He stated that he had sold the vehicle to a man in a pub, I had never heard that said before, 'What pub?' I asked.

'The College.'

Was his reply, well again we were certainly in the right area for our two suspects I carried on and said, 'Do you have a name for your buyer?'

He informed me, 'His name R . . .' and I can show you where he lives because I took the van to his house and I know his missus name and they have got a little boy.'

He showed us the house and yes you are right it was one of our two suspects houses, we now had some more confirmation I was happy we were heading in the right direction at last.

I briefed the controller and asked him to keep the uniform police away from the van which he agreed to, if the uniform started to take notice of this van parked up and insecure and with no tax, it is very likely our suspects would never return to it. All we had to do I believed was wait for a burglary to happen and when we came on duty at 7.00am make our way to the area of the van, and await the arrival of our two men later in the day sounds easy doesn't it just like it happens on the telly.

Week two came and still nothing in fact the van had not moved now for about six days, and you think to yourself had they finished their run of burglaries, no they are too greedy, all burglars are, they carry till they get caught. Friday morning came and I got to the police station about quarter to seven and went straight up to the controllers and I asked, 'Anything Sgt?'

He told me that at about 5.30am this morning the ex-serviceman's club in Aldridge Road was subject of a burglary and cash out the machines was taken along with cigarettes.

This is it, this is my moment this is what we wanted, just then my colleague arrived and we jumped into our car and off we went it was still dark and it was an ideal time to have a drive past to see if the van was there, yes it was and I believed it was time for a walk past to see if we can see inside the van. I volunteered for that because everybody use to say I did not look like a policeman. We parked our car in a grove but we could see the van from where we were, but I am certain they would not see our car if they should return to the van. I walked down the grove across the road past the van towards a paper shop on the corner which had just opened.

I looked inside the van the best I could but it looked full of rubbish, there were old clothes on the front passenger seat so, newspapers everywhere it was a real tip, I did not hang about to long and I went to the shop bought a newspaper and walked back to our car got in the passenger seat and waited. I informed the controller, asking him to keep marked cars away from the scene until we shouted for one, should we make an arrest.

It still looked as if the van had not moved but it must have done the burglary was about two miles away. We sat and waited 7.30am, 8.00am, 8.30am my stomach was rumbling it was past my breakfast time, 9.00am, and

9.10am, 'That's them.' I shouted to my colleague our two main suspects were walking from the newsagents to the van, were they going to walk past, no they both stopped and lit cigarettes and the one suspect opened the passenger door, I thought it is now or never, my colleague drove the car and parked parallel to their van thus blocking the van in, I jumped out ran around the van and detained the passenger my colleague got out the driver's side and had detained the second man as he was about to walk away from the scene.

It was over in seconds both of our suspects were now being unmercifully thrown into the rear of our vehicle and we quickly informed the controller that two were in custody and can we have a double manned marked car as soon as possible to transport the two prisoners. I leant into the back of our car and said top both men, 'We are police officers, you are both under arrest for a burglary that occurred at the . . . ex-serviceman's club this morning.'

Neither made any reply, but of course this was only the start I wanted to look into that van because I wanted to find the cash and cigarettes. The marked car Zulu 7 arrived and took our two prisoners to Erdington Police Station, now we could look in the van.

We opened the rear doors of the van and it was full of rubbish, old clothes, boxes, newspapers it looked like the inside of a bin but what we did find was a Nat West cash bag full of £1 coins and a plastic bag with over 1000 cigarettes inside, this is was what we wanted, this was our evidence we had struck gold.

Back at the police station I telephoned Kingstanding CID and two detectives DC Breakwell and DC Charles arrived it was for them to do the interviews and DC Breakwell knew both of the men in custody. Our part was we went to the canteen and had breakfast and then we assisted the two detectives.

At the end of the day the two men admitted a total of six burglaries and in due course at Birmingham Crown Court pleaded guilty and were sent to prison. Congratulations all round but I still wanted to be a detective but certainly this case did me no harm at all.

For me it was back to Mike 22,but this time not for very long as I had heard that one of the detectives at Erdington was leaving to become a licensee, I needed to know if I was in with a chance so I went to see the DCI, if you don't ask you don't get was my thought. He was very none committal and informed me that there were one or two names currently being looked at and a decision would be made in the near future. Not much good for me I thought, but I did not wait long because the rumours around the police station was that I was going to replace the departing detective.

About four weeks later the DCI called me into his office and offered me a detectives post at Erdington. 'Did I want it?' he asked.

'Yes. I most certainly do.' I said, I nearly kissed him on the forehead but thought that would not be very professional.

My transfer to the CID would be shown on police orders known as 'pinks' because that was the colour of the paper that they used, it contained details of moves, transfers, retirements and promotions, general stuff like that and I could not move until it was on there because it was up to personnel at Lloyd House to rectify any moves and to put that move into pinks. So all I had to do was wait and hope everybody had done their job properly, pinks came out every Thursday so it was just a matter of waiting.

Then it happened I was on 2.00pm x 10.00pm on the Thursday and my Inspector said, 'Have you seen pinks yet?'

'No not yet.' I replied and he handed me a copy of that day's pinks and there it was in black and white, sorry black and pink, 5th April 1981 PC 3055 Wier D3 to DC 3055 Wier D3.

As from the 5th April 1981 I was a detective, all my hard work had paid off and after six years of trying and working and sometimes praying I was now a detective.

CHAPTER SEVEN
The CID

Monday 5th April 1981, my first day as a Detective Constable in the West Midlands Police and apart from a 12 month period between April 1998 and April 1999, I spent the rest of my police service as a detective until I retired in March 2005 a total of 24 years. How lucky was I and I would do it all over again if asked. I loved the job and being a detective had been my goal and here I was.

Day one at Erdington Police Station, I knew most of the detectives by face and some by name now I was going to work with them. I wanted to work at Kingstanding Police Station as a detective, but first things first the opportunity to work at Kingstanding was not going to be too far away. On your first day you meet with the Detective Inspector who in turn introduces you to your DS, who in turn introduces you to the rest of the office. I was given a desk, a chair and a diary and off I went.

At Erdington I was sat facing DC Andy Hipkiss and together we called ourselves the 'Erdington Popular Front' do not ask me why because I do not know, suffice to say that on the television at the time was a programme starring Robert Lindsay and he was known as Smithy of the 'Tooting Popular Front' he was a bit of a rebellious character. I did not think that either Andy or I were in any way rebellious, but perhaps in other people's eyes we were.

You were given your postings for the month and you were given a particular area to work and that was it, as normal you were expected to interview all prisoners arrested for crime, and that unfortunately because it was Erdington, the dreaded word shoplifters sprang to mind and yes you were expected to interview them.

One of my first jobs as a detective at Erdington was the theft of newspapers, so how does the theft of newspapers finish up at Warwick Crown Court. I will tell you, WH Smiths on Erdington High Street were being plagued with people stealing newspapers and the reason being is that the newspapers were delivered at around 4.30am and the shop did not open until 6.00am and when I say newspapers there were probably five or six larges bundles of them covering all titles of newspapers literally hundreds of them.

The job to sort this out was left to the local beat officer WPC Alison Kay (later to become the wife of PC Michael Saunders who I mentioned earlier in the book) and a young probationer PC Ezra Sealy.

I walked in one morning and there were two local youths in custody for the offence. I looked at the evidence that was available, it appeared good, they were observed to remove some of the newspapers from one of the bundles, and they both walked off they were chased and detained but not before they had managed to throw the newspapers into another shop doorway.

Plenty of evidence, including we had the word of two police officers. I later interviewed them and they both denied everything, but because of the available evidence both youths were charged with Theft of the newspapers and bailed to Sutton Coldfield Magistrates Court. I never gave the matter another thought, the papers were submitted to the court by the arresting officers.

However some weeks later I was approached by the same two officers with a request to prepare a committal file of papers for the Crown Court, as these two had both pleaded not guilty at the Magistrates' Court and as is their right they had both elected trial at the Crown Court before a jury. £20.00 worth of newspapers was now going to be heard at the Crown Court.

On the due day the three of us travelled to Warwick Crown Court and after listening to the evidence the court found them guilty and fined them a small amount of money, it was a total waste of time and of course taxpayer's money.

A lot of our work comes from what is known as the night note, this is a typewritten or sometimes handwritten note left by the night detective, and it would normally include all serious crime, and all prisoners for crime who were still in custody and still to be dealt with. So the day staff CID would pick this up in the morning and deal with it, in other words you would either win an investigation or win the prisoners but you would normally win something off the night note.

Nights as a detective I thought was most enjoyable, you would normally work about three or four sets of nights a year, you began on a Monday night and ended seven days later on a Sunday night/Monday morning, you would work from 10.0pm until either 6.00am or later in my service it was 7.00am.

You would as a night detective cover the whole division and that would include for me, D1, D2 and D3 in effect you were there to make and advise on decisions about crime, assist and advise the uniform officers, to interview prisoners if possible, it was a responsible part of being a detective.

Also part of your job was to make sure the night note was delivered to all sub divisions and to leave a copy for the CID, and normally copies for the DI, the DCI and the Detective Superintendent. In other words the view was when you were at home and in bed and day staff CID and respective senior officers came on duty, they knew more or less what had happened on their sub division during the night in relation to crime and prisoners.

I suppose the dreaded part of being a detective was arriving for work at 9.00am in the morning and as you drive into the back yard the night detective is still there, you see his car he is still on duty and as you walk up the stairs you can hear the typewriter clicking away and as you enter the CID office, the night detective is there surrounded by cigarette smoke, brown paper and brown paper bags, and probably blood stained clothing and you knew then you were in for a long day.

And then he spoke, 'Had a nasty rape last night' or 'Got one in hospital badly injured, and three in the cells for it' but hey that's why I wanted to be a detective. You very rarely walked into a murder because normally if it was on your sub division then the DI would have called you out in the early hours of the morning and that has happened to me many, many, many times probably too many to even try to remember.

I always thought of nights like that television programme by the famous author Raul Dahl and that was 'Tales of the unexpected'

1981 was a most unsettling time in England and we were going through a period when the country was in the grip of riots, one of the first was the Brixton riot in London then on 10th July 1981, Birmingham had its own riot in Handsworth a suburb of Birmingham.

The riots were allegedly caused by heavy handed policing and drug related problems in the area, other sources claimed that the local black British felt aggrieved at the increase in Asian owned businesses in Handsworth. Whatever the cause it led to a night of serious public order offences and a clear attack on the police, damage was caused to buildings and property, persons were injured including police officers and many people were arrested, fortunately the riot was all over by the following morning.

What I do remember about being a detective was I think the long hours that we use to work, quiet often you would go to work at 8.00am and not return home until 11.00pm on the night it was not like being in uniform. In uniform when you finished at 2.00pm another shift of officers came on and when you finished at 10.00pm another shift of officers came on and when you finished at 6.00am another shift of officers came on.

With the CID it was not like that you never had another shift of officers, and so if you were on 9.00am x 5.00pm and at 4.30pm say there was an armed robbery, you never went home, you stayed on and dealt with it, you just carried on until you finished, and then of course before you went home you went for a pint, and I remember my wife saying whenever you telephone me to say there's been a murder or a rape or you are going to be late home, you always come home smelling of beer.

I always told her that as a detective, I had to switch off and have my down time and a pint and a smoke was the best way I could do it, I am certain she understood after all we are still married today.

There was to be a change in August 1981, I swopped places with a woman detective she moved to Erdington and I moved to Kingstanding, I will never know the reason why, but hey I was at Kingstanding CID and there to meet me was perhaps the best and most competent policeman, I have ever met in more ways than one during my whole 30 years in the police, it was Detective Sergeant Malcolm Ross all 6' 9" inches of him.

The man was a giant in every way but gentle with it and he rose in this force to the rank of Detective Superintendent before he retired.

In the office there were four detectives including me, DC Brian Breakwell who have already mentioned in this book, DC Ron Carlill who had hair like Elvis Presley and DC Malcolm Wynn an ex-soldier and late joiner to the police and on occasions we would of course have an attached man, I had been there as the attached man if you remember.

I even managed to change my car again, this time I bought a Ford Granada registration number JOM 878W, a real Sweeney car, I bought this from Bristol Street motors and I will always remember it because it had an electric sun roof that leaked when it rained heavy.

I was getting used to working at Kingstanding and enjoying it then one morning I walked in and Malcolm Wynn said, 'I know where there is a stolen motor bike you coming with me?'

Obviously I agreed to go with him, but hold on I hate and detest motor bikes and everything about them the noise, the smell and the leathers I hate the lot. But if it was stolen there might well be a prisoner for it and that is what I am paid for, we got into the car and drove the short distance to Caversham Road, we parked the car and we both got out and walked towards this house, a scruffy looking house at that and Malcolm said, 'It's in the back garden.'

So we walked down the side of the house opened the back gate and there it was a big motor bike staring at me we noted the number and checked it on the PNC, yes it was stolen two days ago from Sutton Coldfield.

A quick knock on the door and one man was in custody, not before we had a look around his house; there were motor bike parts in every room including the kitchen. He was arrested and taken to Kingstanding

Police Station and a police van was called for and all the parts of the motor bikes including the stolen motor bike were loaded up and also bought to the station.

Now at the rear of Kingstanding Police Station was a stable, honest, at this time the force had police horses about 30 or so I think, and Kingstanding was one of their stops a bit like a motorway service station for horses, and its where they could get a drink and some hay, that's the horse and not the rider and that's the truth, but over the next few weeks it was going to become a stable of stolen motor bikes and motor bike parts.

We interviewed the suspect and talk about spilling the beans, he told us everything, how many motor bikes he stole, how many motor bikes other people had stolen and where they were, were all the bits of them were, who bought what and who's got what. So for the next week or so we became the 'motor bike squad' every day sometimes twice a day we were arresting people, interviewing them, charging and bailing them and recovering motor bikes and bits of motor bikes the police station became full of them.

And in total we had charged eight youths with Theft and Handling Stolen Goods and had bailed them to the Magistrates Court and thank god I did not have to do the file of evidence for that case, which was down to DC Wynn.

Everything was eventually sorted and defendants were all dealt with at the Crown Court and I think most got suspended prison sentences, and in due course we either returned the motor bikes to their lawful owners, or if we could not find an owner the property was disposed of under the Police Property Act 1974.

November 1981 was a month to remember for all the wrong reasons, it was during this month on a Friday afternoon that a 13 year schoolboy was abducted on his way home from school as he cycled through Sutton Park, and what happened to the poor lad in the park will now only be known by his two attackers.

When he failed to arrive home from school that evening his father contacted firstly the school to be told that his son was not there and then he telephoned the police.

Of course it was November and by 5.00pm it was dark and so the park keeper for the park had to be called out, we needed to open the park gates to allow the police and volunteers in to try and make as good as search as darkness and time would allow them, the search continued until about 1.00am.

The search resumed the following day then it suddenly ground to the halt with the devastating news that the naked body of a young boy had been found in a field in a village in Warwickshire called Fenny Drayton, and as a result of the finding the body, it had now become a murder enquiry as he had been brutally murdered. The poor lad's cycle was found in bushes not too far away in Bedworth near Coventry.

An incident room was set up at Sutton Coldfield Police Station and the police were certain that they were looking for a dangerous individual, and began to check known paedophiles and perverts but thankfully they did not have to wait long for a breakthrough in the murder investigation.

The following day after the young lads body had been found member of staff at the Princess Alice children's home in New Oscott discovered 30 year old Paul Corrigan, in the grounds of the home had had apparently tried to kill himself by connecting mains electricity to a bath full of water and had failed.

Corrigan began for some reason to confide in this member of staff and he admitted to him that he had previous convictions for sex offences and by now the member of staff was convinced that he had the young lad's killer so he detained him and called the police.

Paul Corrigan was now in custody initially for burglary but later for murder.

He was later interviewed over several days and it was in his ninth interview that he finally admitted what he had done, and his associate in the murder a 16 year old youth was also now implicated in this horrific crime. The youth was very quickly arrested by the police and they were convinced that they now had the killers of the young lad both safely in custody.

I have no intention in this book to outline what the killers did to the young lad but suffice to say it was very, very brutal and very, very violent.

The most distressing part of this murder investigation is shortly after abducting the young lad the killers took him back to the flat, what Corrigan rented and that flat was not far from Kingstanding Police Station where I was working on that very evening.

On 16th June 1982 both Corrigan and the 16 year old pleaded Guilty to manslaughter, Corrigan was ordered to be detained for life, his associate was sentenced to seven years and of course is now out and about.

What one human being can actually do to another human being is beyond belief, and now I had entered into the world of the CID and over the next few years I was going to find out, because it is not a proud fact but I have worked on too many murders to mention and in their own way all the murders were horrific and to this day I do not know the reason why people murder one another.

1982 began with me getting offered a CID course, now all detectives had to complete this course if they wanted to stop on the CID and to remain as a detective and if you for some reason you failed the course you could be removed from your role as a detective and returned to uniform, so for that reason it was an important course and a course you needed to pass.

The course was known as the Junior CID course, and it was for ten weeks it was a residential course and was to be held at the police training centre at Tally Ho, now you try and explain to your wife that you are going away for ten weeks and will only be home for weekends and it's at Tally Ho, that being five miles down the road from where we lived, it did take some explaining but in fairness she has always been supportive of my work.

I remember my CID course well because The Falklands Conflict began on 2nd April 1982, my course began on 5th April 1982 and my course finished on 11th June 1982 and The Falklands Conflict finished on 14th June 1982.

I suppose there were about sixteen of us in the class most were trainee detectives but some like me had been a detective for over 12 months, I do recall one of the detectives in the class who had failed his exams was to be returned to uniform on the following Monday. The class was made up of police from different police forces although the West Midlands had about five detectives in the class

The course was there to teach you law in more depth, learn about the forensic side of our job, take part in practical's, detailed statement taking, I suppose it was the CID version of your initial training at Ryton all those years before.

We had two detectives from the Royal Ulster Constabulary on the course now I thought I had it hard and worked long hours but it was nothing compared to those two, I could sit and listen to them for ages, telling us true stories of policing in Belfast in the 1980's.

Being one of the local officers to the Birmingham area we acted likes guides to the rest of the class, so where they wanted to go we would take them whether it was a pub, curry house, do not forget Birmingham is the home of the balti curry, now some of the detectives had never heard of a balti curry let alone tried one, so of course we had several visits to the Ladypool Road, the home of the famous balti restaurants, most of them could not understand why you did not get a knife and fork with your curry only a big piece of bread called a nam.

We took them to museums, cinemas, shows and football matches we took in a cricket match at Edgbaston, which incidentally is across the road from Tally Ho. We also took them on a black country pub crawl to pubs like Ma Pardoes, The Crooked House also known as the leaning pub, it does actually lean and the more you drink the straighter it gets, honest, the Dry Dock, this is a pub that's actually got a real canal barge in the lounge and they make Dan Dare meat pies the size of dustbin lids.

They all seemed to enjoy the nights out, in particular the two lads from Northern Ireland, I suppose for the first time in a very long time they could actually relax and switch off.

But of course the all-important part of the course was the tenth week, when we had three consecutive days of examinations and you had to pass them all, you had to get at least the class average. Everyone did apart from that one I mentioned earlier.

The Thursday night of the tenth week we had our course dinner which for ease we had at Tally Ho and then on the Friday you said your good byes and returned to your own forces and police stations.

I said I would always remember my CID course because it ran parallel with the Falklands Conflict but whilst I was busy enjoying myself a total of 257 British serviceman and women died and a total of 649 Argentinian serviceman and women died, that's real.

The abduction and murder of a three year old girl was part of my blackest time at Kingstanding, I was involved in this murder from day one and now almost 30 years Later it turns my stomach to think about it.

A young couple from Kingstanding who I will not name for their sake, lived with their three children, one evening they had decided on an evening out and got a baby sitter in to look after the children, he was an 18 year old lad who they knew and who lived local I think they had used him before. The couple arrived home at about 2.30am in the morning and they noticed that the baby sitter had gone, they were annoyed, but they thought nothing more about it and went to bed, the following morning they discovered that their 3 year old daughter was missing.

Instantly they thought perhaps their daughter had been playing up so the baby sitter had taken the girl to his parent's house in Finchley Road so that's where they went. They spoke with his parents but hey had not seen their son for a few days and certainly had not seen the young girl, their son did not live at home as he had his own flat, so quite naturally panic sets in, their daughter is missing and so to all extent is the baby sitter.

The police are called, but what did we know about the babysitter, well we knew from his parents that he had a car which was described as an old Ford Escort unfortunately nobody knew the number of it, and we knew he had a flat down by Birmingham City's football ground. Enquiries soon revealed where the flat was but before we had got to his flat, other police officers had found his car abandoned on waste ground not far from where he lived, and in searching the car our worst fears were realised when it was confirmed the young girl had been found dead in the boot of the car.

I felt that I wanted to kill the person responsible for this completely horrendous crime on a young defenceless child. Not of course the right thing to think, but he was responsible for the death of a 3 year old girl. I do hope some other policeman finds him before I do. They did he was arrested walking back to his flat and taken to Erdington Police Station.

I was not allowed to interview him and I thank god I was not he was interviewed by senior officers because of the sensitive nature of the investigation so I understand it he made no admissions to the crime.

He was later charged with the young girl's murder and in due course appeared at Birmingham Crown Court where after a trial he was found guilty and he was sentenced to life imprisonment.

Why did he do it, we will never know but this murder was quite truthfully one of the worst murders that I have ever been involved in, in my police career.

I have not gone into full details of this crime because as with the abduction and murder of the young lad this crime to was so very violent and brutal and again I will ask the same question what possess one human being to do this sort of crime to another human being.

There is a footnote to this horrendous crime, the father of the murdered girl was later cautioned for stealing a motor car on that fateful night apparently that is how he and his partner had got home after their evening out.

What a very strange world we live in.

At the other end of the age group for murder was an old man who was found murdered in his own house in Norbiton Road, Kingstanding at the back of the police station, I was on 2.00pm x 10.00pm that day and quite literally had just walked into the CID office, DS Ross told me what had happened, he informed me that the old man was an easy touch for the local youths as he would pay them to go and get his cigarettes and other little errands, so the persons responsible would most certainly be local and would most certainly have known the old man and been in his house before, the DS was convinced.

So off we went, house to house enquiries, local shops, pubs, cafes and betting shops and during our enquiries we arrested a couple of the local youths who were wanted on warrant. Did they know anything, you sometimes have to keep asking different people, someone will speak eventually because the last thing people want is the police crawling round asking questions, that is what I use to work on, they did not want you there, so they would say something to get rid of you, sometimes it was a straightforward lie others times when you were talking about murder they would tell you a little bit of the truth, I must say it all helped.

We knew the people responsible were local and the DS said, 'I will be buying the beer tonight.'

He was that confident that a result was not far away. Now when you explain to these people that we are not looking at someone for a bit of damage, it is murder that we are looking at people for, they do tend to talk saying things like it is not my son but I would not trust so and so. I was confident we would get a result it would be one of the young people who had been in the old man's house that I was certain of.

But of course the question was why was he killed, did these locals think he had a stash of money somewhere, it appeared that if that is what they thought they would be well truly disappointed because all he had was his pension.

I think that was the strange thing about the folks of Kingstanding, they would not tell you who broke a window or stole a car but they would tell you who murdered someone, although on most occasions they would not make a written statement I suppose they were like police informants but they did things for nothing.

As a result of gossip and hard police work by mid-afternoon we knew who we were looking for, for the murder it was two local brothers and it was now time to visit the pubs because that's where we would find them that's where they spent their days, so that's what we did however we never found them in the local pubs, but by the time we had visited a couple of pubs and the word had got round that we were looking for them, we had a call on the police radio telling us that two people were at Kingstanding Police Station and they wanted to give themselves up, something to do with the old man.

I was not certain at this stage if they even knew the old man was dead, but they soon did now, because when we got to the police station both men had been arrested on suspicion of murder and placed in separate police cells. They had both been arrested by the attached man, he was in the right place at the right time, he had gone back to the station to use the toilet when the two brothers walked in, lucky or what.

By 10.00pm, interviews finished, certain admissions made, they were both charged with murder and taken by marked police car to the Central Lock Up at Steelhouse Lane for their court appearance in the morning, meanwhile the DS kept to his word and we went for a good drink and yes I was late home again smelling of beer and cigarettes.

The two brothers were later jailed for life for the senseless murder of this old man.

Having now completed my CID course I felt like a real detective, I am not sure why but when you do the course it feels as if you have now ticked all the right boxes for all the right people.

So much happened when I was at Kingstanding, I was on 9.00am x 5.00pm one Sunday, I was the only one on at Kingstanding and I think one detective may have been on at Erdington, it was about ten to five and I walked down the stairs from our office, and walked into the front office to say goodnight to the office man, when the telephone rang, the office man said, 'Its DC Gray from Queens Road are you in?'

I said, 'Yes I suppose so.'

I took the call, DC Gray, who I knew very well for my time at Queens Road told me, 'Nigel, I need you down here now, the uniform have arrested a bus load of boxing fans from the Brookvale, can you get here quick I am trying to contact the DS at Sutton, but I need some help with all the prisoners and witnesses.'

I hardly had time to answer him and he had gone. I thought if he is taking the micky I'll kill him, for he was well known for his weird 'sense of humour' anyway I got into my own car and thought I will drive past the Brookvale pub on the way to Queens Road Police Station to see if there has been an incident or there is any sign of disorder. As I reached the pub and looked at it I thought there has most certainly been an incident.

I could see most of the windows had been put in, there were broken glasses and bottles all over the floor, upturned tables and chairs and some cars with the windows put through, there was a big sign at the front of the pub which said something like, 'Live boxing today, tickets £2 free curry'

Policemen were stood outside admiring the damage. Right I thought damage to the pub, a couple in the cells for drunk and disorderly, perhaps a couple for criminal damage soon sort this out and I will be off home. I confidently went to Queens Road thinking DC Gray has exaggerated this incident and I'll be home in an hour.

I drove into the rear yard at Queens Road and what did I see, yes you have guessed it a single decker bus with most of its windows broken, I am beginning to like this less and less, I walked into the back of the station and upstairs to the CID office where I found DC Gray and two policeman off the theft from vehicle squad, DC Gray looked up from his desk whilst smoking his favourite hamlet cigar and said, 'Thank god you are here I have telephoned the gaffer and he has allowed me to call another two officers in, and we can use a couple of the more experienced officers off the shift, and the DS is on his way from Sutton.'

I am thinking what the hell have we got and he was not exaggerating,

DC Gray explained there had been a boxing match at the Brookvale Public House between two different boxing clubs and near to the end the whole lot has gone up and we have three men in hospital not badly injured and we have sixteen arrested and in the cells.

'Sixteen' I screamed 'Sixteen' I do not think for one moment that I would be going home within the hour.

I walked down downstairs and yes the cell block was full we had two or three to a cell old and young alike, and the front reception area of the police station was full of their relatives and friends and the time was ten to six on a Sunday night, great I thought how great ! Who would be a detective, first things first I had to telephone the wife to say I will be late home again this time because of a pub fight.

The police had responded to a violent incident and arrested all the persons who were in the process of leaving on the bus and away from the public house. All the women and children were dusted down and we ended up with some sixteen male adults in custody and clearly some of them were not involved in the fighting according to the witnesses.

So the main thing in the first instance was witness statements, these would and did include the licensee and his wife who surprisingly we knew as we used the pub, bar staff and anybody else we could find not involved in the fight and of course descriptions and clothing worn would be a big factor so that was made a priority. We had uniform officers at the scene doing just that.

By about ten that night most things were now clear in our minds, the prisoners were bedded down for the night and I would be back at Queens Road at 7.00am on the Monday to begin the interviews, and of course on the Monday we would have more CID staff. Monday arrived and during the day we split into teams and completed interviews, myself and DC Gray worked together and by about 6.00pm we had 11 charged with making an affray and causing criminal damage and the other five were refused charged and made witness statements.

What a 24 hours that was and I never did like boxing.

I am well into 1983 and have completed two very busy years at Kingstanding and I loved every minute.

Time for a bit of history now on 31st January 1983 the wearing of seat belts for the driver and the front seat passenger became law in the United Kingdom, that's a law that has never been broken!!!

One of the group of individuals I disliked the most were the low life who broke into people's houses, they would steal property it could be electrical items it could be personal property, it could be valuables left to them by love ones, by and large burglars quite literally would if the demand arose steal anything, they stole and nine times out of ten they would sell the property cheaply to get money to buy drugs, cigarettes or drink.

These same people would cause wanton damage when inside the house, for no apparent reason or possibly the reason was jealousy of what you had worked for and surrounded yourself with, but some of the lowest scum I have dealt with and I make no apology for using the word would be the individuals who would pull back the bed sheets and leave their excrement there and that did happen I can assure you more than once.

Now you just imagine this you have returned home from work and have discovered that you have been broken into and some of your valuables have been stolen or even damaged. You are totally distressed to think someone has invaded your personal space and they may even have gone through your personal clothing and thrown that about or just wantonly damaged it.

You telephone the police and they attend and do their job and take various details about what time you left the house, and what time did you return, and they need from you a list of any of the stolen property with identifying marks or serial numbers if possible.

In some cases the policeman will tell you not to tidy up but to wait for the scenes of crime officer to attend, and to see if the burglars have left any forensic evidence behind, mainly in the early eighties it would be fingerprints, do not forget this is long before the introduction of DNA.

They leave, the scenes of crime officers leave and then you tidy the house up when you have finished you are totally worn out, so you retire to bed and you would pull back the sheets and I think you know the rest of the story. So every effort was made to catch up with these people but it is like everything in life even the police need luck.

One day the CID staff at Kingstanding had some.

The 2.00pm x 10.00pm detective had just walked into the office and informed us that he had just seen five of Kingstanding's finest walking up Rough Road towards Monmouth Drive, and he named them and guess what they did for a living amongst other things, yes they broke into houses, and they are now walking to one of the better areas on the 'D' division where properties then in the early eighties sold for several hundred thousand pounds.

Where were they going we thought and then decided there is only one thing for us to do, so the three of us jumped into the CID car and off we drove, the intention was for us was to try and follow them as best as we could bearing in mind they knew us and they knew the CID car, but if by seeing us it stops them breaking into anywhere then job done.

We drove up Rough Road into Banners Gate Road down to the traffic lights with Chester Road and then crossed Chester Road and into Monmouth Drive, do not ask me why but they never looked round but they did not, had they had done then we would certainly have been spotted as the CID car we were in was most famous in the Kingstanding area, it was a chocolate coloured Austin Allegro with the registration number of BOP 762V, I can remember it to this day and every criminal in Kingstanding knew it as well.

I suppose they could have been going into Sutton Coldfield to shop or buy their moms something or more likely to go and shoplift, but let's give it a few minutes and see what they get up to. Once in Monmouth Drive we were on the D2 so we informed the controller who we were and what we were doing and could he if possible keep marked police cars out of the area for a bit, but could you ask a police dog handler to work short around the area in case we needed him or more likely his dog.

This lovely group of hard working individuals then turned right into Jeavons Road and left into Markham

Road, one thing was for certain they were not going shopping.

We were about two hundred yards away and when we reached the junction we looked down Markham Road but we could not see them, where the hell had they disappeared to so we sat in the car windows open, smoking, thinking where have they gone. A school up the road was beginning to turn out and parents were driving into Jeavons Road to pick their children up and we all thought we will never find them now, that's what was going through our minds.

But then it happened as the song goes, 'we heard the sound of breaking glass' it was coming from a house in Markham Road, number 12 on the right from where we were now standing, we could see the downstairs front curtains being drawn, this was our house, they the famous five were breaking into this house.

As we got nearer we could see a large pane of glass in the bottom of the front door had been smashed, we informed the D2 controller we had persons on premises and could he send a double manned fast response car and a dog man, the marked car was directed to the rear and the plan was for us three to go in the front door, but they must have been spooked because all of a sudden the front door is thrown open and out they come and with the assistance of the now arrived dog man we detained four of the five after a bit of a chase, they were not going that far because we knew them anyway.

Other police vehicles arrived and the four who had now been arrested for burglary were taken to Sutton Coldfield Police Station. But we saw five, he must have got out the back somehow but the officers at the rear of the house who were still there said quite adamantly that no one has come out this way.

So as we entered the house with the intention of searching for the fifth youth, we could see their goodies lined up by the front door, video recorder, portable TV set, cassette player and cassettes, and the statutory suitcase, most burglars at this time carried their goods away in a suitcase it was so much less obvious than walking along the street carrying a video recorder.

We knew we were looking for a youth known as 'Little Tom' he was barely five foot tall and was made up of skin and bones, so he could be anywhere, so we let the police dog in perhaps he can find him, the dog ran round the house upstairs and downstairs but with no joy, there was only the loft area left unsearched so who's going up there.

Now being the slimmest policeman there I was chosen without choice so up I went, the loft area was light as there was a skylight in there, I had a look round but initially found nothing so I sat down and waited and listened, then I thought there is only one place left so I stood up walked over and on tip toes looked into the cold water tank and there he was 'Little Tom' up to his neck in cold water I dragged him out and passed him down to waiting officers and he too was taken along with the others to Sutton Coldfield Police Station.

All five were later interviewed with the assistance of detectives from Sutton Coldfield and later that night they were charged and bailed with an offence of Burglary Dwelling House and dealt with by the courts in due course.

Told you even the CID has to have some luck.

1983 ended just before Christmas with the Provisional IRA planting a bomb outside Harrods store in London which resulted in the death of six innocent people including three police officers and over seventy five people were injured some seriously.

The season of good will was here.

1984 began with a tragic set of consequences which resulted in the death of a young policeman from Erdington Police Station.

In that year there was a store called Owen and Owen and it was situated on the corner of Newman Road and High Street, Erdington, and on Saturday 4th February 1984, there was a report to the police of persons trying to break into the store by using the metal fire escape staircase at the side of the store.

Police Officers responded and it led to a chase of the offenders over the roof top of the store, unfortunately Police Constable Andrew Stephen Le-Comte who was 21 years old tragically fell from the roof to his death.

The two youths were later arrested and on that Saturday I was on duty at Kingstanding and was called to Erdington Police Station to assist the CID officers there with the investigation into the circumstances surrounding the incident.

High Street itself was full of shops that were regularly being burgled and there was a group of youths who were suspected of committing the crimes including the two who were under arrest. The investigation was led at Erdington by Detective Sergeant Tim Davies and I will tell you this from a personal point of view I would not want this man investigating me he was so thorough it was frightening but what a detective to have on duty on this Saturday.

We never stopped from morning till night and in total there were about nine arrests for Burglary and Handling Stolen Goods and were all charged later that day, stolen property was recovered and a lot of High Street crime was cleared to these individuals but at the end of the day the saddest part was the death of the officer was a tragic accident.

Every year since an award to the best probationer of the year in the police is awarded and is called the Andrew Le-Comte award.

History time again on 12th March 1984 the UK Miners' strike began the strike was to last until 3rd March 1985, it was one of the biggest industrial actions of post war England and its defeat by the Conservatives is said to have significantly weakened the British Trade Union movement.

It was called by the National Union of Mineworkers leader Arthur Scargill and it was caused by the closure of pits some 20 of them that were not deemed viable. The miners' strike hit every police force in the country as they had to supply officers seven days a week and during the term of the strike there were many reported violent clashes between police and strikers probably the most famous being and what was dubbed 'The battle of Orgreave' where police confronted the striking miners' on horseback.

At Orgreave on 29th May 1984 a total of 41 police officers were injured, 28 miners were injured and 81 arrests were made and police officers were using riot gear for the first time in the three month old strike.

The end of the strike came on 3rd March 1985, after certain events which changed people's views of the strike and that included the death of a taxi driver who was taking a working miner to work, and as he was driving by some striking miners who were on a bridge above the road threw a concrete post onto the windscreen of the taxi killing the driver and now this caused massive public opinion to start going against the miners.

During the industrial action the facts are, a total of 11, 291 people were arrested, six pickets died and three teenagers also died picking coal from a colliery waste heap plus of course the taxi driver who was killed and the two striking miners' who served time for his manslaughter.

Near to the end of the strike over half of the miners had given up and returned to work and the Prime Minister of the day Margaret Thatcher claimed victory over the miners and in particular their leader Authur Scargill.

And what of Authur Scargill well he remained President of the National Union of Mineworkers until 2002 when he retired at the age of 64 years.

Was there a winner in this strike I do not think so.

I had been at Kingstanding for nearly three years now and as always in the police things were changing, DS Ross had been promoted to uniform Inspector and went to work at Stetchford and this led to us for some reason having two new detective sergeants at Kingstanding and we also had a new Detective Chief Inspector Mr Heatley.

In April 1984 DCI Heatley asked me if I wished to front up a Burglary Squad to tackle on-going problems with burglaries especially dwelling houses on the D3, there would be a team of four including myself and DC Dave Forrester. I had to select two police constables that I thought would be good for the squad, I was to look at hard working thief takers and I knew two such policemen straight away they were PC Derek Forrest and PC Terry Cleaver, we were to be based in the CID office Erdington Police Station.

I agreed to take on the new role it was once again a new challenge and a week or so later the D3 Burglary Squad was born.

CHAPTER EIGHT
The Burglary Squad

On Monday 16th April 1984 the D3 Burglary Squad was in business and the business we were in was to reduce the number burglaries particularly in dwelling houses and to catch burglars and put them before the court.

We would if we could attempt to visit all scenes of burglaries and keep constant liaison with the scenes of crime officers, to see if they had been lucky enough to obtain any forensic evidence especially fingerprints, to build up a relationship with the Fingerprint Officers based at Lloyd House, so if we did have a fingerprint 'lift' from a burglary then we could speak direct to them and suggest names to them so they could conduct a search of our suggested names against the fingerprint lifts. We were to encourage our informants and liaise regularly with second hand shops and pawn shops in our area.

We were to be based at Erdington Police Station which again suited me as the station was in walking distance to where I was still living at the time and we would be directly answerable to DS Davies at Erdington.

We worked well together and we quickly built up a good working relationship with all the detectives on the D3 and all four units of uniform officers on the D3. We had to look at burglary patterns and try and identify the most vulnerable areas on the D3 and to spend more of a time there and whenever we visited a burglary we would also make house to house enquires and obtain witness statements if they were needed, in the main we dealt with burglaries only and not the normal run of the mill stuff that the other detectives dealt with.

A further part of our job description was to visit convicted prisoners in prison serving time for Burglary or similar offences, to ascertain if they wished to admit to other offences and that the other admitted offences subject of a Superintendents authorisation could be 'written off' to them whilst they were inside, they would face no further charges.

It was a way of them wiping their slates clean prior to being released and also to know that they would not be 'gate arrested' as they left the prison.

I was never a big fan of prison visits and write offs, but the senior officers of the time loved them because it balanced the books, it cleared crime and ultimately made senior officers look good to Lloyd House.

I suppose in my service one of the best thief takers I knew was PC Terry Cleaver, he was like a magnet to thieves, we use to joke that he fell over them but in reality that's exactly what happened, and an example of that was when we had been at Erdington for a couple of days, and he wanted to return some detained property to a complainant who lived on the Lyndhurst Estate about a ten minute walk away, 'I'll only be 10 minutes' he said and off he went.

About five minutes or so later our telephone rang and I answered it and it was the controller, telling me that PC Cleaver had just arrested two youths for breaking into a car and could we go and get him and his prisoners. He had just arrived at the block of flats where he was going to take the property back when he observed the two youths force entry to a parked car and he arrested them so yes he did fall over them but of course that's what we wanted him to do.

He never did get to return his property that day because the two arrested youths admitted several offences of theft from motor vehicles, when we later interviewed so it was down to him that we had such a good start on the Burglary Squad.

I suppose the eighties were the decade of squads, if the police had a problem you set up a squad to deal with it, we had the Serious Crime Squad, Regional Crime Squad,

Drug Squad, Fraud Squad, Cheque Squad, Anti-Terrorist Squad, Immigration Squad, Stolen Vehicle Squad, Robbery Squad, Vice Squad, Bomb Squad, Plain Clothes Squad, Shop lifting Squad, Theft from Vehicle Squad and Burglary Squad to name just a few, as I've said you had a problem you set up a squad and in the main they worked.

Of course that all changed as a result of the Serious Crime Squad being disbanded in 1989 amid rumours of corruption and with that in mind the word 'squad' began to disappear, they assumed all squads were corrupt and the word squad was replaced with words like 'unit' and 'team' more of this later in the book.

Second hand shops were a good source of prisoner and we made regular visits to them in order to check their books, they of course are supposed to take details of the person offering to sell the goods to them including the sellers address, and on regular occasions they would telephone us and ask our advice on something they had purchased that they were not happy with so it worked both ways.

I know most times that the details given by the thief selling the property to the second hand shop was probably false, but sometimes they would leave their correct name but wrong address or vice versa, and as we are the police it was up to us to try and identify them and sometimes we were successful.

We tried to identify handlers of stolen property, because as the old saying goes without handlers you would not have so many burglars, because the burglar always needs someone to sell his stolen gear to.

In this game of police catch burglar you always need luck or nosey neighbours they can be a valuable tool in the fight against crime. One such case I remember was during 1984 we were having a fair amount of day time burglaries in the Great Barr area of the sub division, Great Barr in the main are privately owned properties where their owners are out at work during the day so an easy target for a burglar.

A neighbour had telephoned the police reporting that she thought she had seen someone leave her neighbours house carrying a suitcase, it's that magic word again suitcase, and of course it was in 1984 a favoured way of removing a video recorder from a house.

The job was passed to us as we always worked in plain clothes normally jeans, jumper or T shirts, and it was easier for visiting burglaries when they had just happened because you never know the burglar might still be hanging round seeing if the police had been called. I spoke with the neighbour who had phoned us whilst one of the other lads arranged for a boarding up company to attend and board up the back door that had been smashed to gain access to the house.

I was going to question this lady at length as she had seen the burglar and he might just be the one who is doing all the daytime breaks in Great Barr. I got a bit of a description but it could have fitted half of the residents of Great Barr, he was white and tall, was all I got from the lady and then she said something that was to change the whole investigation and to change the face of day time burglaries on the D3 for some time to come.

I said to her, 'Anything else you can think of that might assist?'

She then told me quite innocently pointing towards the bus stop, 'He waited there for a few minutes and then got in a taxi.'

My next question fingers crossed, 'Do you know the taxi company?'

'She said,' Oh yes, the one on Hawthorn Road I use them to take me to the hospital.'

I thanked her and walked to the car, the next stop of course was the taxi company. I got to the taxi company and asked the radio controller which driver had just collected a fare from Dyas Road at its junction with Birdbrook Road; he looked down a handwritten list and said, 'Car 12.'

I informed him that we needed to speak with the driver as soon as possible and as good as gold the controller asked the driver to return to the taxi base to see us.

We met the driver and asked him to take us to where he had dropped the fare off so myself and PC Cleaver got into the back off the taxi and off he went, we did not drive far before he stopped I suppose about 50 yards away and informed us that he dropped the fare off there, pointing to a house with a car on the front garden, and his fare then walked up the path and into the house, the taxi driver thought that the front door was already open.

I said, 'What can you remember about the fare?'

He said, 'Well he was carrying a suitcase, I remember that.'

I said, 'Can you describe him for me?'

He said,' 'Yes, 6' 2" tall, thin build, long curly dirty looking blond hair, he had a red T shirt and blue jeans.'

We thanked the taxi driver and got out, we radioed the controller for a marked car, and when that arrived we knocked on the front door and as the door opened we walked straight in without introducing ourselves, to find our tall thin man smoking a cigarette, sitting on the settee next to a video recorder and an open suitcase was on the floor, so in one swoop we had our burglar and our handler that being the man who answered the door.

The 6' 2" tall thin man with the long blond curly hair and I was to meet several times over the next couple of years, the problem with him he was so distinctive at the time I do not think there was another young man in Kingstanding who looked like him. All I needed was a witness to the burglary and of course day time burglars took a real risk about being seen.

The myth was that you would get less of a prison sentence if you was a day time burglar as opposed to a night time burglar, the view was at night time people might be in the house in bed so in that set of circumstances I suppose the myth was right.

Being on the Burglary Squad we use to get bits and pieces of information passed onto us by other policemen, we of course had the time to follow the information up in most cases much more than they did.

I remember we had an anonymous telephone call just before Christmas 1984 it might actually have been Christmas Eve itself the caller said, 'If you go to this house in Shady Lane and look in this blokes garage it's full of washing machines, fridges, micro waves and other stuff.'

The caller then hung up, so what do we, do get a search warrant, we do not have enough good information as it is just an anonymous call, what do we know about the people who live in the house, married couple the old man has one previous conviction for Handling stolen goods, going back about three years and they have two young children.

I made my mind up let's go and have a look at the house, so of we went in two separate cars and met up in park in Shady Lane and the idea was for two of us to have a walk past, that was done so what did we know now, there was a light on in the kitchen and a car was parked on the front driveway indicating someone might be at home.

The decision was mine as I was reminded by the other three that it was my burglary squad. So I made my decision myself and big Dave the other DC on the squad would go and knock on the door and we would take it from there, so we did the door was answered by a male aged about 40 years, and I opened the talking by at first introducing us and then telling him we had received a telephone call to suggest that your garage is full of stolen electrical gear, and the best way for me to satisfy myself that the caller is lying is for you to let me have a look inside, we of course got the usual response he said, 'What if I say no'

I carried on and explained that I would get a marked police car to sit outside his house, and I would go to Sutton Coldfield Magistrates Court and obtain a search warrant to search his house and I reminded him that has he had got one previous conviction for handling stolen goods, so I would easily obtain the warrant, but all that will take some time so why don't we just have a look in the garage particularly if you have nothing to hide.

He eventually said 'Go on then its open go and look.'

So we did we lifted the up and over garage door and looked in the garage to me met by several large boxes of electrical goods including fridges, washing machines and micro waves.

He was promptly arrested and he replied, 'I didn't know they were stolen.'

We later charged him and a second man in connection with the offence, it appeared that the goods had been stolen from a lorry that had been parked locked and unattended overnight in the Witton area, I suppose that's where the saying 'they fell of the back of a lorry' originated from.

1984 was coming to an end for the burglary squad and I think we had achieved a lot in eight months so we had a good Christmas. But for the country and for some people they did not have an happy Christmas, because earlier on 12th October 1984, in the early hours of the morning a bomb exploded at the Grand Hotel in Brighton, the IRA target for this explosion was the Prime Minister, Mrs Margaret Thatcher who was staying at the hotel during the conservative party conference.

Five people did however die and 34 were injured. The IRA claimed responsibility the next day. In September 1986 Patrick Magee was found guilty of planting the bomb, detonating it and five counts of murder, he was sentenced to eight life sentences with a recommendation that he serve 35 years. He was released from prison in 1999 as part of the Good Friday Agreement.

1985 for us began how we had left off there were plenty of prisoners coming our way and not all for burglary, we were on a high and seemed to be able to do nothing wrong. An example of that is when two of us were in a white allegro, we followed five youths for the best part of a mile and observed them trying in excess of 15 different car doors in an attempt to either steal the car or steal from it and all the time we are sitting in a car watching them and not once did they look round at us.

We got a marked police car to join us and arrested all five and they were taken to Erdington Police station where after being interviewed they were charged with conspiracy to steal, and bailed to the court, another good day on the burglary squad.

The 3rd March 1985 saw the end of the miner's strike almost a year after it had begun. Some mineworkers had already returned to work which in a way was a victory for the government. Morale was at an all-time low as the miners returned to work. What had the strike gained nothing, because strikes rarely gain anything, the government's view that pits had to close went ahead and to give you an example in 1983 there were 170 working pits and in 2010 there were 6.

I mentioned earlier in this chapter about the 6' 2" tall thin man with long dirty curly blond hair well in 1985 we met again. I had learnt other things about him by now, he was a heavy smoker, he smelt of sweat, he always wore white pumps and he wore dirty unwashed clothes, I mean he sounds like someone who may sleep rough on the streets but he did not, he actually lived with his mom and dad in Kingstanding at the time. He was also unemployed and spent most of his day and evenings in a betting shop in Birdbrook Road.

One day we had a call to a burglary in progress, meaning that with a bit of luck the offender was still inside the property, we arrived I thought within minutes but he had gone, we found the house insecure and went in and clearly the video recorder was missing. I knocked on some doors either side of the property in an effort to find someone who may have witnessed the burglary, I did not find a witness to the burglary, but I found a witness to someone who was seen hanging about near to the house that was broken into.

His description was white male, tall and thin, scruffy clothes with dirty blond hair almost affro style, I wonder who that is. So I went with one of the other lads straight to the suspect's house and we parked past his house some

50 yards further down the road and waited. What you have to bear in mind as well these burglars do not always walk on them main roads they use the gulley's at the back of the houses and even sometimes climb through back gardens, as they need to be on the main roads for as little time as they can.

We had only been there a couple of minutes and through the rear view mirror of the car you could see him walking down the road towards his house carrying a suitcase. He began to walk up his garden path, we got out the car walked back and he was arrested without a struggle.

1985 progressed and we were still successful but being in the main CID at Erdington had its problems, I think and I still think it today that other detectives in that office were jealous of us, as we would normally have problems finding a set of keys for one of the CID cars then they would turn up at 5.00pm when some of the detectives were going home.

Comments were passed, 'I wished I only had burglaries to look at,' or 'I wish I could dress in jeans and a T shirt for work, I have to wear at suit,' silly things like that but it makes your job harder to do and they were so wrong because if there was a serious incident and we were on duty we would always help them, and that occasion arose many times during the life of the burglary squad.

Anyway this all fell into pale significance as on the evening of 9th September 1985 we were to become heavily involved in the second and most violent riot to have come to Handsworth in four years and one of the most violent riots to have come to the streets of Britain in the eighties.

It is now over 25 years since that riot and I can remember it like yesterday, it was probably the most frightening thing I have ever witnessed or been part of it in my career with the police.

Monday 9th September 1985, was a warm pleasant evening that was about to go downhill very, very fast indeed it started about 5.00pm when a traffic officer put a fixed penalty ticket on the windscreen of a car parked near to the Acapulco café on Lozells Road, Handsworth, incidentally the vehicle was parked on double yellow lines and not showing a current tax disc.

The owner arrived and an argument ensued between the police officer and the owner of the car and that was it, it was like lighting the blue touch paper of Handsworth. The owner of the vehicle was arrested and very soon and very quickly a large crowd of mainly African Caribbean men and women gathered and surrounded the police officer who had called for backup, people demanded that the man was released but quite rightly the police refused and the situation quickly deteriorates as more and more people arrive and in minutes the scene is described as a riot, the Villa Cross Bingo Hall is firebombed and the fire brigade arrive and they are ordered by the crowd which is now several hundred strong to let it burn to the ground.

This took a matter of two hours or so and it seemed that the whole of Handsworth was on fire.

1 and 7's were being mobilised all over the force area, a 1 and 7 is a sergeant and seven constables in a police van and in full uniform and on each division and perhaps each sub-division would have one, the Special Patrol Group were being mobilised and sent to various RP's in Handsworth, RP's being rendezvous points.

Within two hours several hundreds of police are now on the streets of Handsworth.

And by mid night the police now some 1500 strong including police from many other forces, were reclaiming and that is the only way I can say it they began to reclaim the streets, from the several hundreds of rioters who were still hell bent on causing as much damage and destruction of property as they could, and to continue to throw missiles at both police and fire officers.

The aftermath after two days of spasmodic rioting was two Asian brothers dead, they were found in their burnt out post office on Lozells Road, they were murdered trying to protect their own property, over 35 people including police were injured, 45 shops were looted by the rioters and then burnt to the ground and a trail of damage running into several thousands and thousands of pounds. The riot had also caused residents to flee their houses some I am told never came back.

The riots were to spark other riots across the country and probably the most infamous was on the Broadwater Farm Estate in Tottenham, North London where PC Keith Blakelock was murdered by rioters who hacked and knifed him to death whilst he was trying to protect fire fighters from the crowd.

The burglary squad had a role to play in the two days of rioting particularly on the first night we were used as 'spotters' as we were in jeans and shirts or T shirts and generally described as scruffy looking, we used to drive and sometimes walk round some of the roads near to the main rioting, our job was to spot likely places of further disorder, likely places where attacks could be made against the police and fire brigade, look for shop premises being looted. Look for petrol bombs which clearly the rioters had in their hundreds and no doubt made some time before the 9th September 1985.

We would then report out findings to the controller who decided on the next course of action to take, we were not in one place long enough in case we were clocked. We had our successes but of course due to the instability of the area the successes were limited. It was a long night and I went off duty about 2.30am in the morning.

The clean-up would take ages and we were involved in some of the post-riot and disorder arrests and in total there was well over 250 arrested and charged with various offences connected to the two days of rioting. An incident room was set up and a dedicated group of detectives continued for many months investigating the riots and arresting the perpetrators of the riots.

We returned to our normal job of catching burglars which we continued to do and as 1985 ended 1986 began and we were still getting results but as they say all good things come to an end, and in February 1986 the same DCI who had some two years earlier been responsible for the formation of the burglary squad was now responsible for telling us that the time had come for the squad to be disbanded, the two PC's were returned to uniform, I returned to Erdington as a detective and Dave Forrester went to Kingstanding as a detective.

We had started in a blaze of glory in 1984, we even had our names and pictures on the front of the local newspaper and we ended in a damp fizz. I do think that perhaps some of the other detectives were jealous of us at times, as we could not do anything wrong we were very successful in what we did and of course success does cause jealousy.

Anyway back to being a detective on a sub division, but I know this is a strange thing to say but I could never feel the same for Erdington after this, I did my job as always to the best of my ability but it is fair to say I was not always happy in my job.

And there was me moaning about not being happy at work when the world woke up on 26th April 1986, to read about the explosion at the Chernobyl nuclear power plant in Pripya, in the Ukraine where it was estimated that in excess of four thousand people died and seven billions of pounds worth of damage was caused, and there was I not happy at work at least I was alive and had a job, things like that disaster puts everything into perspective.

I had two weeks annual leave at the beginning of July 1986, we had nothing planned I think we were just going to have a few day trips here and there when we felt the need, our son now had just had his seventh birthday, but my future with the police service was just about to change when I was at home and I received a telephone call.

CHAPTER NINE
Ladywood Police Station

I was at home when the telephone rang and I answered it and it was my old sergeant from Kingstanding, Malcolm Ross, who was now a Detective Inspector at Ladyood Police Station on the C2 sub division.

It was good to hear the voice of someone who I had always respected, we had remained good friends since Kingstanding, and now he was in charge of the CID at Ladywood.

We had a good chat about the old times and about the future and then he put a proposition to me, did I want to work on the C2 on the CID, he explained me that they had a detective who needed to be nearer to his wife for personal problems that we did not go into, but if I wanted the job we could do a straight swop with one another. I did not need asking twice I said, 'Yes of course, I would certainly like the opportunity to work with you again.'

Here I am again, time for a new challenge.

He went on to explain that the actual vacancy would be at Dudley Road Police Station and not Ladywood and said 'Would that cause you any problems?'

I said, 'No I don't mind, I don't know the area but I'll soon learn.'

He finished by saying, 'I'll get everything sorted with personnel and get back to you in a couple of weeks, I cannot foresee any problems.'

With that we said our goodbyes and I put the telephone down.

Of course my wife thought I was mad, why would I want to leave the comfort of Erdington that was in walking distance and go to work at Dudley Road or even Ladywood that was miles away, the only answer her I could give to her is that it gave me a chance to work with a detective who I admired and respected, she still thought I was mad.

I returned to Erdington after my annual leave and was quickly summoned to the DCI's office, he enquired as to the reason for my interest in a move away from Erdington. I explained that there was an opportunity to work with my old DS again who was now the DI there, a new challenge and perhaps time for a change I had been on the D3 for seven years, five as a detective, he seemed to understand what I was getting at and he informed me the move would be ratified, but asked be to bear with him for about four weeks. I naturally agreed and returned to me desk in the main CID office.

The move to the C2 came through in a matter of weeks and even the detectives I was presently working with thought I was mad. They described it like going from 'the frying pan to the fire' whatever that meant.

Three of us moved away from Erdington much the same time, one got promoted to uniform sergeant, one was moving to the Fraud Squad and I was moving to the C2, so we had a joint leaving do at the Sutton Park Hotel a local pub in Sutton Coldfield.

On a personal front my move was sorted with personnel very quickly and an agreed start date on the C2 was Tuesday 5th August 1986.

The day arrived and at 8.30am on the 5th, I arrived at Walsall Road Police Station to see the Detective Superintendent, Mr Cresswell, who was the Head of CID for the 'C' Division, Walsall Road at the time was the divisional headquarters of the 'C' division which included C1, Thornhill Road and C2, Ladywood.

Our meeting went well, he welcomed me to my new job and he wished me all the best in my new surroundings of C2 and off I went to Ladywood to meet with DI Ross.

In the first instance I would be working at Dudley Road with DC 'Taff' Jones, there was a DS, Ron Nipper in charge of us, but we were told we would hardly see him as he was always doing an acting Inspector role at Ladywood as he was trying to get promoted.

I then drove to Dudley Road Police Station, I had driven past the station in the past but had never been inside, it was actually based in grounds Summerfield Park and I would describe it like a big house in a park.

The CID had two rooms upstairs, one at the front which was the DS's office and one at the back overlooking the park which is where me and Taff sat, and the third room upstairs was where the resident beat officers worked from I think there were four of them, downstairs was the front office, a small kitchen and rest area and two cells and that was it. It was literally a big house in a park.

Introductions over I found myself a desk, a chair and a telephone that's all I wanted and at 4.30pm when I thought I would be going home, Taff asked me, 'Do you want a sharp half?' indicating he wanted a drink before he went home so I said, 'Yes, I'll join you for one.' so we went to one of the local pubs and had a couple of pints and I went home, day one gone.

What I did notice straight away on the C2 was there appeared to be a lot more uniform officers than other shifts at most police stations that I had previously worked at, when you think back to when I joined in 1975 I was on a shift of 10 PC's and 3 sergeants yet at Ladywood in 1986 there would be 18 or maybe as many as 20 PC's and 5 sergeants, it seemed it was as a direct result of the two riots of 1981 and 1985, the area of C1 Handsworth and C2 Ladywood would now always be more heavily policed.

The first week ended without too much fuss, I had got to know most of the detectives on the C2 by face if not name, but over the next few days I was going to get to know them by name as well. I finished work t 4.00pm on the Friday and was looking forward to my weekend off, I arrived home and I think I was sitting down reading the evening paper it would be about 5.30pm and the telephone rang.

Now over the next three years whilst I was at the C2 nearly every time the telephone rang they had got a murder and could I come in, this Friday was no exception, well I answered the telephone it was DC Tony Hunter he was a detective and was based at Ladywood he said, 'Nige, Tony here, the boss wants to know if you want to come in we have a double murder?'

I could not say no I had only been there 4 days so I said, 'Yes of course.'

Tony said, 'The briefings here at half six.'

I said, 'Okay see you then.'

Quick shower, explained to the wife I may be late back again, well she was use to me saying that by now, I got in my car and off I drove to Ladywood Police

Station I parked my car in the rear yard and in I went, I walked into the CID office, there were detectives there from, Harbourne, Quinton, Ladywood, me and Taff and the boss of course DI Ross, we crowded into the CID office and we all listened to DI Ross give the briefing about the double murder and what an horrific murder it was.

The murders had taken place at a house in the Quinton area of Birmingham, it would appear that until recently a couple and their two young children lived there, however the father had moved out of the address and for some reason we did not know at this stage, he was only allowed supervised visits to his children and a social worker would have to be present at all times.

It would appear that on the day of the murder the visit was to be at 3.00pm, but the father had turned up early and was allowed access to the house by his wife and to await the arrival of the social worker, I have no intention to go into all the details in full of the murder as it was too horrific but suffice to say it would appear they argued and he for some reason murdered her and carried her body upstairs and placed in onto the bed.

At about 3.00pm there is a knock on the door and the lady social worker arrives and is invited in, we do not know exactly what happened next in any details apart from the fact that he then proceeded to murder her and he also carried her body upstairs and placed her on the bathroom floor.

As I mentioned earlier I have deliberately left parts of this quite horrible story out.

So he had now got two dead bodies in the house, he had quite deliberately murdered two women in the space of twenty minutes, his wife and the social worker, the social workers car was parked outside the family home and he also had two young children who needed collecting from school in less than an hour's time.

First things first, he took the dead social workers car keys from her handbag and drove the car away and parked it in another road away from the house, he then went and collected the children from school but not before buying a can of petrol.

Later that afternoon the fire brigade were called to a fire at the house, a neighbour had spotted flames coming from the rear bedroom and he took a ladder to the windows and managed with the assistance of the father to get the two young children out through the bedroom window and down to safety, their father then made his was down the ladder and into the rear garden he was burnt but not badly and all three of them were suffering from smoke inhalation.

The fire brigade entered the property through the front door obviously for two reasons, one to put the fire out and one to look to see if there was anybody in the house. What greeted them was something quite horrific, they found two female bodies and from their positioning they believed that had not died as a result of the fire or smoke but had met their death from some other means.

Immediately the police were informed and when the first uniform officers arrived the father was in the back of an ambulance being treated by ambulance staff.

The facts were quickly related to the controller who informed the uniform officers to go with the father to Dudley Road hospital and to make a written note of anything he said and secondly the controller informed the CID.

Welcome to the C2 CID, an incident room was quickly set up, but the DI was right the answer certainly lied with the man in hospital. I worked till 11.00pm that night and 8.00am through to 10.00pm the following day on my leave day, and by the Saturday evening the post mortems on the two women had been carried out and confirmed to us that it was murder and the man in hospital was placed under arrest and under police guard.

The two young children had recovered from the effects of smoke and were now with relatives.

The police would remain with this man until he was fit enough to be discharged from the hospital and then he would be bought to Ladywood Police Station for questioning about the deaths or should I say the murders of his wife and social worker and of course the attempted murders of his two young children.

In due course he was later charged with two murders and other offences and the motive for the murders, well he believed quite wrongly that his wife and social worker were conspiring with each other to make sure he would never see his children again, and the frightening thing was that he was quite prepared to kill his two children by fire.

He was convicted at Birmingham Crown Court and sentenced to an indefinite prison sentence for his crimes.

What a tragic set of circumstances and out of all of his actions that day, nobody won because he has stopped his wife from seeing the children again because he brutally murdered her and because of his crime and the fact that he will be serving a very long sentence he will probably never see the children again.

So there were no winners in that course of action.

Less than a week into my time on the C2 and here I am with 33 hours overtime, more than I did in the last 12 months had I gone, 'from the frying pan and into the fire' I thought well time would surely tell.

The next three years were to prove the busiest of my life, you appeared to go from one serious crime to another and on average over the next three years I worked about 40 hours a month overtime and in one month I did 107 hours overtime, my bank manager loved me. My bank account for the first time in a very long time went from red to black and stayed there.

I cannot even remember all the crimes that I was involved in as there were too many however in one year alone we had 17 murders, one every three weeks now I cannot tell you about all of them because there were quite literally too many but I will mention a couple, perhaps my next book should be called 'A year on the C2'

The C2 sub division, let me tell you about its geographic area it covered Ladywood, Edgbaston, Winson Green parts of Handsworth, Quinton, Harborne and bordered other city divisions and the C2 itself was a vast area and I suppose it had some of the most deprived areas in Birmingham and with that unfortunately you get crime.

I always seemed to be at work, I was eating the wrong food, I never took sandwiches and I ate greasy food both morning and night, the occasional balti curry which I loved, all washed down with a few pints of beer, I was putting weight on and for the first time in my life I had a beer belly.

I was in the office one day when the telephone rang it was the DI he said, 'Can you make Thornhill Road on the

C1, they have a domestic murder and they need some extra staff, it will just be for two days at the most and no more.'

I agreed and off I drove to Thornhill Road, a domestic murder is normally between husband and wife, perhaps girlfriend and boyfriend, or just partners as was this murder. As we know with all murders the first 24 hours are the most crucial. An incident room had been set up and they knew who they were looking for and for the rest of that day I was given some actions to do, statements to take, people to find, witnesses to find, those sort of jobs and at the end of day one I was asked to come in the following day which was agreed.

I returned to Thornhill Road the following day and there seemed more cars about, I thought no more of it and walked into the incident room and thought I do not recognise many of these people, there were loads there CID and uniform I had never seem most of them before, anyway I will wait for the 9.00am briefing all will I am sure become clear, well it did.

The DCI arrived and said that in relation to yesterday's murder the incident room will be moved to Walsall Road and in relation to last night's double murder the incident room will be here, yes you heard right during the night there had been a double murder in Handsworth, again it was domestic and a wife and her sister had been murdered.

Three murders in 24 hours almost a record, the DCI added that if all the Ladywood officers could finish of their actions today and then you will be released back and that is what happened the following day after yet more overtime I was back at Dudley Road, what a 24 hours though, three murders.

Another murder I recall was one Friday night I had just finished work at Dudley Road it was about 10.00pm and I drove home and I had a quick glass of Bells whiskey before myself and the wife retired to bed about mid night. It was to be the shortest night's sleep I had ever had because some thirty minutes later the telephone went it and was the night detective, DC Andy Byrne, from Ladywood, he informed me that there had been a murder on the Dudley Road patch and the boss needs people in, I agreed to go back in and was told there was a briefing at 1.30am at Ladywood.

DI Ross took the briefing and we were told that there had been a young white man stabbed to death at a public house in Aberdeen Street, Winson Green and there had been a second white man also stabbed but not serious and there was an officer with him at Dudley Road Hospital, it would appear to have been an argument between two young white men and three elderly black men, all locals, at the pub which appeared to go horribly wrong.

There are uniform officers at the scene taking statements and what I intend to do is to split this room into three teams led by a DS and you will all have a target each, from the scene these are the three man we are looking for and there are regulars to the pub.

Our teams target was a black male, 50 years old, small build probably know more than 5' 4" tall, very thin, moustache, he was wearing a brown striped suit with a brown check tatty dirty looking beret on his head.

Off to the address we had for him and knocked on the door, the door was answered by a middle aged woman, we introduced ourselves to her and asked to speak with her husband, she shouted to him and he came to the top of the stairs and there he was 5' 4" tall, thin build, moustache, wearing pyjamas and a brown check tatty dirty looking beret, he was arrested and a quick search of the bedroom revealed the clothes he had been wearing at the time which were put into brown papers bags and exhibit 1, of course was the beret which was placed in a brown paper bag.

He was taken to Ladywood Police Station and within fifteen minutes the other teams arrived with their targets and by 4.00am all three men were in custody on suspicion of murder.

Through that Saturday the men were interviewed and all basically said the same that they had been in fear of the two white lads and the knifing was a pure accident. By lunchtime some 12 hours after the murder the three men were charged and they were to remain in custody to appear at Birmingham Magistrates Court on the following Monday.

The court paperwork was completed and by about 4.00pm we had finished, an offer of a pint from the DI was there but I declined as I had a previous engagement; we all said our goodbyes to each other some went for a pint, some went home and I went to a school disco, yes that's right, a school disco.

My day was not finished my son had his end of term school disco on that particular Saturday, which I had promised him I would attend in actual fact I was one on the volunteer barmen for the day. I arrived about 5.00pm absolutely shattered having completely missed out on a night's sleep but I did manage to stay awake long enough to enjoy the rest of the evening and being barman was good for two reasons, one I did not get dragged up on the floor for a dance and secondly I was never short of a drink and it was the drink that probably kept me awake.

It was well into 1987 now and the work just kept coming in and working at Dudley Road we had such a diverse range of work, we covered as detectives HM Prison, Birmingham probably better known as Winson Green Prison, Dudley Road Hospital and All Saints

Hospital, that meant in most cases any crimes or incidents that occur at these premises we would normally deal with, you have to remember there were only two of us and if you take into account annual leave, courses and sickness, sometimes you would be working on your own.

I suppose one of the biggest news stories of 1987 was on 17th August 1987 when Rudolf Hess was found dead in his cell in Spandau Prison, in Berlin he had apparently hung himself with electrical flex, and he was 93 years old. It was alleged that Hess was second in command of the Nazi Party and deputy to Adolf Hitler prior to and during the war.

At the end of World War II Spandau Prison was operated by the Four-Power Authorities (USA, Britain, France and Russia) and it was to house Nazi war criminals sentenced after the Nuremburg Trials in 1946. In total only seven prisoners were ever sent there and from 1966 until his death in 1987 Hess was the only resident, the other six had been released either at the end of their term of imprisonment or of ill health.

In 1987 after the death of Hess the prison was demolished largely to prevent it becoming a neo-Nazi shrine and all materials from the prison were ground to powder and dispersed in the North Sea. It is now a shopping complex and its biggest resident is the German supermarket ALDI.

Dudley Road hospital was a normal accident and emergency hospital and I suppose the most common type of crime there was theft of and theft from motor vehicles from the large car parks that surround the hospital. There were on occasions more serious crime such as internal thefts but in the main they were comfortably managed by the resident beat office for the area and of course their own hospital security staff.

Birmingham Prison was a totally different scenario it was almost a full time job in itself and all crimes of note would be reported to the police and in most cases either Taff or myself would deal, we worked hand in hand with the security staff at the prison and without their help we could not have done our job.

The prison was built in 1849 and is built on what is called the 'Pentonville Model' that is four wings radiating from a central tower, one wing for the governor and all the offices, the remaining three wings for the inmates. On a bad day 1400 prisoners reside there, most are on remand awaiting trials and some are convicted awaiting dispersal to other prisons. Thirty five executions by hanging have taken place at the prison, the last being in 1962 and the room where the hanging took place until recently was the prison barbers shop.

Famous inmates of the prison over the years were to include Ozzy Osborne leader of the pop group Black

Sabbath, Lee Hughes the footballer, Charlie Wilson the great train robber and Fred West the alleged serial killer from Gloucester who committed suicide in the prison in January 1995 before he was brought to trial.

The most common crimes of the prison were assaults, by prisoner on prisoner, assault by prisoner on officer and assault by officer on prisoner, all had to be investigated properly.

Any death in prison and there would have to be a full coroner's inquest so again the investigation had to be completed fully and would include the taking of witness statements from all parties involved, right from the person who discovered the dead body up to and including the pathologists.

The inquest could then take place.

During 1987 I dealt with a male rape in the prison, at the time inmates on remand and not convicted would often be three to a cell and that was the case in this particular incident. The complainant made his complaint of rape to his solicitor on an appearance at Birmingham Magistrates Court, the solicitor then walked into Steelhouse Lane Police Station next to the magistrate's court to report the matter and the front office staff who on discovery of where the incident had taken place, namely Birmingham prison promptly telephoned us at Dudley Road.

I took the call and the brief facts related to me were that his client was in a cell with two others and during the night the one inmate had threatened violence and had raped him whilst the other inmate was allegedly asleep.

We arranged to go straight to Steelhouse Lane Police Station and we met with the solicitor and from there went to the Central Lock up to speak with his client.

The complainant made a detailed written statement to us but then quite rightly in my view stated that he did not want to be returned to the same cell as where the alleged rapist was, we promised we would sort that and from the lock up we went straight to the prison to speak with security.

We asked then that all three inmates were to be placed in separate cells, and the cell where the rape took place to be locked and sealed until we could get scenes of crime officers down to the prison to examine the cell, and obtain any possible evidence and to obtain exhibits for forensic examination, which as time was against the examination of the cell would now take place be tomorrow. Security agreed and all three inmates were to be placed in separate cells away from one another.

Before we went home that night and when the complainant had got back to the prison from the lock up, we took possession of his clothing and arranged a police surgeon to attend the prison to conduct a full medical examination, which on completion the surgeon confirmed that sexual intercourse via the anus had taken place recently. We then notified a relative at the complainants request to bring fresh clothing to the prison that evening as agreed with the security of the prison and with that all sorted I went home late again.

The following morning Taff and I were back down the prison again, we had our statement of complaint, scenes of crime were on their way and we were now shown to where another of the inmates was. We told him why we were here and asked what he knew about the incident, his response was like the wise monkey, heard nothing, saw nothing and most of all he said nothing, 'I was asleep all night' was the best we got, tongue in cheek I thanked him for his time and valuable assistance and we left him to be returned to his cell.

The suspect was next I went with Taff and security to his cell, we put the allegation to him and enquired if he wanted his solicitor present when we formally interviewed about the matter, him he smiled and said, 'Yes get my brief, I am not speaking to you two without one.'

I informed him that I would make suitable arrangements with his solicitor and he would be told by the prison security when the interview was to be held.

In the subsequent interview with his solicitor which had been arranged for a week or so later, he as expected denied all the allegations put to him, he adamantly denied rape, and to most of our questions he just shrugged his shoulders as if he was not bothered and did not care.

He was charged and in due course he appeared before Birmingham Crown Court and the shock was he pleaded Guilty to Buggery on a male, and was sentenced to six years imprisonment, the irony was that at the time of this offence he was on remand for stealing a car for which in due course no evidence was offered.

The prison was a dismal place to be it always seemed to be raining when I had to go there, and with its punishment block and its medical wing it could be a frightening and eerie place as well, but I will end my stories of the prison on a lighter note.

When you were in the prison yard walking perhaps from one building to another, out of love and affection for the police, the inmates would throw out of their cell windows rolled up socks in your direction, but please, please do not catch them as they were full of excrement and most times soaked in urine, it was the inmates way of welcoming the police to the prison, of course they did not do it to the prison officers because that might end up with them losing their privileges.

All Saints Hospital, history lesson first, it was built in 1850 and known as the Winson Green Asylum, it then changed its name to Birmingham Pauper Lunatic Asylum, in 1902 it was called Birmingham City Asylum, and in 1929 it became the Birmingham City Mental Hospital, then the Birmingham Mental Hospital and finally All Saints Hospital, incidentally it closed its doors in 2000 and is now a housing estate.

Within the hospital you had secure wards and insecure wards and you had inpatients and out patients.

Most incidents were dealt with internally by staff, some obviously could not and the one I will tell you about was one of those. One afternoon I had a call from a staff nurse at the hospital requesting police attendance as one of her inpatients had complained of rape.

I attended in the first instance and it was not that straightforward, the complainant a woman of some 40 years old who had been an inpatient for many of them, she had told a nurse that a man with a beard had been naughty with her some two weeks ago, she would not talk with me as I was a man and had a beard and looked like the man who had been naughty with her so clearly I was not the best person for the job. I asked two women detectives from Ladywood to go and interview her by question and answer over the next week or so.

We still asked her to consent to a medical examination even though the incident was two weeks or more old, as you never know what a medical examination might show.

The medical was completed and about two weeks later the question and answer interview was also completed, and I was given the 72 pages of handwritten questions and answers to study as I was the officer in charge of the enquiry.

I read the lot and in brief she knew this man as the man who looked like Jesus who came to the canteen every night for his tea, he was an outpatient and he was known local as P . . ., and one afternoon whilst she was alone on the ward he came in and pulled her underclothes down and raped her, and this was done even though she had refused.

We had no forensics, we had no witnesses, but we did know who the suspect was the staff at the hospital knew him and had seen him about. Firstly I thought I will arrest him from his home address and attempt to keep the hospital out of it, his home address was in fact an empty house in City Road, Egdbaston so that was the end of plan one.

So I decided that I had to arrest him from the hospital, arrangements were made with the staff that the next time he came in for his tea to telephone me at Dudley Road, he would normally arrive about 4.00pm, we heard nothing for about three weeks then as I was just about to go home for the night as usual, when the telephone rang and on the other end was a doctor from All Saints informing me that my man was there having his tea.

I grabbed the attached man and down to the hospital we went and met with the doctor who advised me not to go into the canteen to arrest him, I had every intention to follow the advice of the doctor, he told us that we should go and wait in our car and he would send him out to us we could arrest him put him in the back of the car and away for the hospital before anybody else had seen us.

We agreed and returned to the CID and we sat for a few minutes and just then we were approached by this tall man who actually did look like Jesus with his long beard, walking next to him was a doctor, I got out the car arrested the man known as P . . ., and placed him in the back of the car and the attached man drove all three of us to Ladywood Police Station.

We got him a solicitor and I got him a friend from the hospital to sit with him and we arranged for a police surgeon to examine him, one, forensically, and two, to see if he was fit enough to be detained and interviewed, the surgeon advised us that he was fit to be detained and interviewed.

In the interview he readily admitted having sex with this woman but stated she would do anything for a cigarette and she had consented, but of course we knew by law she could not consent due to her medical condition and we knew that he knew that.

He was later charged with Rape and in due course at the Crown Court he pleaded Guilty to having Sex with a Mental Defective and received four years imprisonment.

Speaking of the hospital for the final time and on a lighter note there was a man there known as 'Zorba the Greek' and whatever the weather he never wore any clothes on the upper part of his body and he would always wash our CID car for a £1 coin, I often wonder what happened to him since the hospital closed.

1988 arrived and again it was a busy time on the C2 CID at Dudley Road and during this year I dealt with a complex criminal investigation that gave me a lot of satisfaction, it was hard work and a long haul but I got there in the end and four men went to prison.

It was a difficult investigation because my complainants and most of my witnesses were self-confessed prostitutes.

It began one Monday morning in September 1988, I arrived for work and sat down with a cup of tea with our new DS, Dave Forrester who had been with me on the burglary squad in 1984, Taff had moved to Ladywood and had been replaced by another experienced detective Tony Hunter. Just then the telephone rang and it was the CID at Ladywood and they informed me that over the weekend two prostitutes had been raped at a house in Winson Green and as we, Dudley Road covered that particular area, could you come over and collect the paperwork.

I drove to Ladywood and collected the paperwork which included statements made by both women and statements made by the police officers who had attended the scene. By nature it is a very difficult crime to investigate so first things first, what exactly did the statements say, I took all the paperwork back to Dudley Road and I had a good mornings read.

What was the story then, well we had two prostitutes living in a house in Winson Green and one of them was only 16 years old, they had been held against their will, assaulted and raped in their own house by two West Indian males who they vaguely knew by nick name, as they had seen the same West Indians looking for prostitutes before in the red light area of Edgbaston. Late on the Saturday evening these two males had broken into the house held the girls there against their will, assaulted them both and raped them.

My first job is that I went to the house to see how they were recovering and if there was anything else that they could recall about the incident or that we, the police could do for them.

Apart from the risky life they had chosen they both seemed level head girls and I remember what the 16 year old said to me minutes after meeting her she said, 'A prostitute can get raped you know.'

I remembered those words all the way through the investigation. So I began, I did house to house enquiries to see if any neighbours had heard anything but the general view was that there were always coming and goings from the house, two brasses lived there, what do you expect?, so I got very little help from the neighbours and to be honest I do not think they cared what had happened.

Scenes of Crime was negative, so from day one we had very little to go on. The best evidence we had was the girls, they had given us good descriptions, they had given us nick names for the two attackers and the 16 year old had the first letter of one of the nick names, the letter 'P' quite literally carved into her leg by a knife, we also knew that both men had arrived at the house driving a dark coloured four door foreign car, and they both appeared to use prostitutes regularly. I thought then this is going to be a long investigation.

Next stop was the red light area where local prostitutes stood on street corners plying their trade, most of them always spoke with the police, we were just an occupational hazard to them, we spoke to some of the girls and gave them the nicknames that we had plus the general descriptions of the two males and of course the vague description of the car.

By now I was investigating this case on my own, as the CID office at Dudley Road had loads of other work to get on with so this particular investigation was unfortunately one of several investigations running at the same time. I did own it and I did spend a lot of time on it because I thought with a bit of luck I could clear the crime, arrest the offenders and get them off the street.

About four weeks into the investigation the 16 year old telephoned me and wanted a meet, I of course went with a colleague and met with her, she handed me a piece of paper with a car registration number on saying that's the car that they came in, one of the girls got the number the other night, of course there was no point in asking for a statement, I thanked her and off we went to do some checks on the car number. A PNC check gave us the current registered owner who lived in Smethwick some five miles from the scene of the rapes, the owner had no previous convictions and to all intense and purpose seemed a reasonable type of person, but this is our first break and he had to be arrested.

The following morning Dave Forrester, Tony Hunter and myself went to the address in Smethwick, we saw the four door car outside and I knocked on the door, the door was answered by a West Indian male who identified himself to use and agreed he was also the owner of the car.

I arrested him for rape and he was taken to Ladywood Police Station, a subsequent search of his house at the time gave us nothing, his vehicle was also removed to Ladywood for forensic examination.

For most of the day myself and Dave Forrester conducted a number of interviews with him and all we had at the end of the interviews was, he was the owner of the car and had many times in the past loaned his car to an associate, what was this associates name, he had no idea but gave us a nickname which did not match the two nick names that we already had. Had he ever heard of our two nicknames before, he informed us he thought he had but was not sure, but he had not got any idea who they were their correct names or where they were from.

So after a day of interviewing, we had nothing, we kept the car for now as a full examination by SOCO had still to be done, but that was still a long shot.

So now we had a third nickname, we had already searched the nick name index at Lloyd House without success for the first two was it worth searching the index for the third nickname, anything is worth a try so the job was back with me and I visited the nick name index and searched the third nick name this time I struck gold.

The third nick name was on the index apparently the offender had given his nickname to the police when he was arrested for an assault but not charged. The nick name also identified to us his associates, he had many but one by one I checked them all on the PNC, and now I believed I had identified the two males I wanted, again they had different nick names not the same as were looking but I was told that this type of individual could have many nick names and also they had street names, they could have as many as ten or so.

But sometimes in the strange world of police work certain things stand out and these two names stood out for me, I felt confident that I may at last be heading the right direction I know I was taking a gamble but I felt very confident and I thought the gamble for the sake of them two girls would be worth it.

I put these two names at the top of my list, they both lived on the C1, Thornhill Road patch in a squat, a room at the top of an old house, we confirmed they lived there because they had given that address for their unemployment giros to be sent so we knew that wherever they stayed during the week sometime on the Thursday they would go and collect their giro to cash at the local post office, it was a true fact that 99 times out of 100 people cashed their giro the same day as it was delivered.

I sat back and reflected and thought what do I have, I have in total two names of suspects who are possible associates of the man who sometimes borrows a four door foreign car off another associate, does not seem a lot really, I needed more.

I wanted a that little bit more, I wanted to know if the owner of the car had lent his car to these two men in particular, I needed to try and pin this man down I believed he knew a lot mote that he was telling me. So I went and spoke with him, now I had information that I did not have when we first interviewed him, we had of course full names, ages, descriptions and different nicknames or street names, to what we had initially asked him about we knew a lot more.

Sitting in his house with his wife and two children in the back living room we saw a different man, I said that we needed to have a further interview with him at the station the following day. He questioned what I was looking for so I told him I have two names and that they lived in a squat in Handsworth, was they the two I was looking for, he did not have to say anything the look on his face told me I had the right names, but I was not going to push the matter further we would conduct a formal interview the following day.

We conducted the interview in the presence of his solicitor but in the interview he made no comment about anything and made no comment to all questions that were put to him so was I back to square one, but not quite I thought, I am going to arrest these two men and if need be put them on a identification parade I had nothing to lose.

I went and spoke with the two girls to see if they were prepared to go on an identification parade and they both informed me that they would, so I informed both of them that I would be in touch in a couple of days, but what they did say was that if I got these two men in custody, more of the girls would speak with us, that was to me a very interesting thing to say.

I was more than happy with the two names I had, so we got to do the job on the following Thursday, we waited for the giro to be delivered and we went straight up to the flat, we had the assistance of other detectives and uniform officers from Thornhill Road, four men were in the flat including the two we wanted, all four were arrested and taken to Ladywood, as search of the flat revealed nothing apart from a few cannabis spiffs.

Dave Forrester and myself interviewed the two main suspects throughout the day, both in the presence of their respective solicitors, the various and of course serious allegations were put to them, and in brief both men agreed they had been at the house as welcome guests and had not forced their way in and any sex with the girls was consensual and not against their will, they went on, we had all smoked cannabis all day and night and yes the one man agreed he had carved his initial in her leg 'because she was my woman' and that in total was the content of the interviews.

What had we got, we have got the right two men who went to that house it's the version of events that differ, the girls say they were assaulted and raped, the others, the suspects say we had sex but it was not rape. We did not need an ID parade at this stage as they were admitting being the two men who had gone to the house and had sex so an ID parade would not take us any further.

I sought advice and it was decided to charge both men, remembering that the girls said more witnesses would come forward if these men were in custody.

I charged them with Rape x 2, unlawful imprisonment x 2, assault x 2, and section 18 wounding x 1and they remained in custody to appear at Birmingham Magistrates Court the following day.

Later that night I went and saw the girls and explained to them what we had done, they to say the least were both over the moon and said that they would get the other girls to come and speak with me.

I informed them that for the next few weeks I would be based at Ladywood Police Station as the DI wanted me to concentrate on this case and nothing else for the time being. The DI was new to Ladywood, it was Kelvin Roberts who use to be my sergeant when I was in uniform at Erdington in 1979, my old DI, Mr Ross had now got promoted to DCI and moved on.

I took the remand at court and both men were remanded in custody for seven days and I went back to Ladywood to continue to put my papers together for the eventual trial at Birmingham Crown Court, then one day I was in my little office which was part of the C2 incident room when I was asked to go to the front office, I got there and saw two women standing there, both saying that they had come to make statements, they were to allege rape but it was slightly historical it was some nine months old, but statements were taken from them and it also led to two other men being put into the frame.

Although at the time whether the offences were historic or not did not bother me they helped begin to build up a picture of the men I was investigating which of course now totalled four.

Over the next few weeks together with the DS, we interviewed all four suspects several times, we put all four men on identification parades and by the end of

October beginning of November we had charged a total of four men with numerous offences of Rape, Indecent Assault, Unlawful Imprisonment. Assault and Wounding. I had taken numerous witness statements from other prostitutes and a witness statement was taken from the man who owned the four door foreign car.

The trial was fixed and would start in the New Year and so it was back to Dudley Road for me again.

1988 was nearing an end and I felt quite satisfied with my year's work and I remember one Friday night I was on 2.00pm x 10.00pm, I was with Tony Hunter and we were talking about Christmas and we had just called into Ladywood to see if everything was alright and we then heard the news of a plane crash in Scotland, and they were asking all police forces to be prepared to mobilise units and go to Scotland.

The date was 21st December 1988 and the plane that crashed was Pan Am Flight 103 and it has crashed into the village of Lockerbie in Scotland with the loss of 270 lives including 11 on the ground. Of course what we do know it due course was that a bomb had exploded on board the flight which caused it to crash. It led to the biggest criminal investigation by Britain's smallest police force the Dumfries and Galloway Constabulary with the assistance of FBI.

On 31st January 2001 a Libyan national was convicted of murder. He was released from prison in August 2009 on compassionate grounds.

1989 arrived and my trial started at Birmingham Crown Court. It was an interesting trial because and I do not know to this day, but we got the four girls to the court to give their evidence but we did and they gave their evidence behind a screen so the defendants could not see their faces.

The first witness was the 16 year old girl and she turned out to be the best witness of all, in cross examination she was continually asked about her profession and that men paid her for sex and that she had been a prostitute for two years so it could never be rape.

She stood up to the questioning very well and the other girls who followed her in the witness box done equally as well, but they as far as I was concerned had done the best that they possible could. I could not have asked for more, it was now time to seat and wait.

None of the defend ants gave evidence or went into the witness box to be examined or cross examined, so the jury took with them to their room the girls side of events and the men's side of events by way of police interviews.

The jury were out for about four hours and came back with a majority of 11-1 in our favour, the men had been convicted, some indictments had been discharged throughout the trial but a lot remained and all four men were sent to prison for a long time, a good end result to a difficult enquiry.

I often wonder what those four girls are doing now.

In March 1989 I went with Tony Hunter for a drink at Tally Ho, he was captain of the West Midlands Police Veterans Cricket Team and he had some arrangements to sort out for the pre-season. We were in the bar and there was a function on in the Lord Knight Suite and I could see a familiar face from years gone by it was Clive Bunn, he was at Queens Road when I was there all those years ago, he saw me and motioned to me to come round which I did.

He informed me that he had just finished his four week Fraud Course and this was the dining in night for the course, I looked round the room and recognised another face, John Woollam he had left Erdington for the Fraud Squad the same time as I had left Erdington for the C2.

Clive told me that he now worked on the Fraud Squad in Birmingham and that it was a fantastic job with very little pressure, he worked mainly 8.00am x 4.00pm with every Saturday and Sunday off and no nights, no murders, no serious crime, no being called out in the early hours of the morning, sounded the dream job, he suggested that I call over to the office and have a coffee with him next week.

I took him up on his invite and the following Tuesday afternoon I went over to see him in his air conditioned brand new offices in a smart office block in the centre of Birmingham, with its brand new desks and chairs, carpeted floors, double glassed windows, separate canteen, your own telephone on your desk, receptionist and computers and well the list went on and on, so by the time he had come back with the coffee I was green with envy.

I had just left my office with a broken desk, second hand or possibly tenth hand chair, one telephone between two of us and with lino on the floor, with a window which never closed properly, which was cracked and an office with no heating, yes I was really green very, very green with envy.

I had my coffee and was shown round the offices and met with the DI, Dave Churchill and the DCI, Arthur Lowe. But fraud we did not get a lot of that at Dudley Road and here Clive was talking about mortgage fraud, banking fraud, cheque and credit card fraud, long firm fraud, carousel fraud, VAT fraud and lots and lots of paperwork that goes with it.

But of course paperwork did not bother me because for years I was doing all the court files for Dudley

Road CID and before that, the Burglary Squad and before that, Kingstanding CID, so paperwork was not a problem.

Mr Lowe then informed me that there was a vacancy for a detective on the Fraud Squad and if I was interested then I would need to submit a report through my DCI as a matter of urgency, I thanked him, finished my coffee and went away thinking I like the look of that, I am going to put that report in, the thought of working normal hours after nearly eight years as a detective appealed to me in more ways than one.

The following day at Dudley Road I typed out the report on our first world war typewriter, requesting that I be considered for an interview for the fourth coming vacancy on the Fraud Squad, I drove to Ladywood to see the DCI and he read and authorised the report and wished me the best, I drove to Lloyd House and handed the report in at Personnel, I could not do anything more I just had to sit and wait.

About two weeks later I got the news I wanted, I was given an interview date and was asked to attend the offices of the Fraud Squad, the interview was with Detective Superintendent Homer, Head of the Fraud Squad and Detective Inspector Harris one of the three Inspectors on the Fraud Squad, the interview went as well as I could have wished for, I seemed to tick the right boxes and when I left I was told I would be notified in the next 24 hours.

The next day Mary Valente, the administration officer for the Fraud Squad at that time telephoned me at Dudley Road, congratulated me and I was offered the vacancy and did I want it, of course I did, she informed that she would contact my administration office at Walsall Road and a suitable date for transfer to the Fraud Squad would be agreed it would of course come out on pinks.

It did come out on pinks and it read Monday 24th April 1989 DC 3055 Wier 'C' Division to DC 3055 Wier 'A' Division Headquarters, Fraud Squad.

And that was it another chapter in my life was coming to an end, I had enjoyed every single minute of my time at Dudley Road and the C2 but it was time to move on, a new challenge beckoned once again.

I had arranged a farewell drink at the White Lion pub in Grosvenor Street West just off Broad Street in the City Centre, the pub was run by a lovely Irish woman called Kath and on my final night she put on a homemade Irish Stew, I can still taste it now.

CHAPTER TEN

The Fraud Squad

I started on the Fraud Squad on Monday 24th April 1989, I arrived at 8.00am in the morning and was introduced to my new colleagues which consisted of a DS, Dave Wallace and two DC's, Graham Rice and Bob Leonard, I was shown to a desk and within an hour or so my DS said, 'What do you know about mortgage fraud?'

I said, 'Nothing, absolutely nothing.' and he then proceeded to hand me this big fat report of many, many pages and said, 'Have a read of that over the next couple of days and we will talk about it then.'

This was great, have a look at a report and we will talk about it in a couple of days, I had just left a department where it was have a look at this report now and we will speak in a two minutes, I was going to like it here, it seemed calm, relaxed nothing like where I had just come from.

The first day in reality is all about find yourself a desk, chair, a telephone, a couple of trays for you work, where the canteen is and where the toilets are, have I parked my car in the cheapest car park by 1989 I was the proud owner of a Ford Granada 2.3L registration number JOM 878L.

In general terms you were allocated a job or jobs and they were yours till the end, the trial in other words, you would work on them on most occasions on your own except for the arrest phase, searches and interviews then the rest of your team and perhaps other teams would assist you.

We were based in a modern office block in Birmingham City centre and within walking distance of police headquarters and situated within the Fraud Squad was a cheque squad which dealt with all the West Midlands Police cheque and credit card fraud it was second only to the Metropolitan Police cheque squad, also within the office was an intelligence unit which gathered intelligence on all fraudsters that came through the West Midlands Police systems, it was manned by two detectives, one who looked after the fraud side and one who looked after the cheque side.

The head of the Fraud Squad was a Detective Superintendent and he had a DCI, three inspectors, 8 sergeants and about 40 detectives under him, we also had four typists and an administration office, so it was quite a big squad.

We had work referred to us from a variety of different sources which included the local West Midlands Police and other Police Forces, the Official Receiver, the Department of Trade and Industry, the Office of the Supervision of Solicitors, Accountancy firms, Banks, Building Societies, all the frauds that were taken on by the office were of a complex nature and were shrouded with mountains of paperwork.

Going back to the report that was handed to me I read it twice and really did not fully understand but thought now's the time for a discussion with the DS.

The scenario for the fraud was this, we had three main suspects, a property developer who I shall call Mr C, with his own company in Wolverhampton, a property valuer, Mr V, and a third man who I will describe as the odd job man or 'gopher' for the other two, and I will call him Mr L.

The fraud was based in the Wolverhampton area and the end result was that loans were being obtained by various parties fraudulently but being controlled solely by the property developer.

It worked liked this, the property developer would buy a rundown terrace type of property in the more poorer areas of Wolverhampton, he would quite literally smarten the building up with the assistance of the odd job man and when I say smarten I mean a coat of paint and not much more.

Then the valuer would value the property at an inflated price, normally at a price agreed with the developer, the developer would then put tenants in and get them to sign various forms which they thought was a tenancy agreement, but it was in fact mortgage application forms, so the tenants ended up buying the property. The mortgage advance was made by the mortgage/loan company and with the assistance of two totally innocent solicitors, the loan would go the seller/vendor of the house who of course was the developer, it was as simple as that.

The tenants would now be in a reasonable type house and quite unaware that they had bought it with misleading information contained on the mortgage application forms, and that they would soon be falling into more debt. The tenant would then be left with a mortgage he/she knew nothing about and the developer would end up with a nice profit.

In 1989 we were talking of a profit for the developer in the region of £20,000.00 per house less expenses that included solicitor's fees, other fees, paint and payments to the valuer and odd job man

The tenants who I could only describe as educationally lacking and I do not mean that disrespectfully, but they were signing various forms and clearly not understanding what they were doing, but to them it gave them a roof over their head at least for the time being, the developer would collect 'rent' off them every month, sometimes it would go towards the mortgage advance via bank accounts that he had opened in the tenants names, again they knew nothing of this, but in most cases he would normally keep it.

So the mortgage would not get paid all the time or regularly and the debts soon mounted and it would be the tenants who got the demanding letters and threats of eviction from the mortgage/loan companies and not of course the developer. This is of course the first they knew that they might own the house that they were living in but it was too late then.

It came to the police through Mr L, the odd job man who felt that what the developer Mr C, in particular was doing was morally wrong and of course what I then found out is, that some of the tenants involved were his friends and he had in his own way introduced then to Mr C, but he had no idea what was about to unfold and I for one do not and have never blamed him.

As Mr L was still a possible suspect in the fraud he was informed that we may need to interview him formally and under caution in the near future.

How was I going to tackle the fraud, we had potentially between 20 and 30 tenants who had signed for mortgages/loans when they all thought they were signing a tenancy agreement, the stumbling block here was all the tenants were allegedly unemployed but on the mortgage application forms they were all put down as employed by various companies with one common address, the home address of Mr L.

So my first thought was, have these tenants played a more active role in this fraud that what was being at first suggested, so my mind was made up all the tenants I could find, because some had of course been evicted by now or rehoused by the council, would be arrested and interviewed under caution.

I thought well I like a challenge, and at the end of the day all frauds are thefts and deceptions but more complicated.

The arrest and interview under caution path was on the advice of the Crown Prosecution Service, and so with the assistance of the DS, over the next three months or so we managed between us to arrest and interview the majority of the thirty tenants.

In the interview they all said basically the same, that was they were asked by Mr L who they knew, if they needed to rent a newer house, a better house than what they were currently living in. The quickly agreed and in due course they were asked by the developer Mr C, to sign various forms which they all thought was for a tenancy agreement.

Phase two was the arrest and interview of the three main suspects, Mr C, the property developer was arrested and interviewed and he could see no wrong, all he was helping people get on the housing ladder and it was the odd job man, Mr L who found all these people for him and gave them all the forms to sign and all the employment details. And that the valuations on all the properties were fair valuations completed by Mr V, a well-respected valuer in Wolverhampton.

Which of course I knew to be a lie as we had all the properties re-valued and the difference in some of the properties was frightening, the best example was a terraced typed house in the red light area of Wolverhampton bought by the Mr C for £35.000, it was smartened up with a coat of paint, valued by Mr V and sold for £69.900, it was re-valued some six months later and it was £30.000 tops something wrong there.

In relation to the bank accounts and various employment details, he put that firmly down to Mr L even to the point that it was Mr L who collected any monies from the tenants that was due and he had nothing to do with it.

Mr C was bailed from the police station to return at a future date.

The valuer, Mr V, was next and all he kept saying is that he gave a fair valuation for the type of property that he valued and that the Mr C had not asked him to over value any of the properties and in fact he informed us that he would never do such a thing for anyone let alone a man he only vaguely knew.

He was also bailed from the police station with the same proviso as Mr C, in that we would see him at a future date.

Mr L told us everything, he was a friend, associate and in some cases a relative of the people who had 'bought' these properties, he agreed Mr C gave him money to paint the house and generally tidy them up, but he was convinced and actually told all of these people that they were only tenants because none of them could get a mortgage because they were all un-employed and he added at the end of the interview, 'I will plead guilty. Mr Wier and I will make a witness statement and I will tell you everything.'

He too was released from the police station to a future date.

An interim report went to the CPS, who advised that all the original people in this investigation, the so called tenants would now all be asked to make witness statements and that they would not face court proceedings in relation to any possible offence they may have committed.

The three main suspects would be re-interviewed when the witness statements had been obtained from the tenants and they would be charged and go for trial at Wolverhampton Crown Court in the New Year.

So all their interviews under caution made by the original tenants would now be transferred onto Section 9 witness statements, and I would re-visit each and every one of them again and ask them to read the statement and if they agreed with the statement to sign and date it.

Also to inform all the tenants and of course their respective partners, that they would not be facing criminal charges, but might be called to give evidence at the Crown Court in due course as a witness. This was completed as quick and possible.

The three main suspects were interviewed for a second and final time and none of them added anything further and they were charged with various offences of criminal deception and bailed from the police station to Wolverhampton Magistrates Court.

Towards the end of the year I submitted my file of evidence, complete with witness statements and other relevant documents to the CPS and the three defendants in due course were committed to Wolverhampton Crown Court for trial.

Before I move onto 1990, I cannot close 1989 without mentioning the terrible Hillsborough Disaster that occurred on 15th April 1989 at Hillsborough football stadium, it was home on that fateful day to a FA Cup semi-final match between Liverpool and Nottingham Forest, the game itself was abandoned after 6 minutes.

The human crush took place at the Leppings Lane end of the ground where the Liverpool supporters were allocated and due to the large number of Liverpool fans outside the ground estimated at 5,000 or more trying to gain access to the ground through the turn styles, the police decided to open a set of exit gates which had no turn styles, this was done because it was feared that someone would be killed outside the ground, but now with the gates open it resulted in thousands of fans running through and into two already overcrowded central pens of fans, which was now causing a huge crush at the front of the terrace, which of course in 1989 all pitches were surrounded by high metal fences.

People were now being pressed up against these fences, but of course the fans at the back had no knowledge of this and so the human crush happened eventually the fence broke under pressure so fans could now get on the pitch but not before many had lost their lives, they basically died standing up of compressive asphyxia in other words crushed to death.

A total of 96 people died and over 766 were injured.

Also it was in 1990 that I once again I bought another motor car this time I purchased a Vauxhall Senator 3000cc automatic registration number C848 UPE, what a fantastic car that turned out to be I owned that car for over ten years it was a truly comfortable car.

The beginning of 1990 and the trial began, day one, Mr L pleaded Guilty, the other two defendants pleaded Not Guilty, counsel for the prosecution addressed the court and said that defendant number one, Mr L, who had pleaded Guilty was prepared to make a witness statement to the police, that the prosecution together with other witness statements would rely on for the trial.

The trial was put back seven days for me to take the statement. I started the following day and every morning I would drive to his house for 9.00am and listen and write until 4.00pm then drive back to work, the statement took five full days to write, one day to type and consisted of well over 140 pages.

The trial began and the first witness was Mr L, he gave his evidence over three days and was brilliant, so detailed it was unbelievable, he was followed by twenty two of the original people, the tenants, we failed to find about six and they too all gave excellent evidence, so at the end of two weeks the prosecution had given all of its evidence.

The third week the two remaining defendants were called to give evidence and on the Wednesday the jury had retired to consider their verdict, I thought it went well but as we know it's for the jury to decide. Midmorning on the Thursday the jury were back, they found the valuer Mr V, not guilty and he was discharged and left the court immediately.

They found the property developer, Mr C, guilty, Mr L, joined Mr C in the dock for sentencing, Mr L was given a six suspended prison sentence for eighteen months, however Mr C was sent to prison for nine months an excellent result all round.

There was a sad end to this investigation as some months after the trial finished Mr L died as a result of a short illness, I felt so very sorry for him, I know he did do wrong but he was a lovely man and one man I will not forget.

I thought nearly 12 months to conclude one fraud but not to worry it was not long before I got my next fraud. I was in the office and the telephone rang it was the internal audit department of Birmingham Midshires Building Society based in Wolverhampton and they wanted to meet with the Fraud Squad, as they believed that they had uncovered a fraud involving a solicitor.

I had a new DS by now Steve Groves and I discussed with him my conversation with the building society that I had just had, and we both agreed to go and meet with them to see if there was a fraud for us to investigate, which we did.

The fraud that they had uncovered involved some 125 houses, a solicitor, the manager and deputy branch manager of the Birmingham Midshires Building Society in Coventry, a property dealer, a chartered surveyor, a life assurance expert who was the current boyfriend of the deputy branch manager were all believed to be involved in the fraud.

The meeting went well and they were able to supply to us in the first instance, with hard copies of all the documents in relation to the 125 houses and details including full names, addresses of the suspects.

We came out of the meeting and sat on a bench with our recently purchased pork and stuffing sandwich and the DS said, 'Looks like you have won another mortgage fraud Nigel, but in fairness it looks a good one.'

I said, 'Thanks, and you are right this will be a good enquiry'

Time now for a little piece of history in fact two pieces of history was made, on 31st January 1990 saw the very first McDonalds restaurant open in Moscow, Russia.

On 11th February 1990 Nelson Mandela was released from the Victor Verster Prison in Cape Town South Africa after serving a total of 27 years in prison.

After about 6 weeks I had all the paperwork for the properties that were under suspicion, I quickly looked through them all, but I decided at a very early stage to only select an sample amount of properties for further investigation and the figure I had decided on was 25, and that was because it was 25th March 1990 when I made the decision, frightening isn't how us detectives think.

Most of the properties were based in Coventry but that was always going to be the case because apart from the solicitor every one of the suspects lived in Coventry, so looking at these 25 houses what was the obvious things that stood out.

All had the same solicitor, all had the same valuer, all had the same life assurance man, all mortgages were authorised by either the branch manager or the deputy branch manager at the Coventry branch of the building society, the introducer of the mortgage to the society was either the property dealer or a company registered at the home of the solicitor and with its directors being the solicitor and the life assurance man. So it was all very nicely put together.

What you have to remember, the introducer of a mortgage to a building society would have commission paid to them based on the loan advanced and of course the man involved in life assurance would have commission paid to him based on the loan insured for the life of the mortgage, so the scope for making money was enormous.

The property dealer who I shall refer to as Mr M, his fraud was different to the other main players his involved the buying and selling of the same property 3 or 4 times in a 12 month period and on each occasion the value of the property rose, it was estimated that he made over one million pounds profit and to date he has never been brought to justice because when he knew the police were after him he disappeared to Southern Ireland.

Mr M owned four properties in Coventry, he sold each and every one of them to say Mr X, who then sold them to Mr Y, who then sold them to Mr Z, however in real terms the properties were never sold because it was only the names of the owners that changed because, Mr M was in fact Mr X,Y and Z, but on each transaction, he made money and the solicitor acting for both Mr M and the society was of course the solicitor we were looking at in our fraud. The fraud was never discovered in the first instance because no papers were ever filed at HM Land Registry.

The fraud of course should have been detected but the solicitor deliberately stalled on sending relevant documents to HM Land Registry, so to all intense and purpose the property had never been sold at all.

The second part of this fraud involved everybody apart from Mr M, at the time in Coventry there was a saying, 'that if you wanted a 100% mortgage go to the Midshires because they never turned you down' and they did not. They openly encouraged re-mortgages and first time buyers wanting 100% mortgages, you name it you could get it from them.

The applicants would normally attend the branch in person and were seen by the branch manager who I will refer to as Mr J or his deputy Miss H, in most cases it was a matter of them signing forms, no enquiries were made as to the suitability to re-pay the loan, no enquiries were made at named employers and off they went with the applicants knowing that were going to get the loan they wanted.

The introducers name was normally handwritten in the top right corner of the application form, the introducer in most cases being the company run by the solicitor, Mr S and the life assurance man Mr A, that guaranteed a fee for them and then surprise, surprise all the applicant's wanted life assurance from the company that Mr A, was quite lawfully employed by and that generated another fee.

Incidentally the Coventry branch of the Birmingham Midshires Building Society won branch of the month on more than one occasion.

Everything went well until the bottom dropped out of the housing market in the late eighties and interest rates were rising, a lot of the applicants could not pay their mortgage so the society would try and make contact with the mortgagees but often got no response. So after many months of trying they would select the worst case scenario and go and visit the property in the hope of attempting to rectify the now obvious problem of mortgage arrears, but their visits revealed some shocks that they were not expecting.

A good example of that was a terraced property in Cross Street, Coventry this was bought for £110,000 in 1989 with a 100% mortgage, the property was now worth £65,000, but because of the less than regular repayments on the mortgage, the society was now owed about in excess of £125,000. The applicant in this case had disappeared now and left behind an empty property and a big debt, that was probably the worst case but there were several like that.

This is where the valuer Mr V, came in, his valuations in most cases were too high and it was firmly believed that he valued the property at the agreed mortgage loan so in the case of Cross Street the mortgage loan or advance was £110,000 he would value at £110,000 possibly only doing a door step valuation.

By that I mean he probably did not even go inside the property he was valuing and on occasions, he was a valuer from Coventry valuing property in Birmingham and as far away as Telford that would not normally happen, the society would always select a valuer who knew the area but in this case they had little choice because Mr J or Miss H were selecting the valuer, the same one in most cases.

Whilst I was investigating this fraud I was given another fraud, this too was based in the Coventry area and it centred on a so called financial advisor, who

I will refer to as Mr Joban and it was so simple it was unbelievable, the financial advisor ran his own company on the Foleshill Road and it was a company that dealt with life assurance.

He being the advisor and introducer of new business to the various Life Assurance companies was paid a commission based on the term of the policy and to give an example, if I signed up for a life policy for 30 years and the pay out on death would be £100,000 the introducer would get in the region of 1% of that, a £1,000 as an upfront payment or commission on receipt of the first monthly instalment received.

Mr Joban after writing to numerous life assurance companies eventually got a license to sell life assurance from two of the companies after completing a successful training period. Now in the space of six months this man introduced the same 100 people to the same two companies, claiming his commission from both companies, now to make the fraud easier to handle he would pay the first months instalment for the customer, remember after the first instalment he got his commission and low and behold no further instalments were made.

The companies got suspicious in relation to the non-payment of further monthly instalments so they made their own enquiries and after speaking with several of the customers they came up with the view that many of the them had only signed up as a favour for this man, who most of course knew well, and without exception none wanted the policy.

But the main man, Mr Joban in charge of all this had made approximately £200,000 in a very short space of time, and by using the rules as they were then the life assurance companies could not claw his commission back, this of course has changed now and commissions can be clawed back.

Both these cases were now being dealt with solely by me and for the next 6-12 months I was gathering documents, interviewing witnesses, obtaining several hundred witness statements, I think for both frauds in excess of four hundred statements were taken so 1990 is now the end of 1991. But I was now in a position to start making arrests in both frauds.

On 24th November 1991 Freddie Mercury the lead singer with the pop group Queen died peacefully at his home in London. The Queen were one of the greatest pop groups of the 1980's.

1992 for me was a year full of arrests, interviews and preparing court papers, in relation to the Birmingham Midshires Fraud the five main suspects were arrested and interviewed several times, over the forthcoming months, there was as you would expect no admissions of guilt and all had the same story merely stating that what they were doing was not criminal and merely very good if not sharp practice.

And in the case of the two from the building society again as you would expect, all they would say is that there were doing their best for the society and if there was mistakes they were honest mistakes and not criminal.

All five defendants were charged and bailed to appear at Birmingham Crown Court at a date in the future.

The financial advisor was somewhat easier he was interviewed and said all the people who took out the policies were helping him to build up his new business and that's why he made the first monthly payment, he believed that they would continue with the payments and if they did not it was nothing to do with him.

I for one did not believe him and he too was charged and bailed to appear in due course at Coventry Crown Court.

The next 12 months for me was court appearance after court appearance from Birmingham to Coventry and back again and then towards the end of the year the financial advisor, Mr Joban appeared before Coventry Crown Court and pleaded guilty and was sentenced to 6 months imprisonment.

We did not recover one penny of the commission he had made and according to bank statements that we had recovered during the investigation he sent most of the money to his parents in India, we could never get that money back.

In relation to the Birmingham Midshires trial, because the defendants had been charged with several conspiracies they as is there right elected separate trials, so these separate trials and there were five in total, took place over many months because a lot of the witnesses had to give evidence in all of the trials and that included me.

Having such a lot of separate trials does take up a lot of time as you had to keep giving the court inconvenient dates, including annual leave of your witnesses but during 1992 and early 1993 this is exactly what happened.

The Birmingham Midshires saga concluded on 1st September 1993 after several trials all before the same judge, His Honour Justice Farrer and the end result was, the branch manager Mr J and the life assurance man Mr A were convicted, the deputy branch manager Miss H was acquitted, no evidence was offered against the valuer Mr V, and the biggest shock to me was that after three trials the solicitor was acquitted of all charges.

That is one decision I could never understand, it seemed as if the jury would not except that a solicitor could be guilty of committing crime.

HHJ Farrer said at the end of all the trials that myself and DS Steve Groves should be awarded a commendation for the hard work and commitment over many, many months that we had put into this complex and difficult criminal investigation and further to get the matter before the court.

We were both awarded a Chief Superintendents commendation's shortly afterwards.

What happened to the solicitor well two years later he was involved in another fraud that was investigated in our office and which involved the criminal abuse of the legal aid system and for this fraud he received six years imprisonment and of course he was struck off as a practising solicitor, so we got there in the end.

My next fraud was a fraud that involved the asset stripping of companies quite common in the 1990s as more and more companies struggled for business and they are left open to the vultures that come in and asset strip, sorry they tend to call themselves company restructure experts.

They will look for ailing companies who are in deep debt problems and will offer you a way out, they move in and they will suggest to you the best way that your company can solve its money problems, they will suggest that they put their own people in who will become the new directors thus taking the hassle away from old directors, and these new directors will need to be in control of the finances, in other words they get their name on the company cheque book, and in return they will reduce your costs and outputs and allegedly make huge savings and keep the naughty creditors away so you can continue to trade.

Utter rubbish they are asset strippers or thieves to put it another way, they are there to steal.

Anyway you reluctantly agree that these people seem like angels, having been sent by the Lord to help you, you are fed up with arguing with banks and creditors and loan companies and now someone is going to do it for you, to do all the dirty work and what do they want in return £1,000 a month salary, that's nothing its small fry, they are going to get rid of my problems for me.

Now whilst you are reading this you may think, well they have not done anything wrong, well they haven't yet but they will soon. For example you have six company cars and six company vans, they tell you we will reduce that to two of each vehicles and they will sell for you the remaining eight vehicles and the money will go into the company account and it does, but remember whose names are now on the cheque book, the asset strippers sorry the angels names are on the cheque book.

The two remaining company cars a nice Jaguar or a nice BMW, will now be driven round and used by the new directors of course. Now asset stripping what do I mean by that, it is another word for theft of course, now the sale money of the eight vehicles sold at auction has gone into the company account that the new directors control, so will either the old directors or the company itself see any of that money of course not it will go on alleged expenses, so the eight vehicles which were assets of the company have now gone, sold and the money has gone to.

The asset strippers like selling off machinery, they like refinancing machinery, with the support of false and misleading valuations, they like selling off parts of your building or your land, the thing you have to remember is that you do not control anything now these people will run your company, strip your assets and go leaving you in a bigger mess.

My next fraud enquiry was to be one of those involving asset strippers, these so called vultures had moved into a little company in Digbeth, in Birmingham and took over its running, this was a good enquiry and I learnt a lot and met many a good criminal who incidentally still live and 'work' in Birmingham today.

These individuals and I suppose in total there were about ten of them would be my investigation for the next 18 months or so, in the meantime I would have little jobs given to me but this was a large and complex enquiry and I loved every minute.

1994 began of course with the arrest of both Fred and Rose West from Glouceste,r and the police began the task of digging up their house and gardens, it led to Fred West being charged with 12 murders and Rose West 10 murders.

Fred West committed suicide in HMP Birmingham on 1st January 1995 before his trial took place and his wife Rose was sent to prison for life on after a trial on 22nd November 1995 for her part in the horrific crimes.

Out of the ten main suspects in this investigation, two stood out as leaders and the one in particular was into everything, asset stripping, mortgage fraud, company fraud the lot and he lived in a lovely five bed roomed detached house in the country, he also had a side line, a genuine building company that refurbished old properties and in real terms he did not have to commit fraud to survive but I suppose there is more excitement in fraud than laying a few bricks here and there.

The second man was more of an enforcer, he looked the part he was short, stocky, and built like a brick toilet, and together they worked well, but it was my job to try and stop them. It was a difficult enquiry because every time you went back to the original directors and said to them, 'Did you give them permission to sell 'a' and 'b'?

The answer would always be the same, 'Yes, they said it would assist in keeping the company running.'

'Did you give them permission to refinance 'a' and 'b'?

The answer again would be, 'Yes.'

So it made my investigation very difficult, but my instructions were to investigate it as much as you can, to investigate them as much as you can, then submit a detailed report to the Crown Prosecution Service and they would make the final decision to whether any or all of the main suspects would face any criminal charges of in fact that none would face any charges.

One of the two main men had flown to America why I will never know, he was not running from the police as far as I was aware, but I needed to interview him and on the advice of the CPS, they would request that the West Midlands Police authorise me to go to America to conduct an interview under caution with this suspect.

The force actually agreed without much of a fight and in actual fact I was lucky enough to travel to America twice, with my inspector of course, to complete this part of the investigation, that included conducting an interview under caution with the suspect at the FBI office in Tampa, Florida and later on my second visit to America and again at the request of the CPS, I obtained a detailed witness statement of some 120 pages from the same man.

It was an excellent experience and in general the FBI looked after us fantastically well, our main contact was a

Drugs Enforcement Officer and he too was brilliant and looked after us very well.

Can I just make some readers a little bit jealous, the hotel we stopped in for the duration of our stay was the The Reddington Hotel, Reddington Beach, Florida and the hotel overlooked the gulf coast and that is genuine

I have even been back to the hotel for a holiday with my wife, as it was that good.

When I returned to normality I submitted a large detailed file of evidence to the Crown Prosecution Service for them to consider. In total I submitted evidence against ten people for various offences including theft, handling stolen goods and criminal deception, the CPS considered my file for several months and in the end they decided that there was not sufficient evidence to secure a conviction and therefore nobody was charged. It all seemed like a waste of time but I had done my best in difficult circumstances.

1995 was a changing year for the police service in the West Midlands and particularly detectives, because of something that happened in 1989. It certainly had a big impact on me because on 6th January 1996 I was made subject of the force 'tenure of post policy' and returned to a sub division as a detective. I did not want to leave the Fraud Squad but the West Midlands Police decided that six years was long enough and I had no choice whatsoever the force had made their mind up for me.

So the end of 1995 ended in sadness as I was to be moved from the job I had so enjoyed and was good at, but as I have said in this book before let's bring on the new challenge.

1995 ended on a good note for some people because on 3rd October 1995 O.J. Simpson the famous American footballer was found not guilty of murdering his ex-wife and friend.

CHAPTER ELEVEN

Tenure of Post Policy

Firstly I need to turn the clock back to 14th August 1989 when the then Chief Constable of the West Midlands Police, Mr Geoffrey Dear disbanded the forces Serious Crime Squad amid a number of alleged complaints . including corruption, the making up of suspects statements and false confessions

Between 1986 and 1989 it is alleged that 97 complaints were made against the squad.

The origin of the Serious Crime Squad can be traced back to 1952 when the old City of Birmingham Constabulary embarked on an experiment to tackle organised and serious crime in the Birmingham area and they assembled a group of 'seasoned and experienced' detectives and the Birmingham Special Crime Squad was born.

It proved to be such a success that it provided the inspiration for the Serious Crime Squad that was formed in 1974 when several forces including Birmingham City joined together to became the West Midlands Police.

In August 1989 when the squad was disbanded an investigation was set up by the Police Complaints Authority and conducted on their behalf by the West Yorkshire Police, in total 97 complaints were investigated and between March 1991 and October 1991 the enquiry team past a succession of files to the Crown Prosecution Service for consideration of criminal charges against some but not all of the officers concerned.

In May 1992 the Director of Public Prosecutions, Dame Barbara Mills concluded that there was insufficient evidence to prosecute a single officer from the squad.

But the damage was done in November 1991 the Birmingham Six, six men who had been convicted of the 1974 Birmingham Pub bombings which killed 21 innocent people and injured over 170 had been freed by the Court of Appeal after an investigation in which it is alleged that the squad had played an important part which had now been shown to be flawed.

Remember no Serious Crime Squad officer was ever charged with anything.

But whatever the ins and outs of the Serious Crime Squad and what may or may not have occurred the face of the West Midlands Police was to change.

The first thing to go was the word 'squad' all squads now became 'teams' or 'units' we had to get away from the word squad because it could be perceived as being possibly corrupt, it was now a tainted word within the West Midlands Police.

The Fraud Squad for example became the Major Fraud Unit. But the thing that hit me personally was the force 'tenure of post policy' the force had now decided that nearly all detectives on these squads who had in most cases completed at least five years' service or more, and in a lot of cases on the same squad would now be returned to divisional CID. This was to be done so that staff could be changed and interchanged regularly so giving a fairer movement of staff.

For me I had been a detective on the Fraud Squad for six years I was finished I had to move.

The policy in due course would tell you how long you could stop on a particular squad the Fraud Squad or Major Fraud Unit as it was about to be called was a 5 year tenure.

To return and remain as a detective back on a division you would have to sit an 'exit board' and if you passed this board you would normally be returned to the division of your choice. In 1993 we moved house to go and live in Sutton Coldfield which was on the 'D' division, so when applying for my exit board the 'D' was my preferred choice.

If you elected not to go for an exit board and a lot of experienced detectives did not, then you would be returned to uniform duties.

This was the police, or should I say senior officers tarring all detectives with the same brush, they had chosen not to look at you as an individual, you were looked out as a detective on a squad and that meant you were to be moved.

It was perceived that all detectives working on squads were or could become corrupt, absolutely no evidence whatsoever in this but it did not matter, their minds were made up.

It would appear in the early stage that the only officers that were spared tenure were uniform officers and detectives working on divisions and or sub divisions, as they were described as frontline officers, in other words more likely to be meeting members of the public at more regular and consistent times.

Why were they deemed to be less potentially corrupt than someone on a squad, I do not know, that of course was never explained to us.

My own story well I applied for and got an exit board, the purpose of the board was to find out if you were up to date with what was happening on the outside world, because for the last six years you had been specialising in fraud, not rape, not murder, not burglary, not theft, not assault, just fraud so you had to do a fair share of studying and visiting people to see how the force had changed, what new procedures had been bought in and of course DNA had come along way.

The divisional CID had changed with the introduction of the Divisional Crime Support Units which was a large group of detectives on a division dealing with all serious crime, Crime Bureaus were bought in to standardise the reporting and management of recorded crime on a division, large purpose built Intelligence Cells supporting the DCSU were bought it.

So I had a bit of researching to do and various visits had to be made, one of those visits was again to my old friend Mr Ross who by now a Superintendent, so that's what I did in the latter part of 1995, the one thing I was not going to do was to fail an exit board.

The forces reasoning behind tenure was to 'allow greater movement of officers throughout the various departments and to spread experience throughout the force.' That's the forces view, not mine and not too many other police officers share that view. To my mind tenure was bought in because of poor and inferior management and nothing else.

I suppose I was quite unfortunate really because I was actually tenured twice, once at the end of 1995 beginning of 1996 and again in 1998, so this is why I probably feel so strong about it, I believe to this day that it was a mistake and a complete waste of time and money. I felt when I was tenured that I was being punished for being a detective or investigating fraud.

Incidentally when the force had a new Chief Constable in 2002, his first job was to scrap the tenure policy because it was not working' specialist departments particularly the CID were losing all of its experience by this policy.

It was replaced by the Performance Management and Organisation Effectiveness Policy for police officers and this came into force on 1st September 2003, too late for me because not only was I subject of tenure in 1995/1996 I was made subject of tenure once more in 1997 moving in 1998, when the then Chief Constable decided not only were specialist squads and departments subject of tenure so would divisional CID and Traffic, but I will discuss the second hammer blow in a latter chapter.

My exit board was set for November 1995 and it consisted of Detective Superintendent Newbury, someone from the Police Federation and someone from Personnel. Various questions about procedures were put to me and various little scenarios were put to me like, you are the Night DC and a rape occurs what action would you take, I was happy with these questions because before the Fraud Squad, this is what I was doing this was bread and butter to me and any other experienced detective who was going to have to go through this process.

I answered to the best of my knowledge and now I had to wait for the result of the board, I was told the same day that I had been successful and had passed the exit board, that was great a great relief for me.

And as tenure was not retrospective nearly 90% of all squads in the force would be losing their most experienced detective officers very quickly.

I was notified by personnel that I would be leaving the Fraud Squad on 3rd January 1996 and beginning a new life as a detective at Bromford Police Station on Monday 6th January 1996, and so another new chapter in my life as a policeman begins and of course another new challenge but this time I had not chosen this challenge.

CHAPTER TWELVE

Return to the CID

On Monday 6th January 1996 I drove to Bromford Lane Police Station to begin my new job as a detective on one of the newly formed Divisional Crime Support Units or DCSU's as they were more commonly known.

The units were formed to deal with all serious crime on their respective divisions mine of course being the 'D' Division, which included the D1, D2 and D3, they would also cover nights and this was to allow local CID to deal with the less serious crime.

The basic make up was a large group of experienced detectives and police constables which could very quickly respond to most serious crime, the make-up of each unit varied from division to division but in the main you had a Detective Chief Inspector, two Detective Inspectors, and six teams made up of six sergeants and 30 detectives/ police constables. The idea was for us to cover the whole of the division 24 hours a day leaving local policing to be delivered by local officers.

They had been running about 18 months before I joined them and there was already rumours of them being broken up, but on day one when I joined them they were well and truly there and working.

Each and every day there would be a duty crew working 8.00am x 4.00pm and a duty crew working 2.00pm x 10.00pm, the other four crews in them main did their own work and generally picked their own hours, situated at the top of the office was the office manager, he kept everything in order and he was the technician of the DCSU.

Day one introductions out the way and off we went to Queens Road Police Station, there were several persons in custody for a violent disorder that had occurred late the night before, the DS gave us all our instructions some stayed at the police station to interview the suspects, others like me went out and took witness statements and made door to door enquiries, we dealt with the matter and by the end of the day a total of seven defendants were charged and bailed to the court.

I finished at 8.00pm on the night, a 12 hour day on my first day, I had a funny feeling on day one that I was not going to enjoy the work.

Prison visits were another part of the job profile, I mentioned these earlier in my book it's when someone has received a custodial sentence and you visit him, to see if he wishes to admit other similar offences, that because he is serving a sentence can be subject of a Superintendents authority be 'written off' to him. I did not like them all those years ago and I did not like them now.

Also on most days that you walked in to the office various people had been arrested overnight for serious offences and you were expected to deal with them, almost like a glorified 'prisoner handling unit,'

The local CID were moaning about their increase in workload and some days on the DCSU you were waiting for things to happen, so clearly someone somewhere had got their figures wrong and you could sense that any day now the DCSU would finish.

But in the meantime we carried on until sometime in April/May 1996 came the good news that the DCSU's were to be disbanded throughout the force and the staff returned to either divisional CID for the detectives or a return to uniform for the police constables, you can guess who were the saddest and most disappointed to see the unit disbanded.

Anyway the detectives were given a choice, Queens Road, Stechford or Sutton Coldfield, I put Sutton Coldfield down on my form as my preferred preference. I thought Queens Road been there and done that, Stetchford never worked there and never fancied it so it had to be Sutton. I was interviewed by the DCI and one on the DI's to find out your reasons why you chose were you did I suppose I lived in Sutton, it was nearer to travel and I had previous knowledge of the Sutton area when I worked at both Erdington and Kingstanding I could not really say much more.

I must have said the right things because a couple of days later I was informed that by the end of June on a date to be agreed I would be working on the CID at Sutton Coldfield.

I have to say I for one was glad to see my time on the DCSU had come to its end, I did not enjoy my six months there and I would put in on par with a favourite saying 'ambulance chasing' in that I mean you were always chasing prisoners, chasing crime figures, chasing detections, it just was not me so I was looking forward to my move to Sutton Coldfield.

1996 would also be remembered for the Dunblane Massacre when on 13th March 1996, Thomas Hamilton entered the Dunblane school and shot dead 16 children and one teacher before turning the gun on himself and killing himself, remembered as one of the worst post war massacres in this country.

So on Monday 24th June 1996 I paraded myself in the CID office at Sutton Coldfield for my welcoming chat by the inspector, Detective Inspector Mullen, Sutton

CID was three teams one covered Sutton Coldfield, one covered Castle Vale, and one covered Erdington and Kingstanding. After a couple of days desk hopping I eventually found myself assigned to the team that covered Sutton Coldfield, there were three other detectives that made up the team and at this stage we had no DS.

The first job allocated to me was funny enough a fraud which I think had been round the CID office a few times before it landed on my desk, it was clearly covered in dust.

The fraud in itself was quite simple a company in Sutton Coldfield had promised to deliver cheap cigarettes from an East European country to this country on a large scale but did not deliver, two business men had paid out over £90,000 to this company and the company had failed to deliver the goods.

Of course I had not got the luxury of the Fraud Squad where I was only running with one or two jobs at a time, I was now in a CID office where work was being booked out to me on a daily basis.

The work at Sutton was certainly a good mixture from burglaries, sexual offences through to wounding's and assaults. We had a large shopping centre on us and with large shops and plenty of them crime that went with it, things like the credit and cheque card frauds too small for the Fraud Squad to deal with so they came to the CID.

We were joined in late August 1996 by the new DS, Bob Harley who I knew from Bromford Lane during my short stay there, he had been in charge of the Intelligence Cell.

We were having some good results between us, we had recently charged four youths with a Robbery on a young woman in Sutton, all we started off with was a part registration number of a mini car but through good detective work and of course an element of good luck we identified the car and arrested four youths, surprisingly three of them admitted the offence and put the blame on the cannabis they had taken.

All four were later charged with an offence of Robbery and were dealt with at Birmingham Crown Court; surprisingly none of them went to prison they all received suspended prison sentences.

I was actually enjoying my work for the first time since I left the Fraud Squad and as 1996 ended I had the chance to work two bank holidays, now bank holidays for policemen are good news because you earn double time 16 hours pay for one day's work, so names in a hat and I got two, 2.00pm x 10.00 Boxing Day, and 8.00am x 4.00pm New Year's Day.

I think these were the first bank holidays I had worked since before my time on the Fraud Squad and that was going back to 1989 some seven years or so.

Boxing Day was not a problem by the time you arrived for work at 2.00pm, the morning staff had dealt with most things and I think on this occasion we just assisted them to tidy up some court papers for the prisoners that had been arrested overnight. The remainder of the day was pretty quiet and it allowed you to get through of some of your outstanding paperwork.

I worked over the rest of the Christmas period and it was pretty quiet all round it seemed that even the criminals had taken time off to celebrate Christmas but that was about to change it the biggest way possible to prove that criminals never take time off.

New Year's Day Wednesday 1st January 1997, I woke and got ready for work, I was working the 8.00am x 4.00pm shift at Sutton, I looked out the window and there was a covering of snow it looked lovely, so I drove to work and that morning there would be Bob Harley and two DC's on duty, John James and myself.

First things first we had to check with the custody sergeant to see if there was any prisoners left overnight as a result of the New Year's Eve parties, no it was all quiet in the custody block and there were no outstanding enquiries from nights to be followed up. It was going well by 8.30am we were sitting in the main CID office, the three of us discussing who would win the Manchester United v Aston Villa game that night; it was also to be televised on Sky television. I obviously went for Villa as I was a Villa season ticket holder at the time along with my wife and son, so I wanted Villa to win.

It would be about 10.00am the telephone rang in the office, John James answered and it was the control room at Queens Road and after speaking with them for a few minutes he put the telephone down and said, 'They have found the body of a woman in the grounds of Holy Trinity church, the duty Inspector wants us own there.'

There was no time to finish our tea, I drove down there as quick as possible with John and met with the Inspector. He explained to us that the vicar's wife, incidentally the Vicar and his wife had only been in situ at the church for about a week, and on this particular morning she was showing friends around the garden of the church and when they came to the curates house which at the moment is empty, they could see what they thought was the body of a woman lying on the floor near to the door.

They of course did not walk up to the body they returned to the vicarage then immediately telephoned for the police.

The inspector further explained that if you come to the front of the curate's house and look over the wall you can see signs of an obvious struggle.

I looked over the wall and could see what appeared to be blood on the floor and on a rocky kerb within the front garden of the curate's house, I then went next door to the vicarage and was shown into the rear garden and I walked up to the rear of the curate's house where the body had been discovered.

I walked in the same footmarks that had been made by the first officer on the scene and when I reached the curates house I could quite clearly see lying on the snow covered floor near to the back door the body a young woman, her clothing was dishevelled and there was what appeared to be matted blood on her head and hair, it was clear that she had been subject of a violent attack.

I came back out again stepping in the same foot marks as before as best as I could and I then walked back through the vicarage and round to the front of the curates house where I again met up with the John and the Inspector, also there was a young police officer, he was keeping a running log of who was at the scene.

What a welcome to the New Year, a young girl lying dead in a snow covered garden, what the hell had she done to deserve this, I felt sick to the stomach.

Clearly we had a scene of a disturbance in the front garden of the curate's house and the body was found at the rear of the house, so whether the offender had dragged her around the back which would mean people walking down Trinity Hill would not be able to see the body, or whether the attacker had just left her there and she dragged herself around the back of the house, at this stage we had no idea.

I will make mention at this time that the curates house had only one door to it and it was situated at the rear of the house, and was not in view from Trinity Hill where people may have walked past during the night, and that is why the young girl may have dragged herself around to the back of the house, because she could see the door and could have thought someone was at home, unfortunately the house had been empty for a week or so.

So we had two scenes that needed protecting as soon as possible as the snow was still falling, the front garden of the curates house, where the attack had occurred, and the rear of the curates house where the poor unfortunate victim was found.

I stood for a moment thinking to myself, that ten hours ago people were drinking, laughing, enjoying themselves and seeing in the New Year at midnight, whilst this poor young girl was being battered to death.

The uniform Inspector who I knew well and was an ex-detective sergeant who had recently been promoted to Inspector, and when I joined up with him at the front of the curate's house he informed me that the wheels had been set in motion and the control room were informing the relevant parties to attend at the scene.

The duty Chief Superintendent was on his way to Sutton Coldfield Police Station. Tents and covering for the two scenes was being arranged from Park Lane and scenes of crime officers had been informed as had a police surgeon.

The duty DI and DCI were also now in attendance. A uniform officer would remain at the scene completing a running log of everyone who attends the scene.

My first thought was lets knock on some doors you never know, somebody might have heard something so together with the other DC, we began at some flats facing the church, but in the main what we had was people telling us that they had been out for the evening or we had loads of friends around so we didn't hear anything, and I suppose if someone had been screaming most of us would have put it down to New Year's celebrations.

If only these people had known that some fifty yards away a poor innocent girl was being brutally murdered.

So now it was back to the police station to find out what was to be done next. Certain procedures are put into place, a DS would be in charge of house to house enquires and a DS would be in charge of allocating jobs or actions as they are called, at this stage and being New

Year's day it was decided in the first instance to ask both D1 and D3 for staff and to arrange a briefing in the CID office, so at least we would all know what everyone else knew and we would all be in the same position.

This was arranged for 2.00pm and by that time the body which of course at this stage was still unidentified had been removed from the scene and was at the Central Mortuary where a Home Office Pathologist was about to complete a post mortem.

The two scenes were now adequately covered by tenting and scenes of crime officers were in attendance and they were looking for absolutely anything that the attacker may have left behind that would assist us in solving this vicious murder.

The briefing was given and to be truthful at this stage we knew very little, as we had no obvious witnesses forthcoming, we would of course know more after the post mortem, missing persons files were being checked to see if any missing person fitted the general age and description of our body.

The front office then took a telephone call and the caller wished to see the police because he thought he might have some information for us. I obtained the name and address, told the DS, Bob Harley about the call and the need for the police to go and see this potential witness, I grabbed hold of the DC, John who had been to the scene with me and off we drove to meet with the caller.

The caller was a man in his forties, married with a teenage daughter and teenage son we were invited in, he informed us that the family had just returned from the shops in Sutton Coldfield and had seen all the police action by the church, and that is why they had telephoned.

The next fifteen minutes or so was about to change the course of this murder investigation, I listened intensely as first as the man explained that he and his family were at the Good Hope Sports and Social Club, to see in the New Year and that some of his daughters friends were there, not particularly in their company but at the club and obviously as the evening progressed they all chatted and everyone was looking forward to seeing in the New Year.

His daughter then informed me that one of her friends had left the club about 10.00pm to walk to a local pub, the Station in Sutton town centre where her friend was going to meet some other of her friends, and she would be walking in the same direction and on the same road as where all those policemen are now, she carried on, so I have tried to telephone my friend to see if she is alright, but there is no reply and that's why we are all a bit concerned, and this is the reason we wanted to speak with the police, we all feel something may have happened to her.

My heart was beginning to sink very fast indeed, I was speaking to a good family and it is obvious that they were concerned for their daughter's friend, so I decided to be truthful as I could with them without upsetting the family any further.

I told them that a body of a young lady had been found in the grounds of the church, and that's why the police officers were there, now the next question did not come so easily, do not forget I have been to the scene, I have seen the body on the ground and I knew exactly what the young girl was wearing, so the question was directed to the daughter, I said,

'Can you think carefully and can you tell me if you remember what clothes, what colour and style of clothes your friend was wearing last night.'

I again sat and listened as she told me in great detail as to what her friend was wearing last night, even down to the colour of her nail vanish. I knew then that we had possibly identified our unfortunate murder victim.

I thanked the daughter for all her help but said nothing further to her, I then spoke to the girl's father outside the house and on his own, and I explained to him that there is a possibility that the girl found battered to death, is your daughters friend and I reminded him not to say anything further to anyone at this stage.

I informed him that I was going to report back to senior officers and later today some other police officers will be back to take full witness statements from you and your family.

I could not really say much more that that at this time. I left with the John James and drove back to Sutton, I needed to speak with the police officer at the mortuary and in this case it was the DCI, Kelvin Roberts. The call was made and the first question was asked of him, 'What colour nail varnish was she wearing?'

I was told, and then colours and style of clothing were then discussed and more and more I thought I think that we have identified our body.

The Chief Superintendent and duty DI were informed and an officer was sent direct to the victims house as we had established that her parents were due back later that night after visiting friends up north for the New Year.

An incident room was to be set up the following morning, but I did not work on it because for the next few days after I had booked annual leave so by the time returned to work the incident room was fully staffed.

I felt sad and disappointed at this, as I believed I had helped considerably to assist in the possibly identity of the girl and I would have liked to have worked on the incident room and naturally to catch the killer.

It turned out that the victim did leave the social club about 10.00pm to visit friends in a local pub in Sutton Coldfield, and her walk would have taken her close to the church and I can only assume that is where she was attacked and then dragged into the garden of the curate's house.

The whole episode does not bear thinking about it was a horrific end to a young girls life, the killer needed to be caught. What a horrific crime, a 17 year old girl was dragged off the street, raped and battered and left for dead.

This was one of the worst offences of murder that I had seen in my time as a policeman and it took until November 2003 to bring her killer to justice and it was a breakthrough in DNA that bought this person to the court.

The killer had been arrested for an unconnected assault and DNA was taken from him a search was made on the DNA data base and a match was made, at his trial it was stated that it would be a billion to one chance that it was not him.

The jury quite rightly convicted him after a trial and he was sentenced to life imprisonment.

Why did he kill her? I do not think we will ever know because even with the over whelming evidence of

DNA against him and despite several interviews with the police he has never admitted the crime or showed any remorse.

1997 was a mixed year at work for me, as we now had a new Chief Constable in the West Midlands Police and he was a great supporter of the forces tenure of post policy, so much so he was going to amend the policy and bring tenure in to include all divisional detectives and force traffic officers.

Both of these roles had been excused tenure prior to this on the basis that they were front line policing and not a squad, so in my case as well as being tenured off a squad, the Fraud Squad, I was now about to be tenured off divisional CID, so I was about to be tenured for the second time in 18 months, this possibly was the lowest point in all my 30 years with the police, talk about low morale I had never felt so low in all my police service.

I think it is fair to say I am only one of a handful of detectives to have been tenured twice in his or her career, I personally do not know of anyone else but I am sure there is somewhere.

How was this new policy going to work, well divisional detectives and traffic officers were now subject of a five year tenure, I had been a detective for 16 years so I was struggling to remain in post. In the first instance every detective or traffic officer with more than 14 years in post would be returned to uniform duty as soon as possible, that's me then, after that it worked down until anyone with five years or more would be tenured in the next 12 months and returned to uniform.

I bet some of the senior uniform officers in the force were wondering what was happening, suddenly there were going to be surrounded by ex-detectives who would all be carrying the same 'long miserable face' who of course did not want to be there in the first place.

The idea was that you would be returned to uniform duties for a minimum of 12 months, and then you could re-apply for a detectives post or traffic officer's post, of course that is presuming there were any vacancies.

What a total waste of time what do the police gain from this well nothing of course, this course of action certainly caused the morale in the police to fall to possible its lowest point for many years a fact always denied by the then Chief Constable.

The same month I was informed by the same Chief Constable that having completed 22 years' service, I was entitled to my Long Service and Good Conduct medal and it would be presented to me at an Awards Evening at Tally Ho.

It was also decided at this time that Kingstanding Police Station would once again have its own CID staff based there, something that we had not had for many years and because of my previous working knowledge of the area I was asked to go and set it up with my DS, Bob Harley and this is what we done, incidentally there had been no CID at Kingstanding for about two or three years and they were missed.

It is whilst I was back working as a detective at Kingstanding that I made the decision that if I was going to go back to uniform then I would ask if I could be based at Kingstanding, if I am going to walk the streets with a uniform on then I would like to walk the streets that I know so well, also my parents lived in Kingstanding, so there was always going to be a tea spot.

1997 ended and 1998 arrived and at this time I was still on the CID at Kingstanding but pressure was on me to agree a date with personnel for my return to uniform.

Of course to do that I had to make several journeys to the stores to get myself kitted out in a uniform, because at this time the police were now wearing white shirts instead of blue, I got six of them, two pair of trousers, two jumpers, gloves etc . . . a utility belt to put my baton, handcuffs, first aid pouch, torch and CS spray on, of course I had not been trained in the use of any of them as I had been on the CID for 16 plus years, but hopefully my stay in uniform will only be for 12 months.

I put my report in with an agreed date and met with my new uniform Inspector, Tony Shuck, I had known him prior to this meeting and I had got absolutely no problems with him at all and got on very well with him.

He appeared and certainly was a very understanding person and considering what the force was asking me to do, to go back to front line uniform duties after nearly 17 years as a detective and without of course proper training, I needed this man's support and I got it.

So a date was agreed for me to return to uniform duties for the first time since 1981.

CHAPTER THIRTEEN
Return to Uniform

So the day had arrived, Monday 27th April 1998, I had put on a uniform for the first time in many years and off I went to start my new job at Kingstanding Police Station.

I was posted to the reactive team at Kingstanding Police Station and what this meant in reality is, that I would not be working nights as only the proactive teams worked nights, the reactive teams were like the old style resident and permanent beat officers used to be, it was just a new name for that sort of work, they call them neighbourhood teams today.

You would still be expected to drive police cars and cover the proactive teams at vulnerable times or when they were on leave or even when they were dealing with a serious incident or perhaps had several prisoners.

A new style of policing had now come to the West Midlands Police, it was called sector policing, the new Chief Constable believed in sector policing and within these sectors police would work their own beats called micro beats.

On the D2 we had four sectors, Sutton Coldfield, Castle Vale, Erdington and Kingstanding and each sector was responsible for its own policing so in affect me being based at Kingstanding, meant I would not deal with any incident on the other three sectors unless it was urgent or they had a lack of resources to deal.

So here I was Monday 27th April 1.45pm, on parade at Kingstanding Police Station with my brand new uniform on feeling and no doubt looking totally lost and out of my depth.

The sergeant read out the postings for the afternoon shift, 'PC Wier, Mike 22, take your refs at 7.00pm.'

Hang on is this a spin, I have not driven a marked police car for 17 years and no it was not a spin, I was expected to take out a marked police car on day one. And not only that at 2.30pm I had my first job I was sent to a domestic dispute, god how I had missed them after all these years. I got there and noticed that another police car had just arrived and had parked further down the road so I was quite happy to see that just in case there were any problems.

I walked up to the door and it was answered by a young woman who appeared quite upset, who explained that he ex-partner had been back at the house causing trouble but thankfully he had left now.

I gave her the usual advice about taking out civil proceedings such as an injunction to stop him coming her, just then he walked in through the open front door and started shouting at the occupant, I am standing here thinking what the hell has the job done to me, why am I here dealing with domestic disputes after 17 years of dealing with serious crime.

I felt pretty low it was 2.30pm in the afternoon and I am standing in the middle of a young couple who were arguing about something I could not even tell you what they were arguing about or actually cared about.

I thought here I am 47 years old they are barely 25 years old and they are standing there in the middle of the afternoon arguing about something and nothing, and here am I standing in the middle of them trying to keep the peace why I asked myself, all I knew is that I was not going to stand her all afternoon listening to them.

I had listened to enough I said to the young female, 'Do you want him out this house?

She said, 'Yes, I do please I don't want to see him again.'

So I turned to the male and said, 'You have heard what she has said; now I am asking you to leave this house before you are arrested.'

He looked straight at me almost as if I was not there and shouted at me, 'What if I don't go.'

I replied in a slightly raised voice as I was now getting extremely board with him, 'You will leave otherwise I will remove you.' as I looked up to him, he was about 6' 2" tall, muscular build, no doubt a regular at the gym, thinking I wonder what his thinking about now, anyway to my surprise and without any more shouting, he turned round and walked out muttering something like all policeman are the same, they do not understand us, I have not got a clue what he was on about.

Job one of the day finished I was then sent to a second job, a distraction burglary, this is where the occupier is at home and in nearly every case elderly people are targeted in these types of burglaries.

The burglars will knock on the door and tell the occupier they are from the water board, and they are checking water pressure in the area, or from the gas board we need to check your meter, and we need access to your property and the elderly people unfortunately let them in, these individuals then steal cash and jewellery and will then make an excuse and leave, the occupier will then later discover their property missing.

That is a distraction burglary, a despicable crime against in the main elderly people and that's where I was sent to on the Kings Road in Kingstanding, the controller also informed me that she was the elderly mother of a serving police officer.

But this was more my time of work I could sit down with her and take a written statement and get a description of the offenders and get that circulated to the other police officers. Any follow up work would be done by the CID, probably the detective at Kingstanding who had replaced me when I went back to uniform, was I bitter, yes, but it was not the new detectives fault.

I took a statement off the lady and recorded all the details and went back to the police station, I completed a crime report and submitted it to the sergeant along with the witness statement that I had taken.

Whilst I was there the Inspector called me in and enquired how my first day was going, I explained to him that I was so out of touch being out of uniform for 17 years and that you are going to have to send me on a lot of courses to update me with all the new procedures. He reassured me in saying that when the courses became available then that is something he would discuss with me, but he had other ideas and I sat and listened and I was impressed, he went on to offer me the role of Kingstanding Police Stations intelligence officer, he explained the role to me, that I would have to check the briefings every day and I would have to prepare briefings for nights.

He carried on saying that I would have to highlight to him any problems on the sector, and work with both the reactive and proactive teams to sort the problems out; I would have to attend weekly meetings at Sutton Coldfield with the Superintendent and the other sector intelligence officers. I could work in plain clothes but I may have to work the odd Saturday or Sunday on a police car and cover the odd demonstration if required to do so.

I said, 'You are offering me that job?'

'Yes.' He said and continued, 'You will be much more useful in that sort of role than just driving a police car around the sector for 8 hours a day.'

I said, 'Yes, I will take it yes please; I will certainly have a good go at it anyway.'

I never looked back after that, and I was actually enjoying my new role, I was liaising with both the reactive and proactive officers and between us we put together some good operations with very good results. I worked mainly 8.00am x 4.00pm and when called upon to work either a Saturday or Sunday driving a car and in uniform then I did so.

I was feeling quite pleased with myself, the year in fairness was flying by and although from a personal point of view I never agreed with the decision to put me back to uniform, I now thought of it as a new challenge once more and my next goal would be to get back onto the CID.

But first things first 1998 was World Cup Year, it was held in France and the eventual winners were France who beat Brazil in the final 3-1, but the World Cup will be remembered for out last 16 match with Argentina where the match after 90 minutes had finished 2-2, but we had David Beckham sent off for kicking out at an Argentina player.

I wonder how may remember that and the match was decided on penalties and once again we lost, as David Batty's spot kicked was saved, well there's always another World Cup and of course we are still waiting.

15th August 1998 was a horrendous day for the people of County Tyrone in Northern Ireland, this is when the Real IRA detonated a bomb in the shopping area in the village of Ormagh in County Tyrone, and 29 innocent people were killed and over 200 injured some serious. It is still to this day the greatest loss of life throughout the years of Northern Ireland's troubles.

I was liking my new role as an intelligence officer and I even had a prisoner, one day I was in the office when the telephone rang and I answered it and it was the manager at the local off licence, who had just realised she had been given a forged £20.00 note and the person who gave it to her was outside standing by a car, I grabbed hold of the nearest uniform officer bearing in mind I was in plain clothes and ran out the police station down to Kingtsanding Circle and grabbed hold of this man who was still standing by this car, we bought him back to the police station and searched him and found three more forged £20.00 notes.

I arrested him and he was later interviewed and dealt with by me at Sutton Coldfield Police Station and later charged with offences of Possession and Using a Forged Twenty Pound note, he was dealt with sometime later at the local magistrate's court.

Was there no end to my talent but deep down I wanted the CID back, I had to wait 12 months to return to the CID but I could submit an application before that. In October 1998 a report came out from Sutton Coldfield indicating that they would be looking for detectives to fill detective posts that may become vacant in early 1999 and applications from suitable candidates could be submitted now.

I discussed this with my inspector and he informed me that I should put the application in now and he would fully endorse it, so that's exactly what I did. The completed application went firstly to the Inspector who wrote a lengthy recommendation as to why I should return to the CID and then it went to the DCI and Superintendent, they too both endorsed it favourably and now all I had to do was sit and wait for an interview.

All interviews for the detective posts would take place in the New Year at Sutton Coldfield Police Station and they would be taken by a uniform Superintendent and a DS off the CID, so for me I sat and waited.

1998 was also the year my son bought his first car, a Rover Metro 'F' registration, automatic and blue in colour, I went with him to look at it at a house in Kings Heath, we took the vehicle out for a test drive it and he was adamant he wanted it, so a price with the owner was agreed, £450, and the following day we got a taxi there so we could drive the car back home, what a nail it was but you always remember your first car and my son loved it.

It was also the year I started to wear glasses for the first time, I was now using a computer at work more and more and found I could not focus on everything as good as I could before so I had my eyes tested and began to wear glasses for the first time.

1998 came to an end and 1999 began with me getting a date for an interview for the CID, the interview was late January 1999 and was held at Sutton Coldfield Police Station, the interviewees were Superintendent Green and DS Bob Harley and for the first time in ages I was actually in full uniform.

The interview went as well as I could have expected and later that week I was told that when a vacancy arose and I had completed my 12 months in uniform then I would be transferred to the CID. I was over the moon, I only ever wanted to be a detective and I had now got the chance again, I suppose in retrospect I had enjoyed the last few months but I still thought it should not ever have happened but never mind I was on the road back.

I had my start date for the CID it was to be Monday 26th April 1999, so the last few months of my time in uniform at Kingstanding flew by and there was a spring in my step, I was going back to the job I love as a detective.

At the back of my mind I wanted to get back on the Fraud Squad or the Major Fraud Unit as it was now called but one thing at a time, I had made many friends in my time in uniform and hopefully passed on some of my experience to the younger members of the police force. I suppose the only disappointment I had was when I was told that the vacancy for my detective post was at Erdington and not Kingstanding.

I said my good byes at Kingstanding and in particular to Inspector Schuck, as without his assistance I think I would have struggled during those 12 months or so and now I looked forward to a new chapter in my police life.

CHAPTER FOURTEEN
CID Again

Monday 26th April 1999, I was to start on the CID at Erdington sector on a 2.00pm x 10.00pm shift, I will never forget this day because it was the day the BBC presenter Jill Dando was shot dead outside her house in Fulham in London and although someone was later arrested and charged for the murder he was eventually acquitted after a retrial.

The D2 Erdington CID shared Erdington Police Station with D1, Queens Road and the CID was based in the old single men's quarters at the back of the police station, I walked upstairs to the CID office and found it locked never mind I will have a nose round the building after all I used to work at this police station many years ago, the first thing I noticed was that the bar had gone and also the canteen had gone, I have had some good times in that bar, but the police force was changing and a lot of the bars and canteens in police stations were now being closed.

I recognised a few faces and spoke with them whilst I waited the arrival of my new CID team which was to consist of a DS, three DC's me being one of the DC's and an attached man, he was doing his six month attachment to the department although they now called them TDC's, temporary detective constables.

They all arrived and introductions over, I found myself the usual chair, desk and telephone and almost immediately my new DS gave me some jobs to get on with, they obviously was aware that I had been a detective before so they was not going to tell me what to do, I was the most experienced police officer and detective in that office but what I did find was the office was a bit clicky, the other two DC's and DS went everywhere together leaving me with the TDC, I did not mind that because he was keen and eager to learn, but so much for working as a team.

I did not like it, but I teamed up with the TDC and we got on with the work oblivious to what the other three may or may not have been doing. The main thing as I was back on the CID but I still had itchy feet I wanted that job on the Major Fraud Unit.

I had six years left before retirement so tenure was probably never going to affect me again so I had to plan out the next six years and the plan was simple keep my nose clean, do my job to the best of my ability, and look for a vacancy on the newly named Major Fraud Unit in the months ahead.

The sector at Erdington was strangely quiet, Kingstanding, Sutton and Castle Vale were always busy, the High Street side of Erdington was covered by the DI and all we were left with was a large residential area covering parts of Erdington, Perry Common and Boldmere, but never mind I had my fair share of prisoners during my time there but there was no excitement, I had only been away for a year but everything about the CID seemed to have changed.

New people, new rules, new procedures, and no fun, no excitement and no laughs, what was happening to the CID as I had known it.

I cannot really put my finger on it but years ago the CID had round pegs in round holes, now it seemed like they had square pegs in round holes, policemen and women who you would never associate with the CID were suddenly working there, the older experienced detectives had gone to be replaced by younger inexperienced detectives and I will give you an example of what I meant, I could give you many but I will give you the one that sticks in my mind the most as to what was wrong with the so called modern CID.

Each day one of the sector CID teams would be duty CID, and that meant you would literally pick everything up that came through the door, particularly overnight prisoners and anything else that came in during the day and part of that role was you had to parade at the Sutton CID office.

This was not particularly good because Sutton CID itself might be on the same 8.00am x 4.00pm shift as you, but you as a duty crew would be expected to share their small compact office with them that in itself produced problems. You could have as many as ten officers sharing maybe four telephones and trying to use five or so desks.

One day I went straight to Sutton as I had a prisoner answering bail at 9.00am, so I walked into their office and sat up a corner out of the way drinking a cup of tea waiting for my prisoner to arrive.

Sutton CID were duty that day, I was then joined in the office by the newly promoted DI, who I knew well he was in fact my attached man way back in 1981 when I was at Kingstanding, we had a lot to chat about it was also his first day at Sutton.

Just then the telephone rang and one of the Sutton detectives answered the call and spoke for a few minutes and then said to the caller, 'I am just going for breakfast so give me half an hour and I will come down,' and put the phone down, the DI enquired with the officer what the call was about to be told that that uniform officers were at the scene of a hanging and they wanted CID presence.

The look on the DI's face was a picture he was a bald man anyway and now the whole of his face, neck and head was boiling red with rage, was he going to explode, yes I think he was. He looked at the detective and in not so many words suggested to the detective that she should go to the scene of the hanging now and not after breakfast.

The detective grabbed a coat and a set of car keys and disappeared out the door and never looked back.

Now that's what I meant when I said that the CID had changed, you would never talk like that to a DI, you would never tell the control room you are going to have breakfast first before going to the scene of a hanging, you would most certainly deal with the job first then eat, what had I come back to, I had only been away 12 months yet it seemed like years.

The detective involved left Sutton CID the same day to work on a unit at Bromford Lane Police Station dealing with child abuse.

October 1999 arrived and I was to go on annual leave for three weeks with my wife and son to Florida and how I had looked forward to that but when I arrived back home on the Saturday, I had several messages on my home telephone, I played then back and they were all off my DS at Erdington he was telling me that there was a vacancy for a detective on the Major Fraud Unit but all applications had to be in by 9.00am on Monday 25th October 1999, is was now Saturday 23rd October not much time I thought.

This had all happened in the space of the three weeks I had been away but what can I do, I cannot do much until Monday morning anyway so I decided I would rough out some notes in order to complete the application form on the Monday at work, I knew that the Superintendents secretary was always at work early about 7.30am and I knew I needed her assistance in this.

I could plead with her to assist me with the typing of the form, and then I needed the DI, and Superintendent to endorse the application form and to recommend me, now they were early arrivals for work so if I could do that get the form fully signed up and endorsed, grab some keys, I could get the completed form to personnel in town before nine, of course I would telephone them first to make sure everything was in order. It all sounded so simple, I thought it had to work I need that form completed, signed up and in town before 9.00am.

Would my gamble work it has got to be worth a try, so I arrived at the secretary's office at 7.30am on that Monday and she was already there. I pleaded with her to type the form out for me she agreed and within ten minutes it was done, I thanked her and went along the corridor in search of the DI with form in hand, phase one complete. The DI arrived just before eight and I was standing by his office door with form in hand and I said, 'Morning Sir, can I get you a coffee.'

To which he replied sarcastically, 'What do you want?'

I explained to him that I was applying for a job on the Major Fraud Unit and I need his recommendation for the job and I had to be in town by nine with the completed form.

By the time I had made him a coffee he had written a recommendation on the form I thanked him and off I went, phase two complete, back along the corridor to await the arrival of the Superintendent. I had by this time already made contact with personnel up town to explain that I may be 30 minutes late with the form and I was told there was no problem with that.

The Superintendent arrived, 'Sir I need a word please.'

He growled, 'Be quick DC Wier, I have a meeting in five minutes.' I explained what I wanted and he sat down and wrote his recommendation out on the form, he wished me well and now downstairs I ran to the CID office for a set of keys, phase three complete.

I drove to town and went straight to personnel and hand delivered my application form in relation to the vacancy on the Major Fraud Unit, a young girl in personnel took the form from me and placed it into a draw in a metal cabinet, and me being extremely nosey enquired if there had been much interest in the job and had many people applied, she said, 'Yes you are number 13, but of course it is closed now so there will be no more applications'.

I was number 13 was that going to be an omen, I have said it on a number of occasions but all I could do was to sit and wait, but I did not have to wait long because later that week I had a telephone call from the admin lady at the Major Fraud Unit, Mary, it was the same lady who worked there when I left in January 1996.

We talked about old times for a few minutes and then she asked, 'What time and day do you want to attend for the interview with DI Churchill?'

I said, 'Not being superstitious I will go last please, is that still number 13?'

She said, 'Yes' and added '12.30pm Friday 5th November 1999 is that alright?'

I said, 'Yes that's fine thank you, I will see you then.'

So that was the date of my interview for the Major Fraud Unit, was I going to get my wish and go back to the department where I did not want to leave in the first place.

I arrived for the interview about midday and waited in the front office to be called in, of course I knew lots of the people there, including the admin lady Mary and a lot of the detectives, my interview was to be held in the DI's office and my interviewees were DI Churchill and a DS off the Financial Investigation Unit. I had known the DI for several years and he was my DI when I was first on the Fraud Squad many years ago but would that be to my advantage or not.

I would approach the interview as if I did not know anyone in that room, I wanted that job and this could possibly be the last chance I had so I had to be very professional in everything I said and did, and I always remember my old DS, Malcolm Ross saying, 'Do not sit down until you are told to and do not cross your legs.'

I thought the interview went very well, I believe I was direct but professional in my answers to the various questions and at the conclusion the DI informed me to telephone him back that same afternoon, at about 3.00pm and I would be told either way as to whether or not I had been successful, I left reasonable satisfied how it went but there was 13 of us to interview so I had a 13 to 1 chance at the job.

I got back to Sutton Coldfield at about 2.00pm, and literally hung around the CID office I just wanted to know if I had the job or not. I had been working at Sutton for about a month now as I had been given a job to do by the DI and I even had my own office. The job well it was all about a murder that had occurred some years before.

On 7th February 1995 a private detective who lived in Walmey, Sutton Coldfield was beaten to death in his own house and left naked in a bath full of water. His wife who was a South African lady was out of the country at the time, she was in actual fact back home in South Africa, she immediately returned home after hearing of the news of her husband's death.

But nothing as you know is straightforward in this life as this case was about to go on and prove.

The private detective feared that his life was in danger after receiving some strange and unusual telephone calls from people he did not know, so he did the 1471 on his telephone after one of these calls and he obtained the telephone number that had called him and he proceeded to write it down.

He then told his sister that if anything happened to him to give the details of the telephone number to the police and hand her the piece of paper containing the telephone number, which of course is what she did after he was found murdered. Nobody seemed to know why he had this feeling that something might happen to him but he did and by writing down that telephone number he actually helped to solve his own murder.

The telephone number gave police the lead they needed and very quickly his wife was arrested and charged with her husband's murder, her part being that she hired two 'hit men' to travel from South Africa to kill her husband unfortunately by the time the police discovered the body they were back in South Africa.

However in July 1996 his wife was convicted of his murder at Birmingham crown Court and was sentenced to life imprisonment.

The two South African men were located and were now serving prison sentences in South Africa for minor crime and efforts were now in place to have the two men extradited back to England to face trial for murder.

My role in all this was to locate and trace all the witnesses involved in the earlier trial of 1996, and to see if they were still prepared to go to court and to give evidence at such a time that the two South African men were extradited and were back in this country and standing trial for their part in the murder.

There was in excess of 220 witnesses and those I traced would have to make a further short witness statement confirming what they told the police in 1995/96 is the truth and that in 1999 or later depending on when the two men were extradited that they would still be willing to attend court and give that very same evidence.

I really was enjoying this job as having my own office was nice and the fact that I was away from that clicky office at Erdington was good.

The two were eventually extradited in October 2002 and there is another horrific twist in this story, six West Midland Officers went to South Africa to bring these two violent men back and on the way to the airport in South Africa one on the cars was involved in a road accident in torrential rain and one of the West Midland officers, DC Rob Ling from Sutton Coldfield tragically died as a result of the car crash.

The two South African men stood trial at Birmingham Crown Court and on 25th July 2003 they were found guilty of the murder of the private detective and were both given life sentences.

In April 2007 the wife of the private detective was released from prison on compassionate grounds and died in October 2007 of cancer in a hospice.

There were certainly no winners in that murder.

But my job at the time was to trace the witnesses and that's what I was doing and when 3.00pm came round on that bonfire night in 1999, I rang the Major Fraud Unit spoke with the admin lady who said, 'Just before I put you through to the DI, you have got the job but do not tell him I said so.' and then she put me through, the DI answered in the way he always answered the telephone, 'DI here.'

I said, 'It's me Nigel, boss.'

'Congratulations,' he said, 'you were successful and have the job.'

I said, 'Many thanks what happens now?'

We then had a general chat about things and it was explained that Mary would contact Sutton personnel and the DI and a date for your transfer back to fraud would be agreed. I was over the moon I was going back to where I thought I should never have left.

That was sorted by all parties and a start date of Monday 6th December 1999 was agreed and to me it was a great day as I was back in fraud which I left on tenure some 5 years and 11 months ago, and in that time I felt as if I had been around the world twice.

CHAPTER FIFTEEN

Fraud Squad Again

Monday 6th December 1999 and here I was again back on the Fraud Squad or Major Fraud Unit as it was now known, not a great deal had changed in my 5 years 11 months away we were still in the same building and we were still short of staff, the basement still let in water and the canal next to the building still smelt, but the main thing was I was back doing the job I never wanted to leave in the first place.

As you can appreciate not a lot happened prior to the Christmas break, apart from me going to the local Chinese restaurant for the Major Fraud Unit Christmas function. I had a good break at Christmas because being on this particular unit you do not work any bank holidays. So I was looking forward to 2000 to get my new jobs allocated to me.

I returned to work on Tuesday 4th January 2000 and within a couple of days I was given two new jobs, one involved the theft of computers and the other involved a bank manager of a famous bank in Birmingham stealing in excess of £90,000 from the bank.

I never cleared up the computer fraud and the two men wanted are as far as I know still outstanding today. It was an easy planned fraud, these two men set up a company based in the jewellery quarter in Birmingham and bought in computers via catalogue companies which were then delivered to their shop, in the first instance they paid for the computers and then they build up a good working relationship with the various suppliers of the computers, they would then order more than before but on this occasion would fail to pay for them in the due time, It really was as simple as that.

The supplier would naturally make an enquiry when the payment was due normally 30 or 60 days after delivery of the goods, so in the first instance they would contact the company probably by telephone and when they got no reply they would call round at the company premises and low and behold they found an empty shop premises.

Our two men had vanished without trace and with them several thousand pounds worth of computers and computer equipment in this case in excess of £100,000 and to this day they have never traced. Every address and telephone number was checked but it all led nowhere and it was quite disappointing not to have successfully concluded the matter.

But I did get to travel all over England to various computer suppliers obtaining statements so that was a good side to the investigation from my point of view.

The story of the bank manager was successfully concluded by me after a relatively short investigation, he was one of a number of managers who worked at this particular bank and held a good position with a good salary, what made him turn to fraud and theft I never did find out.

But in brief his modus operandi was that he use to log onto to other staff members computers, normally when they were out at lunch and apply on line for a loan using false details and in his position of manager he would then authorise that loan and direct the loan be paid into a named account, he would then log out and return to his own office.

How simple is that, so simple and effective that over a period of 18 months or so he stole over £96,000 using this method and when details of non-payment of the loan came to light, he being a manager would be asked to sort the problem out, so then he would either borrow more money using false details or close the account off altogether as he had the authority to do so.

He could not lose, but yes he could because another member of staff suspected something and so the banks internal fraud department was contacted and he was monitored and obviously detected.

I dealt with him from start to finish and on arrest and interview he admitted the crime straight away and in due course he appeared at the Crown Court, where not surprisingly he was sent to prison for 18 months.

Of course the year 2000 was the year that Doctor Harold Shipman was found guilty of murdering 15 patients between 1995 and 1998 and on 31st January 2000 he was sent to prison for life and of interest on 13th January 2004 he was found dead in his cell at Wakefield Prison he had committed suicide by hanging with a noose made from bed sheets.

He is of course is the only man who knows how many people he killed but whilst he was a practising doctor between 1971 and 1998 a total of 459 people died whilst under his care so we can only guess how many of those that he killed. And why did he kill them again he knows the answer but it is known that in some of the cases he was left money and jewellery by his patients so perhaps he killed for gain.

Because he killed himself at the age of 58 his wife was entitled to his NHS pension something of course he could never have collected and something that she would not have received had he reached the age of 60 years, so that makes you think.

During the summer of 2000 we had a new DS and DC join us and they were to become my working partners over the next few years, the DS I had known for many years, the DC Pete Jones I had never met before and early in 2001 he retired from the police but he came back as a member of police staff and we worked together on an enquiry that was to last some four years and we became very good friends in that time. Me personally, well I was about to step into the minefield of pensions.

I remember the one sided conversation I had with the DS, he said,

'You got much work on at the moment?' that means you are about to have a new fraud booked out to you, he then said, 'What do you know about pensions funds and the regulations that surround them?' that means the new job is a fraud involving a pension fund of some description.

He carried on, 'We can get you some help for you if you need it' that means it is going to be one hell of a big job, and he finished with, 'The DI thinks you are the best man for the job.' oh that makes it alright then I thought.

Now I am like most normal people, I do not really understand pensions and the regulations that surround pensions and in truth I find the whole subject rather dry and boring, so I was not relishing the fact that my new job was all about pensions and no doubt involving a fraud as well.

I certainly did not have to wait that long to find out what the new job was all about.

CHAPTER SIXTEEN
The Cheney Pension Fund

On Wednesday 1ˢᵗ November 2000, I attended a conference where I met with representatives from the Occupational Pensions Regulatory Authority (OPRA) and a representive from the Independent Trustee Services (ITS) the DI and DS were also there, and the biggest and most complex case I had ever worked on in my 30 years as a policeman was just about to unfold in front of me and was going to keep me fully occupied for the next four years.

The fraud entered around a company based in Birmingham and the company was called C W Cheney and Sons Limited, (CWC) with their registered office in Factory Road, Hockley, Birmingham.

The business was an old long standing and established lock making company that had been trading for over 100 years, it manufactured hose clips or jubilee clips as they were better known and locks for suitcases and other bags. In 1980 the company was having on-going financial difficulties, as the demand for locks in the suitcase and bag industry was changing and the need for them diminishing.

Therefore the company was put up for sale and late in 1980 it was purchased by a German owned company. But once again despite the company being restructured, the new owners were having the same on-going financial difficulties as the previous owners so the German owned company decided to sell CWC and they successfully sold it in 1999.

But as before the new owners soon found they had the same problems as the previous German owners and with the continuing financial difficulties and the demand for this type of lock now virtually non-existence due to companies now using plastic instead of metal, so they too reluctantly decided to sell the business this time with the assistant of a local and established business broker.

Enter the fraudsters, the history of CWC was now about to change for ever, after over 100 years of trading.

On 28th April 2000, CWC together with the plant, machinery, shares and assets was sold to a London based company known as CLCL, for £175,000.00, a company fronted by two men who I will refer to as KS and MM, of course one of the biggest single assets of the company was the CWC pension fund which at the time of the sale of the company to CLCL had a balance of almost three point one million pounds. (£3.1 million)

The CWC pension fund was set up in 1993 as a final salary pension scheme for the employers and had at the time of the sale in April 2000 had about 230 members.

On completion of the sale of CWC to this London based company, the original trustees of the pension fund who were of course employees of CWC then resigned to be replaced by new trustees, in the first instance it was the live in partner of KS, someone who I will refer to as AM and her company known as TP and also a London based law firm known as MMS.

Incidentally MMS was another company that was fronted by KS and MM and it had given the impression that it was looking after the day to day running of the pension fund. Of course you needed trustees to run the pension fund because it was only the trustees who could move money from the pension scheme to invest elsewhere.

So in effect by close of play on 28th April 2000, the fraudsters KS and MM controlled CWC the company and the Cheney Pension Fund.

The entire pension fund's assets were at the time invested in a legitimate investment company in Scotland and on this particular date, the 28th all relevant documents which included the signed copies of the Deeds of

Appointment and Removal of Trustee document signed by MMS (the company) and AM were forwarded to the investment company and accompanying these documents was a request from the new trustees, the fraudsters to transfer £700,000 from the fund into the account of TP which we know is controlled by AM.

The money was transferred from the investment company into the company account of TP later that day. Once the money had arrived it was quickly dispersed by AM. In effect the pension scheme had been used to fund the acquisition of CWC and to pay off a large loan that was owed to a German bank by CWC, obviously not what a pension fund should be doing.

Once acquired by CLCL, the company of CWC continued to operate as a business however the employers were kept in the dark and were certainly not aware about the withdrawal of £700,000 from their pension fund or of its intended use.

On 23rd May 2000 a further £50,000 was withdrawn by the trustees from the investment company and that money was used to purchase another company known as LP, a Wolverhampton based company which at the time of sale and purchase was not even trading so why this company was purchased using pension funds I never did find out unless it was done as a favour for someone.

There was no security or provision made for the repayment of interest and they had purely used pension money to buy what turned out to be a non-profit making company, that never traded after its purchase clearly this was not a valid reason to use pension money in this way.

The next step and relevant date in the fraud was on 23rd May 2000, MMS (the company) was replaced as trustee of the fund by someone who I will refer to as R, the relevant documents were again prepared and signed and forwarded to the investment company and along with those documents was a new document that was now going to give KS complete control of the pension fund.

No doubt on his, KS instigation R and MM (the current trustees) granted KS power of attorney to act in their name as trustees of the pension fund. KS had complete control of the fund.

The Department of Trade and Industry, a government funded body that investigates breaches of company law and its directors were about to compulsory wind up the company known as CLCL and for that reason CWC had to be sold again and in July 2000 CWC was sold by CLCL to PAML another company completely controlled by KS, MM, and AM.

On 11th July 2000, AM resigned as director of CWC and was replaced by a man who I will refer to as CAP, who I will make mention of later and another business associate of KS a man known as IDS became company secretary of CWC.

Whilst all this was going on the poor pensioners had no idea what was happening to their pension fund and that it was in actual being plundered by KS, MM and their friends and business associates.

IDS owned another company known as HRDL, and CWC along with its pension fund of nearly £2.2 million pounds was sold to HRDL, this was a company controlled by IDS and CAP who I mentioned earlier now became a director of both CWC and HRDL.

Two new trustees were appointed and they were completely innocent of any offence and were merely used by the main conspirators of this fraud. In fact the one trustee became power of attorney and in later interviews with police admitted at the behest of KS and MM, he signed many pieces of blank paper but obviously they purported him to be a trustee of the CWC pension fund.

What control did our fraudsters have over these two innocent men to persuade then to do what they did, that was something else I never did bottom out throughout the investigation.

Two other people who have not been mentioned yet are TF and AS and they ran a property investment company known as BE, that company alone owed creditors several million pounds through failed property investment, they were very close friends of both KS and MM, but some of the creditors they and their company owed money to, wanted their investments back now and were not prepared to wait.

TF and AS were already on bail for a mortgage fraud to the Metropolitan Police and they in their fraud had attempted to raise money to pay off these creditors, so all in all they were in dire financial problems and this is where the CWC pension fund came in.

It would appear that the CWC pension fund in part would assist TF and AS to pay off some of the more aggressive creditors who were putting them under immense pressure with even threats to their lives.

Whilst this was going on KS was under pressure because the CWC pensions funds actuaries who make sure the pension fund is being looked after and managed correctly and for the benefit of the pensioners kept requesting information from KS which was not forthcoming. We know why he kept stalling as he was using the pension fund for whatever purpose he wanted and none of it was for the benefit of the pensioners.

However this did not stop what happened next, on 11th September 2000 KS contacted the investment company to state it was his intention to make a visit to them in Scotland and deliver all the original signed documents in relation to the change of trustee, it seemed unusual because he could have posted them but there was a sense of urgency to the visit because the same day the new trustee requested a transfer of £701,000, this time the money was to go to the account of HRDL as this was the company that now owned CWC.

This money was dispersed within days most going out of the account in cash, some in cheques and some in banker's drafts to a company registered in Switzerland.

Between 11th September 2000 and 10th October 2000, £2.2 million pounds was transferred out of the investment company and into the company of HRDL, and even by now to further complicate our investigation that company had now changed its name from HRDL to HPIL and they too received some of the transferred monies.

Almost a million pounds was taken out in cash and disappeared, no doubt into the hands of the main conspirators, the other £1.2 million went out in cheques and bankers drafts to individuals and companies throughout London and the South East, all this took place in a space of four's weeks most of the companies and individuals were creditors of the company known BI that had been run by TF and AS.

So by now the fraud was well in advance, the funds stolen were in my mind being used two fold, one for the benefit of the main fraudsters, KS, MM and the like and secondly for the benefit of TF and AS and their company.

The funds actuaries who were still not getting much assistance or response from KS, decided to make their own enquires with the investment company in Scotland, which of course revealed that since April 2000, £2.9 million pounds had been transferred out of the fund, allegedly for the benefit of these other companies and all the investment company had to show for all this was several alleged draft loan agreements for the investment of the pension monies prepared in the main by KS.

The actuaries now fearing the worst approached OPRA, who spoke with the investment company and found there was only £70,000 left in an fund that had nearly £3.1 million in April 2000, they also attempted to make contact with KS and although they did meet with him and speak with him they were clearly not happy with what he was saying and also what was happening to the pension fund.

OPRA then removed the last remaining two trustees of the fund who of course time would tell that they were completely innocent, and replaced them with an independent trustee, the company known as the Independent Trustee Services (ITS)

OPRA then contacted the police, and this is where I came in, 'You got much on?' and folks it was as simple as that, I came out of the meeting, loaded down with copy files and reports and with the various representatives of OPRA and the Independent Trustee Services (ITS) thinking where do I start.

I sat down and thought what do I have, I have the theft of £2.9 million pounds, upwards of ten conspirators to the fraud, hundreds of people who have had money from the fund albeit probably quite innocently because they thought they were getting their investment back, loads of companies, solicitors, the DTI and last but certainly not least 240 pensioners.

We also had current employees, who would be future pensioners who would be looking forward to a pension in their retirement and by the look of it would not be getting the pension that they thought they would have after contributing for many years.

What a nightmare, what a mess, what a job, where the hell do I start?

The DI informed me that he would be contacting the Serious Fraud Office in London to assist and you can tell by its name what it deals with and particular to them is that they would deal with all pensions frauds amongst other serious fraud, they of course dealt with the biggest pension fraud this country has ever known and that involved The Maxwell's, way back in the 90's, incidentally the Cheney Pension Fraud was to become the second biggest pension fraud the county had known and still is I think.

I had never worked with the Serious Fraud Office but over the next four years I was to see a lot of them and I found all of them to be most professional in every way and I enjoyed every minute of my working relationship with them and I hope them with me.

Anyway day one of four years and where do I start, first things first, such an investigation will have to have a name so the Cheney pension fraud became Operation Delstone.

I was the officer in charge of the investigation and when I wanted help I ask otherwise it is most definitely down to me, I have said this many times in this book, I like a challenge and I now had the greatest challenge of my police service and hopefully I will succeed and bring the criminals to justice.

The start of the enquiry for me was to go to the factory premises of CWC in Factory Road, Hockley about 2 miles from the office where I was working and speak with the workers to see what they could tell me, if anything, because one of the main fraudsters, KS had been to the factory several times and spoke with the work force, so what had he said to them and what could they tell me.

The workers in fact told me very little they had obviously been kept very much in the dark, KS to them was the new owner and he was a very plausible person as most fraudsters are, he told various stories about the problem the company faced, that he was the best man to sort these problems out and he would continue to run the company as long as he was able to do so.

And all these nasty rumours about missing money were wrong and there was no missing money, because any of the pension funds that had been used by the trustees had been properly used and properly invested, he went on to tell that that their pension fund had been properly invested by way of loans, to other companies and when the loans were paid back there would be interest on the loans, so the investment would make the fund more money.

I arrived at the company at about 9.00am and was met by the new company accountant, a man who I will refer to as AF, a larger than life friendly man he told me that KS was actually on the premises and he was in the board room.

Shall I arrest him I thought, the allegation is that he may have conspired with others to steal £2.9 million pounds, no I thought let us have a chat see what he has to say first of all I can always arrest him later.

I found the board room and there he was sitting at the table surrounded by papers, he certainly looked the part,

I thought let us start at the top and work down instead of the other way round after introductions, I said, 'I am here because it has been reported that £2.9 million pounds has been stolen from the pension fund of this company, the company that I believe you are involved in'

I then listened to about fifteen minutes of utter bull shit, I cannot describe it any other way, he went on, and on and on, he said, 'I can tell you now quite categorically that the money has been invested and loan documents are in place and the money plus a bonus will be repaid to the pension fund in April 2001.'

And on, and on he went, he said 'The pension fund is safe on my life, I would have nothing whatsoever to do with any criminal offence involving the fund.'

His face with his wispy long blond hair, was getting redder and redder and for me I was bored I had listened to bull shit all my life and I was now sitting in a room talking to the master of bull shit, I could not take it anymore and I finished the conversation like this, I said, 'KS if the £2.9 million pounds is back with the investment company tonight, you will never see me, Mr Wier ever again, if the money is not returned then you will become to hate me. I want a fax off you as soon as possible with the full story of your alleged innocent involvement in this,' and I added 'to include all names of the persons you have personally dealt with, I now bid you good bye.'

I left knowing that the money would never be returned and I knew that I had just met with my number one target and the main man Mr KS, and I had left him with his mouth wide open.

I got back to the office and thinking like a detective, I knew in my own mind the money would not be returned because it had gone, but KS and his associates in whatever form still own CWC, the company which was clearly struggling and what would they the company do next. I was quickly going to find out from a source I had at this time that up till now I had very little to do with apart from one quick meeting, it was of course the SFO.

We of course was coming up to Christmas 2000 and I was looking forward to some annual leave but then something happened that needed some immediate attention, I think it was the 22nd December 2000 when I received a telephone call which meant I had to do some quick thinking and call upon the expertise of other people at very short notice.

Now of course by this time we had referred the matter to the SFO and it would in due course be a joint investigation, but these plans were going to come together in the New Year and not three days before Christmas, but between us we had to think on out feet quickly and indeed we did just that.

That afternoon KS acting for and on behalf of the law firm MMS, was going to the county court in London to put CWC into receivership, in other words to fold the company up and close it down, now although that was likely to happen in the future as the company were no longer trading profitably, we certainly did not want KS to get his hands on it as he would then have total control over everything, the building, its plant and machinery, work in action and other assets including the land the factory sat on.

So the last thing either the SFO or the police wanted was him in complete control of everything connected with CWC.

Now we had to appreciate that the largest asset, the pension fund was all but gone but the factory building its self with the land would be worth thousands after all it was a very large building not far from Birmingham City Centre and we believed it had potential for future investment.

I believed that if anything was going to happen to the building, the land and its contents it should be for the benefit of its genuine creditors possible the pensioners, I did not want KS or his associates to have control because I believe he would not have the creditors or pensioners interest at heart, he would only have his own, so we had to act quick.

The decision was that we, and by that I mean the SFO and the West Midlands Police would instruct the Official Receivers Office to compulsory wind the company up, then if we were successful then it would be the OR and not KS putting new locks on the front door.

Both hearings were to be heard at the same court and on the same the same day, but the decision thankfully was made in our favour and by Christmas the factory premises of CWC were secured by padlocks by the Official Receivers Office and not thankfully KS and his associates.

KS and his friends no longer had control either of CWC and its now small pension fund, in other words they were not going to steal anything else from the company.

2001 arrived and so did a 17 page fax message from KS giving me a potted history of events from April 2000 until October 2000, he was of course still protesting his innocence of any wrong dealings in connection with the purchase and sale of CWC and its pension fund, but what I did know was that £2.9 million pounds was missing presumably stolen with the assistance and corroboration of KS.

It was now down to me as the investigating officer to try and bring the whole matter to a successful conclusion, I was confident that persons would be charged but less confident of ever recovering any money.

I believed early on that there appeared to be two distinct set of circumstances surrounding the fraud, the first set of circumstances from April 2000 to September 2000, and in the main involved MM, KS and AM when £750,000 was transferred out of the pension fund and the second set of circumstances from September 2000 to October 2000 and in the main involved MM, KS, IDS, TF and AS and their company BI, when £2.2 million was transferred out of the pension fund.

This is how I decided as the investigating officer that I would investigate the matter.

One of the first jobs was to go to Birmingham Crown Court to obtain Production Orders under the Police and Criminal Evidence Act 1984, to be served on all the banks that were holding various accounts in relation to my group of suspects and any of their associated companies, and once I was in possession of copies of the relevant bank statements, I could then start identifying the movement of the monies and start to look at an audit trail.

The second job was to travel to Glasgow to the head office of the investment company, and from there recover all the original documents submitted by my suspects since April 2000. In relation to this I must have caught the DI on a good day because he allowed me to fly from Birmingham to Glasgow and to use taxis for any other part of my journey.

So we both of those jobs completed I began to speak with past directors and officers of CWC and past trustees of the CWC pension fund, to see if they could throw any light on what had happened but unfortunately as hard as they tried they could not really offer me anything I did not already know.

The conspirators had done an excellent job of keeping the entire workforce in the dark, I likened it to Operation Mushroom, 'fed bull shit and kept in the dark' and that's exactly what had happened to them.

So literally taking the bull by the horn I decided to arrest and interview the two trustees, who had become trustees of the fund in September 2000, I looked upon them as the weaker link in this complex fraud.

During February 2001 and later in August 2001 both men, the trustees were arrested and interviewed by myself and the DS, and as we first thought and certainly at this stage in the investigation they appeared to have been used by the main conspirators.

It would appear that both men had met the main suspects through their respective different types of work, one was a decorator and the other supplied limousines, and both had been asked in return for payment to sign various forms that were put in front of them at KS and MM office in Central London and that is what they did with no thought as to what they were signing and for what reason.

They had absolutely no idea what they were signing for and have absolutely no knowledge that there were both soon to become trustees of a pension fund.

But this was a very early stage in the investigation so no final decision could be made in relation to them. But my initial thought was they are not thieves they are idiots.

The same month February 2001, I was contacted by the solicitor acting for IDS and he stated that his client wished to speak with us, because his client thought he had been used and conned by MM and KS and he wanted to come and tell us his side of the allegations.

Not one to look a gift horse in the mouth I arranged to meet him by appointment at a police station on 21st February 2001, where I then arrested him and later interviewed him.

During his interview he informed me that he had been used by these two individuals, referring to KS and MM, and that any money that he had taken from the accounts was legitimate fees for work completed, and at all time he had acted under strict instructions. He agreed that he had supplied the company known as HRDL which later changed its name to HPIL because KS had asked him for a company with an associated bank account already in place.

He produced to me various documents allegedly supporting his version of events and he like the earlier two trustees who had been arrested and interviewed he was also released on police bail whilst further enquiries continued, there was a long way still to go in this investigation.

Other enquiries were going on and I had taken statements from the previous German owners of CWC and was regularly attending meetings with both the SFO and the ITS and its representive Mr Chris Martin.

Of course the ITS was now managing what was left of the CWC pension fund which in total was about £70,000, or about six months pension so ITS at this time were in the middle of negotiating with the Government backed Pensions Compensation Board.

The PCB was bought to life by the problems that the Maxwell's pension fund fraud had left in relation to pensions and pensioners, so the government of the day put into place the PCB which would assist and partly fund all legal pension schemes that had been subject to fraud or some other similar crime, but of course everything was down to negotiation.

The Independend Trustee Services (ITS) was successful and from January 2001 the CWC pension scheme would be supported by the PCB, but certain things would have to change for the pensioners of CWC, there would be no more lump sum tax free payments when you reached pensionable age and the weekly payments would be less but at least it was something for the pensioners of CWC.

What was known at this stage is that almost 1 million pounds in cash was taken out of the accounts of HRDL and HPIL during September, October and early November 2000 and our enquiries led us to a man who I will refer to as DM, the delivery man.

His role was to collect cash normally from IDS, as he was the account holder and he withdrew the money from the bank, and deliver it to where he was instructed to and in most cases it went to KS or MM at their offices in London. It was decided to arrest DM and he was arrested and interviewed on 28th March 2001, he was later released on police bail. I was fairly satisfied that he was not a thief stealing pensioners money, he was just doing what he was told to do and of course being paid to do and that was to collect envelopes or packages from IDS and to take them to where he was told which normally was to normally KS and MM.

That was his sole contribution, in fact he was a nice friendly person and not a thief, he was never charged with any offence in connection with the fraud and he became a very important and good prosecution witness in the subsequent trails that followed.

On 18th April 2001, I decided to arrest and interview a man who I will refer to as CAP, I could never fathom out what he was all about, for some reason in September 2000 when CWC was being sold to HRDL, CAP became both the director of CWC and HRDL and his name and signature turned up on a lot of documents and I do mean a lot.

In several interviews and on more than one occasion he declined to answer any questions put to him, and it was something I could never understand because if you are totally innocent you shout from the roof top you do not keep your mouth firmly closed, but for the time he kept his mouth shut and he too like the others was put on police bail.

On 21st April 2001, I arrested KS who I believed was the main man, the main fraudster along with his business partner MM, several interviews were completed with him on this day and I have to admit that I thank god, that the interviews were tape recorded because this man could talk, he could talk the hind legs of a donkey.

He sat there like a businessman and spent the next four hours or so trying to tell me and the DS, that he of course was totally innocent of all crime, he had most certainly not stolen any pension money and everything was above board and he has always done his best and everybody had used him. He had put these documents together for the loans in particular on the sole instructions of the trustees and the loans were of course genuine and would make money when they were repaid.

KS had informed me that the loans with interest would be repaid to the pension fund in April 2001, well I interviewed KS on 21st April 2001 and had the loans been repaid, of course not, the money had long gone and was never coming back. I nearly believed him at one stage but fortunately I saw sense and woke up, he like the others was placed on police bail.

KS was in fact a friendly and charming man and he always dressed immaculately in an expensive suit and collar and tie and I could understand why people had been conned by him. But in truth he was full from head to toe with bull shit but remember the old saying 'bull shit baffles brains.'

He was of course a charming man with manners and immaculately dressed but a typical fraudster, he was as smooth as a brick and in my opinion along with his friend MM, he was the brains behind this fraud, it was a clever and calculated fraud and I believe he was one of the few people who I had met who could carry this out, he could sell ice cream to the eskimos.

On 15th May 2001, I arrested AM and she was later interviewed and as expected being the partner of KS, everything that she did was at the behest of KS and she believed that she had done nothing wrong because KS had done nothing wrong. We really did not get anywhere when we interviewed her and how does the famous saying go 'butter would not melt in her mouth,' AM to was put on police bail along with the others as enquiries continued.

Around this time I had received a telephone call from the solicitor acting for MM and what followed was quite a strange conversation, he basically said that MM wanted to speak with us and tell us his side of this whole messy affair, but if we arrested him he would advise his client to make no comment, but if we interviewed him but did not arrest him he would speak quite freely and openly to you.

Well as you can guess I went for option two and on 18th May 2001 by appointment and without arrest I interviewed MM.

MM was totally different to KS in everything, I immediately believed him to be the more senior, the more aggressive and the more powerful of the two men, everybody was lying apart from him and if there had been any wrong doings it was the work of KS and his friends.

I found MM difficult and to deal with and he was very confident during the interview that he would never be charged in connection with this crime, he was almost 'big headed' in his replies to questions. However he had now given me a version of events surrounding the pension fraud and what he knew and did not know about it, so his interview would allow me to look further into the part he played in all this, being a good liar you also had to have a good memory, I was confident that in due course I would charge him.

At the conclusion of the interviews he was released from the police station and not placed on police bail like the others at this stage.

The investigation continued and now I had copies of all the bank statements from all the relevant bank accounts, and I began the task along with the financial investigator from the SFO of identifying people who had received monies, probably quite innocently from the pension fund in particular monies from the account of HRDL later known as HPIL, because between them these two accounts had received £2.2 million pounds of pension money.

I knew almost a million pounds came out of the accounts in cash and we never ever traced that money, but we believed it went to pacify the more aggressive creditors of TF, AS and their company BI.

Also I believed that part of the missing money went to the fund the extravagant lifestyle of KS, MM and AM.

KS and AM with their regular trips to America, in particularly Los Angeles, they got married there with the ceremony being conducted by an Elvis Presley impersonator. Not forgetting MM's regular trips to Thailand sometimes three times a year, the purchase of an exclusive car paid for mainly in cash and also the cash purchase of a very nice gents watch for £5,000. So I believed that the main instigators of this crime also had some reward from it but of course it was up to me to prove.

The remainder some £1.2 million pounds went to individuals and various named companies probably creditors of BI, that being TF and AS now defunct property investment company. It was my intention to locate every penny of the missing money and with the assistance of the SFO and in particular the financial investigator we started to identify the recipients of some of this money.

It was fairly exhausting work because it involved banks and or building societies but of course the SFO had certain powers that I did not, I know that sounds strange but they had a power called a Section 2 Power, and they could serve that on a bank or building society and they in turn would have to give information to the SFO on demand.

It was certainly quicker than me going to court to obtain a production order under the PACE 1984, so their section 2 was extremely useful and in total during this investigation I think it was used in excess of 50 times, it got the information I wanted quicker so I could act quicker.

It is perhaps better if I gave an example of how it worked, I have in front of me copy statements in relation to HRDL and HPIL and on such and such date £3,000 was debited out of the account, my production order would allow me to ask the bank where the £3,000 was transferred to and they would tell me it has been credited to for an example Lloyds/TSB bank in Finchley, North London.

In normal circumstances I would then have to go back to the Crown Court to obtain a further production order to serve on Lloyds/TSB bank to ascertain who the account holder was who had received the £3,000.

How long would that normally take perhaps seven, fourteen or maybe twenty one days, a section 2 order would be served and the information would follow probably arrive the next few days so that is why that power was useful to me in order find out who had received monies from the accounts of HRDL and HPIL much more quickly.

It was however extremely time consuming because I would firstly identify the account holder then try and find out if they were on the telephone, to speak with them tell them, explain what my enquiry was and then arrange at some suitable time to visit them and take a statement from them, outlining the circumstances of how they were owed the money, how they were eventually paid and of course more importantly by whom.

If there were not on the telephone I would have to contact the local police station to ask them to call round to the address and in turn ask the occupier to either contact me or give me a telephone to contact them.

So just to make an initial contact with someone after first identifying them could take days or even on some occasion's weeks.

Now one thing you have to remember, I worked in Birmingham and the individuals I wanted to see and speak with apart from the odd one or two all lived and worked in London, so every time I took a witness statement it meant me travelling to London and back, a full day's work for one statement and during this investigation I took in excess of 300 statements.

By the way I am not moaning it was still a great investigation, all I am trying to do is explain the difficulties of the investigation.

After many of these statements had been taken a particular pattern emerged it was clear that people had invested money with the property investment company BI and their directors TF and AS, with a promise of a good return which clearly never happened.

The smallest amount invested I found was £3,000 from a lovely old lady in the East End of London, up the way up to £100,000 from a car dealer in North London, and all these people were promised a wonderful return on their investment in a very short space of time, in most cases only months and it never happened.

So now was the time to arrest and interview the directors of BI, TF and AS and on 22nd and 23rd August 2001, both men were arrested and interviewed and both men made no comment to any question put to them by me, after their interviews they too were released on police bail.

This was a big disappointment to me as they had the answer to where £2.2 million pounds of pension money had gone to but they declined to tell me, and I believe the reason they did not tell me was that both men were on Crown Court bail for a mortgage fraud and were awaiting trial at Southwark Crown Court, so they decided the best course of action was to keep their mouth shut, perhaps I do not blame them.

I really loved this enquiry I was travelling to London most weeks sometimes twice a week because the SFO, Chris Martin from ITS and 99% of my witnesses were all based in London. One day I would travel from Snow Hill station to Marylebone station and perhaps the next time I would go New Street station to Euston station just for a change.

I was enjoying myself travelling up and down to London on the best criminal investigation that I had ever been involved in then suddenly the world changed forever.

11th September 2001 or 9/11 as it is best known happened with a series of coordinated suicide attacks by al-Qaeda upon the United States of America, on that morning 19 al-Qaeda terrorists hijacked four commercial passenger jet air liners and the hijackers intentionally crashed two of the air liners into the Twin Towers of the World Trade Centre in Manhattan, killing everyone on board and many hundreds within the two buildings and both buildings collapsed within two hours.

The hijackers crashed a third airliner into the Pentagon in Virginia and the fourth airliner crashed into a field in Shanksville, Pennsylvania after some of its passengers and flight crew attempted to retake control of the plane, there were no survivors from any of the planes.

In total 2,977 innocent people and 19 hijackers died as a result of this terrorist action and this included 343 fire fighters and 60 police officers it is also known that over 200 people jumped to their deaths from the burning Towers.

The World as we knew it would never be the same again.

Within hours of the attack the FBI was able to determine the names of the hijackers, identifying a Mohamed Atta from Egypt as the ringleader and one of the 19 hijackers, the FBI investigation codenamed Operation PENTTBOM was the largest and complex investigation in the history of the FBI involving over 7000 agents.

They quickly determined that al-Qaeda led by Osama Bin Laden bore responsibility for the attacks and what came with that was the United States of America war on terror which led to the invasion by force of Afghanistan and Iraq, the war on terror continues today.

I was actually at work when news of the airliners crashing into the Twin Towers was coming through and I have to say the mood in our office was very sombre, as we sat and watched the devastation happening before our eyes and we were ourselves in a state of shock, that's when you know your problems are nothing compared to the problems that occurred during and after 9/11.

On 4th October 2001, the West Midlands Police lost one of their officers a PC Malcolm Walker, a police motor cyclist from Sutton Coldfield who was on his motor cycle travelling along Walsall Road in Birmingham when a Nicholas Walters who was driving a stolen Peugeot motor vehicle registration number P348 WWO deliberately collided with the officer, the force of the collision threw the officer off the motor cycle and over some iron railings and onto the pavement.

The officer suffered horrendous injuries and later died in hospital, and in due course Walters was convicted after a trial of the officers murder at Nottingham Crown Court.

During December 2001 I re-interviewed the two trustees, DM, the delivery man, IDS, CAP, KS and AM where after their various interviews they were again all released on police bail. Once again the interviews were tape recorded as with the previous interviews earlier in the year and as before all of them continued to protest their innocence.

One thing I do recall is that IDS stated that in the New Year he wanted to see me again but on this occasion he did not want his solicitor present, I reminded him that it was a matter for himself and if he wished to speak to me then in fairness to both him and me it would be under caution and would be tape recorded.

On 14th January 2002 as arranged I again saw IDS and a further interview took place, but I learnt nothing that I did not already know in fact he was just trying to minimise his part in the fraud. IDS was again later released on police bail.

On 17th January 2002 I again saw KS and further interviews took place and I have to say the bull shit coming from him continued with pace. I think he got to the stage that he believed all the lies that he was telling me. He like the others was once again released on police bail.

Just turning the clock back to 18th October 2001 at Middlesex Guildhall Crown Court both TF and AS were both sentenced to lengthy prison sentences of four years for various fraud offences involving their company BI, which of course is where I believed a lot of the stolen pension money went to and it went to pay off the creditors of their company BI.

I was now in a position with my enquiry that I needed to interview both men again even though they were now serving prisoners. I was getting to the stage in the investigation that I was ready to charge some of them in relation to the theft of £2,918.915.00 from the CWC pension fund.

On 20th March 2002 I went to HMP Wandsworth, South London with the DS and in the presence of their respective solicitors both TF and AS were interviewed and as before both men elected not to make any comment to questions put to them. Once more this was a bitter disappointment to me, because I believed that once that had been convicted of the mortgage fraud they would talk to me and tell me about the pension fraud but I was wrong.

I formally charged both men with Conspiracy to steal £2,918.915.00 from the CWC pension fund between April 2000 and October 2000.

On 27th March 2002 at Steelhouse Lane Police Station KS, AM, IDS and CAP were all charged with Conspiracy to steal £2,918.915.00 from the CWC pension fund between April 2000 and October 2000.

We now had six persons charged with the offence but enquires into the matter continued and even now I was still identifying witnesses and liaising with other law enforcement agencies.

On 5th April 2002, KS, AM, IDS, CAP, TF and AS all appeared at Birmingham Magistrates Court and were committed to the Crown Court for trial. With the exception of TF and AS who were remanded back into custody as they were both serving prisoners, the other four were remanded on court to court bail.

By now I had been joined by Mr Pete Jones in the Cheney investigation, as I said earlier he had retired from the police after serving 30 years and had now returned as a member of the police support staff but it was suggested by the DS that he would be better suited assisting me in my current investigation, so at long last I had someone to share the workload with and as it was a complex fraud and investigation the old saying of 'two heads are better than one' certainly was correct, because almost from day one we hit it off and worked extremely well together and never looked back.

On 29th May 2002 at Marylebone Police Station in North London I again interviewed MM in the presence of his solicitor; again he made no comment to questions put to him. Once again he was the most difficult man to interview and whilst I asked the questions he just sat there looking at me or looking through me and he would not even tell me his name or address, what a difficult character.

I do not know if he was trying to intimidate me in any way but it failed miserably because later that same day he was also charged with Conspiracy to steal £2,915.918.00 from the CWC pension fund between April 2000 and October 2000 and was bailed to Birmingham Magistrates Court.

I now had seven defendants charged with this offence and they would be appearing at Birmingham Crown Court in due course for trial.

No further action was taken against either the two trustees or the delivery man who I have referred as DM, they were not to be prosecuted for any offence, however they may be called as prosecution witnesses during the forthcoming trial.

I was still working with Pete Jones and we were still travelling the length and breadth of the country, interviewing witnesses and taking statements off them. Even though people had been charged there was still a lot of work to be done in order to get all the papers ready for the trial.

We had two prosecuting counsel, one being a Queens Counsel, Mr William Coaker, QC and one being his junior, Mr David Wallbank and I have to say at this stage it was a pleasure to work with them, they were both very experienced, keen and knowledgeable men. It was of course their job to put together this complicated case for the Crown Court.

We had regular meetings in London with the SFO and one or both of them were always present, as they were putting the case together to be trial ready there was always work that they wanted doing so that fell to me or the SFO to do, but everything was coming together well, as they say, it was taking shape.

I had taken a few witness statements from some of the CWC pensioners, but had written to all 236 of them by way of a detailed questionnaire asking them to write down what they expected from the CWC pension fund.

At this time the government backed PCB was still topping up the pension fund every six months or so, but as I said earlier in the book there was no tax free lump sum payments being made to the pensioners when they had retired, and the weekly pension payment was greatly reduced but at least there were getting something.

I recall speaking to one pensioner who had been in the CWC pension scheme from day one and he was looking for a tax free lump sum payment of £38,000, as he and his wife were going to pay off their mortgage and move into the country and what did he get in the end, he got nothing. They were horrendous stories from people who were looking forward to retirement with the security of a pension and that pension now lay in ruins for the mindless act of the seven defendants now charged in relation to the theft from the fund.

On 6th November 2002 I attended Nottingham Crown Court; the defendants submitted to the Crown Court that they wanted the trial to be held in London and not Birmingham; because they believed that they would not get a fair trial in Birmingham. The reason behind this was that because the company of CWC and its 236 pensioners were mainly Birmingham based, they thought that any person that would be picked to sit on the jury for the trial would be over sympathetic to the pensioners so not allowing the seven defendants a fair trial.

The Judge at Nottingham listened to several arguments all through the long day from various counsel for the defendants, but ruled that the trial would remain at Birmingham and not London.

It was towards the end of 2002 that I bought my last car before I retired, I actually bought this car off my son, how things have changed normally it was the son buying if his father, my son had owned this car since 1999 and was about to sell it so I decided to buy it, it was a Vauxhall Cavalier 2.0cdi automatic registration number G21 EOJ, and this car actually broke down on the Aston Expressway two days after I retired from the police force, spooky or what.

2003 began the same as 2002 ended I was still working with Pete Jones taking statements and attending regular conferences with the SFO, the prosecution case against the seven charged seemed to becoming stronger and stronger as each week passed.

We were identifying new witnesses but the most annoying thing was that we could not recover was the cash, we believed that almost 1 million pounds was taken out of the accounts of HRDL and HPIL in a very short space of time but who had received the cash, had our defendants had it and hidden it away in bank accounts we did now know of.

Had they just spent it on the good life there was certainly evidence that KS, AM and MM were used to the good life, they were always travelling abroad on holidays we know that MM had bought a nice car and an expensive watch but this did not all add up to 1 million pounds, clearly some had gone to the aggressive creditors of TF and AS company BI, but perhaps I will never know where all the cash went to maybe some of it has been hidden away for a rainy day.

During 2003 there was several appearances at Birmingham Crown Court in relation to the forthcoming Cheney trial, one such appearance was on 2nd May 2003 when to my surprise TF entered a guilty plea to the offence of conspiring with others to steal £2.9 million pounds from the CWC pension fund.

He would now no longer stand trial with the others and would be sentenced at the conclusion of the trial involving the other defendants. He was still serving a sentence for previous matters and this guilty plea came as a bit of a shock but it certainly proved we had the right people.

For me 2003 flew by we had several appearances at the Crown Court in relation to the remaining six defendants and we completed numerous other enquiries and by the end of 2003 we were ready to go to trial, but it was never going to be that simple on 14th November 2003 at Birmingham Crown Court there was an application by KS and AM to have a separate trials to the other defendants.

This was because KS at the time was on a suspended 18 month prison sentence for offences that had been investigated and prosecuted by the Department of Trade and Industry, and if there was a joint trial of all six remaining defendants, he believed that reference would be made to the DTI investigation and suspended sentence and he believed that he would not get a fair trial.

The trial Judge agreed to this request and allowed separate trials and the first trial would begin on Monday 12th January 2004, and it would involve AS, AP, IDS and MM, the trial of KS and AM would follow the first trial.

And you will never believe this I missed the first week because I was on a course in London, I was to be trained as a Financial Investigator for the West Midlands Police and between 12th and 16th January 2004, I was on my Financial Investigators course at Hendon Police College. I was however telephoned every night by someone from the SFO to keep me updated with what was happening in the trial at Birmingham.

The trial at Birmingham Crown Court against AS, CAP, IDS and MM lasted from 12th January 2004 until 7th May 2004 some 4 ½ months by far the longest trial I had ever been involved in, and apart from the odd day here and there I was there every day. I was the officer in charge of the investigation and of course I was expected to be there, the trial went well and without exception the witnesses stood up to examination and cross examination.

On 7th May 2004 after three days of deliberation the jury returned with its verdicts, there were as follows, AS, IDS and MM Guilty, CAP Not Guilty and for this reason he was immediately released from the court, he left the building without saying a word, so I still do not know why he remained silent during his interviews and I suppose now I never will.

Of course on the day of sentencing, TF was also back before the court and the four defendants were sentenced as follows, MM seven years, IDS four and half years, AS three and half years, and TF three and half years.

Trial one of phase one completed, trial two of phase two still to come. At this stage there was a news blackout and nothing was to be reported by the press.

Although I was happy that the first part of the CWC saga had ended particularly well for me, the weekend that followed will be remembered for all the wrong reasons. At 2.30am on the Saturday morning my mobile telephone rang at home and on the other end of this call was a man who introduced himself as a paramedic. He went on to inform me that my father in law had been found dead in the bathroom of his house and could we make our way over as soon as possible.

At the age of 78 years my father in law Harry Cook was dead, I tell you what, you soon come down to earth from the highs of my success on the Friday to the lows of the Saturday after being told that someone who was close to you has suddenly died.

The second trial was to begin later that year but in the meantime as part of my continuing training to become a Financial Investigator, between 21st and 25th June 2004 I attended the CAS Business Centre in East London and completed my Confiscation and Restraint Course.

Although no trial date had been set it was agreed to list the case of KS and AM before the trial Judge at Birmingham Crown Court, so that all parties could tell the court their position, i.e. how many witnesses were to be called, how long is it likely to last, commitments from all parties, it is not unusual for this to be sorted before a trial starts, because in the first instance we fully expected the same witnesses to be called in this trial as in the last trial, so we were again looking at a lengthy trial perhaps three months in duration.

The directions' hearing as they are quite commonly called was listed for 29th and 30th July 2004. I was there as normal as was the prosecution team and SFO and what happened next took us all by surprise. KS and AM took their places in the dock, the indictment was put to them both and KS then pleaded guilty to the offence of conspiracy to steal the pension money on this date, now we did not know that was going to happen but there he is in front of the trial Judge saying,

'I am guilty of stealing £2.9 million pounds but my partner AM is totally innocent of all this and anything she did was on my direction.'

A quick adjournment whilst prosecuting counsel, SFO and police discussed what we are going to do with AM now that KS has pleaded guilty. In view of his plea it was decided that the prosecution would now offer no evidence against her, so that was agreed and back into court and that was a course of action that was taken in which all parties agreed including the trial Judge.

AM walked from the court a free woman, KS was remanded on bail for sentence on a date to be fixed.

One thing you can say about KS is you never know what is coming next and about a month later we were back at the Crown Court, KS wanted to vacate his guilty plea and enter a not guilty plea. After listening to various arguments the trail Judge said the guilty plea was to stand, no undue pressure was put on KS to plead guilty, it was his choice and his choice alone so the application to vacate the plea was dismissed.

On 7th October 2004, KS was back before the Crown Court for sentence and he received six and half years for the offence of conspiracy to steal the Cheney pension fund and the 18 month sentence in relation to the previous DTI matters was invoked so in total he received 8 years imprisonment.

What a character the man was full of surprises and how would I describe him, 'a likeable fraudster' if you can have such a person.

The Cheney saga was over after almost 4 years, since it all began on 1st November 2000 with a visit from OPRA and ended in October 2004 with a pint of beer in the Square Peg pub opposite the Crown Court.

2004 for me was not over for me because I was still training to become an accredited financial investigator and between 25th and 29th October 2004, I was back in London to complete a Money Laundering Course, I was now on my way to becoming a financial investigator with the West Midlands Police.

2004 well it was my 29th year in the police force and by far it was my busiest but I did not mind because one thing was for certain there was not a day in 2004 when I was bored, I did not have time to be bored and I was loving every minute of it, but should I not be slowing down by now, obviously not.

And 2004 was also the year I received a Chief Superintendent's Commendation for my work on Cheney pension fund fraud or to give it is correct name Operation Delstone.

What happened to the pensioners because really this chapter is all about them and the horrible crime committed against them and their pension fund, well in late 2004 the PCB made a final and one off payment to the Cheney pension fund and although the payment will not last forever it will at least help all the pensioners of CWC past and present in getting some payment each and every month.

They said after the Maxwell pension fraud that they hoped no other pension fraud would happen but unfortunately one did, but at least in the Cheney pension fraud five people were sent to prison in the Maxwell pension fraud nobody was.

This was a complex fraud as you can see but it must also rank as one of the most difficult of investigations that I had been involved in but I would not have missed it for the world.

The trials bought with it, its own tragedies, the biggest shock was not too long after the completion of the both trials, the trial Judge HHJ Stanley died of cancer.

One of the defence counsels also died whilst the trial was on going along with a financial investigator from the SFO.

MM who was one of the defendants in the trials, he also suffered a loss his mother tragically died, I had met her once during the investigation and I would describe her as a lovely women.

So yet again with most crime there are no winners just losers.

But just turning the clock back slightly on 21st May 2004 a detective constable from Queens Road Police Station, a DC Michael Swindells who was 44 years of age, was stabbed to death as he responded to a assistance call from uniform officers, who were on a canal towpath by Spaghetti junction trying to arrest a male with a knife, who had just threatened council workers who had come to repair his fence.

An absolute tragedy his attacker a local man who suffered from a mental condition was arrested and later at Birmingham Crown Court was detained indefinitely for the police officers manslaughter.

But 2004 was not finished on 26th December 2004 we had the Indian Ocean Earthquake what we tend to know as the Tsunami, which hit Southeast Asia it was the third biggest earthquake the world had ever known and was the strongest in the last 40 years, it registered 9.3 on the Richter scale it was estimated that in excess of 186,000 people died and over 40,000 are missing.

The last thing to mention is that I packed up smoking on Boxing Day in 2004 and have not smoked since; I began smoking cigarettes just after I joined the police in 1975 and I packed in smoking cigarettes just before I retired.

And over this particular Christmas and New Year break what was I was thinking of yes, retirement.

CHAPTER SEVENTEEN

Retirement

The beginning of 2005 was to be my final three months of my police career spanning 30 years, my actual retirement date was 9th March 2005, I had served under six Chief Constables and never met one of them is that good or bad I do not really know.

On your retirement you always have the opportunity to meet with the Chief Constable but I declined the offer as I thought what would I say to him.

I started to think about my retirement probably during the last two years or so but with fervour in 2004 and when did it actually hit home that I was to retire after 30 years, I think that was when my DI suggested I go on a pre-retirement course, that was held at Tally Ho on 6th and 7th December 2004, that's when you spend two days in a classroom and are spoken to by invited people who discuss, pensions, savings, so now you know retirement is not far away.

It seemed so strange that here I was getting ready to say goodbye to the police force and it was at Tally Ho all them many years ago where I actually said, hello to the police force, I had by now completed the full circle.

And how do you retire from the police force which has been your life for 30 years well it's so easy you submit a report to the personnel office of the West Midlands Police giving them you retirement date, a copy of the report is sent to finance because in my case I was asking to commute the full tax free lump sum payment that I was entitled to, and that is it.

As I had declined to meet with the Chief Constable, I attended Lloyd House and collected a plaque and a framed certificate signed by the Chief Constable thanking for my 30 years' service.

People often ask me if I have any regrets in my police service, should I perhaps had gone for promotion, but if I had a done that I would not have been a detective for over 23 years which to me was the best job in the force, so to quote the famous song by Edith Piaf *'Non, je ne regretted rien'* I have no regrets.

All what was left now was to have a farewell drink with a few friends and colleagues in a local pub, I then walked out the front door into the rain with a bunch of flowers for my wife and a bottle of wine for me and that was the end of my police service with the West Midlands Police.